The Book of Revelation

The Expositor's Bible Study and Commentary

DR. MAXWELL SHIMBA

Shimba Publishing LLC

Printed in the United States of America

First Printing Edition 2023

Table of Contents

Introduction

The Book of Revelation, often simply referred to as "Revelation" or "The Apocalypse," is one of the most intriguing and enigmatic texts in the entire Bible. It is the final book of the New Testament and stands as a literary and theological masterpiece that has captured the imagination of scholars, theologians, and believers for centuries. Revelation is a book of profound mystery, vivid symbolism, and prophetic visions that offer a glimpse into the divine plan for the future and the ultimate triumph of good over evil.

Attributed to the apostle John, who wrote it while exiled on the island of Patmos, Revelation opens with a remarkable encounter. John is granted a vision of the glorified and resurrected Christ, who commissions him to record the revelations that he will witness. What unfolds from this point is a dramatic and awe-inspiring narrative that explores the cosmic battle between the forces of light and darkness, the return of Christ in glory, the final judgment, and the promise of a new heaven and a new earth.

One of the distinctive features of Revelation is its extensive use of symbolic language and imagery. The book is replete with seals, trumpets, bowls, beasts, dragons, and heavenly beings, all of which convey profound spiritual truths and eschatological events. These symbols are a hallmark of apocalyptic literature, a genre that was prevalent in the ancient world and often used to convey messages of hope, resistance, and divine intervention in times of crisis.

Interpreting Revelation has been a source of theological diversity and debate throughout Christian history. Some readers approach it with a literal lens, seeking to decipher its prophecies in a chronological and future-oriented manner. Others view it as primarily symbolic, emphasizing its moral and spiritual lessons, while still recognizing its relevance to the human experience.

Revelation also addresses the circumstances of its original audience – early Christians facing persecution and uncertainty. It offers them words of encouragement, warning, and hope, reminding them of God's ultimate sovereignty and the assurance of their ultimate victory in Christ.

In this introduction, we embark on a journey into the Book of Revelation, inviting readers to explore its pages with an open heart and a willingness to grapple with its complexities. Regardless of one's theological perspective, Revelation speaks to universal themes – the longing for justice, the triumph of faith over adversity, and the promise of a renewed creation. As we delve into its chapters, may we find inspiration, solace, and a deepened understanding of God's plan for humanity, even amid the mysterious and enigmatic visions that characterize this remarkable book.

CHAPTER ONE

Introduction and Greetings to the Seven Churches

Introduction:

Chapter 1 of the Book of Revelation serves as an introduction and sets the stage for the prophetic visions that follow. It opens with the revelation of Jesus Christ to the apostle John. In a vision on the island of Patmos, John encounters the glorified Christ, who appears to him with dazzling brilliance and authority. Jesus is described as clothed in a robe with a golden sash, and His eyes are like blazing fire. His feet are like polished bronze, and His voice is like the sound of rushing waters. In His right hand, He holds seven stars, symbolizing the angels of the seven churches, and a sharp, double-edged sword comes from His mouth, representing His powerful Word.

John's reaction to this awe-inspiring vision is one of fear and reverence. He falls at Jesus' feet as though dead. However, Jesus comforts him with the words, "Do not be afraid. I am the First and the Last. I am the Living One; I was dead, and now look, I am alive forever and ever!" These words affirm Christ's divinity, His victory over death, and His eternal nature. Jesus then commissions John to write down what he sees and send it to the seven churches in Asia Minor, initiating the prophetic revelations that make up the rest of the book. Chapter 1 serves as a powerful reminder of the majesty, authority, and eternal nature of Jesus Christ, the central figure of the Book of Revelation, and sets the tone for the prophetic messages that will follow.

Verse 1: "The revelation from Jesus Christ, which God gave him to show his servants what must soon take place. He made it known by sending his angel to his servant John."

- The opening verse introduces the book of Revelation as a revelation from Jesus Christ, given by God to show His servants what will soon occur. This revelation was communicated through an angel to the Apostle John.

Interpretation and Commentary:

1. Revelation from Jesus Christ: The book of Revelation begins by emphasizing its divine origin. It is not merely a human composition but a revelation directly from Jesus Christ. This underscores the authority and importance of the message.

2. What Must Soon Take Place: The book's primary purpose is to unveil future events, emphasizing their imminence. While the timeline of "soon" may be debated, it conveys the sense of urgency and readiness expected of believers.

3. Transmission Through Angel and John: God chose to communicate this revelation through the mediation of an angel to His servant, John. This angelic involvement underscores the importance and sacredness of the message.

Verse 2: "Who testifies to everything he saw—that is, the word of God and the testimony of Jesus Christ."

- John testifies that he faithfully recorded everything he saw, including the word of God and the testimony of Jesus Christ.

Interpretation and Commentary:

1. Faithful Witness: John, as the human author, asserts his role as a faithful witness. He emphasizes that his account is reliable and truthful, inspired by the Holy Spirit.

2. Word of God and Testimony of Jesus: The content of Revelation comprises both the word of God (God's divine message and purpose) and the testimony of Jesus Christ (His role, teachings, and redemptive work). This underscores the centrality of Jesus in the book's themes.

Verse 3: "Blessed is the one who reads aloud the words of this prophecy, and blessed are those who hear it and take to heart what is written in it, because the time is near."

• This verse pronounces a blessing on those who read aloud the words of Revelation, those who hear it, and those who take its message to heart, emphasizing the imminence of the events.

Interpretation and Commentary:

1. Blessing for Engagement: A blessing is promised to all who engage with the book of Revelation, whether by reading, hearing, or internalizing its message. This underscores the transformative power of God's Word.

2. The Time Is Near: The verse emphasizes the expectation of the imminent fulfillment of the events described in Revelation. It encourages readers to live in readiness and anticipation of Christ's return.

Verse 4: "John, to the seven churches in the province of Asia: Grace and peace to you from him who is, and who was, and who is to come, and from the seven spirits before his throne."

• John identifies himself as the author and addresses the seven churches in Asia, extending grace and peace from God the Father (the eternal God) and from the seven spirits before His throne.

Interpretation and Commentary:

1. Author and Recipients: John, the Apostle, is the author, and his message is directed to the seven specific churches in Asia Minor. While these were real historical churches, they also symbolize the broader Church throughout history.

2. Grace and Peace: The standard Christian greeting of "grace and peace" reflects the blessings and well-wishes conveyed from God to His people. It's a reminder of the spiritual riches found in Christ.

3. The Triune God: The mention of "him who is, and who was, and who is to come" refers to God the Father, emphasizing His eternal nature. The reference to the "seven spirits" signifies the fullness and perfection of the Holy Spirit.

Verse 5: "And from Jesus Christ, who is the faithful witness, the firstborn from the dead, and the ruler of the kings of the earth. To him who loves us and has freed us from our sins by his blood."

• John extends greetings and praise from Jesus Christ, emphasizing His roles as the faithful witness, the firstborn from the dead, the ruler of kings, and the one who loves and redeems His people through His blood.

Interpretation and Commentary:

1. Faithful Witness: Jesus Christ is described as the faithful witness, signifying His reliability and faithfulness in revealing God's truth and purpose.

2. Firstborn from the Dead: This title highlights Christ's resurrection, which is central to Christian faith. He is the first to conquer death, paving the way for believers' resurrection and eternal life.

3. Ruler of Kings: Jesus' authority extends over all rulers and kings. This emphasizes His sovereignty and ultimate governance over earthly powers.

4. Redemption through His Blood: Christ's sacrificial death on the cross is emphasized as the means by which believers are freed from sin and reconciled to God. It underscores the central theme of salvation through His atonement.

Verse 6: "And has made us to be a kingdom and priests to serve his God and Father—to him be glory and power forever and ever! Amen."

• Believers are acknowledged as a kingdom of priests, serving God and the Father. This verse concludes with a doxology, attributing glory and power to God.

Interpretation and Commentary:

1. Kingdom and Priests: Believers are not only recipients of God's grace but also participants in His divine plan. They are called to be a kingdom and priests, emphasizing their role in representing God and interceding for others.

2. Worship and Glory: The concluding doxology recognizes God's glory and power. It reflects the central theme of worship and the sovereignty of God throughout Revelation.

Verse 7: "Look, he is coming with the clouds, and every eye will see him, even those who pierced him; and all peoples on earth will mourn because of him. So shall it be! Amen."

• This verse anticipates the glorious return of Jesus Christ, emphasizing the universal visibility of His coming and the mixed response it will evoke.

Interpretation and Commentary:

1. Second Coming of Christ: This verse announces the future return of Jesus Christ, described in apocalyptic language. His coming "with the clouds" echoes similar descriptions in the Old Testament (e.g., Daniel 7:13) and signifies His divine majesty.

2. Universal Visibility: The phrase "every eye will see him" underscores the universal and unmistakable nature of His return. It affirms the literal, visible return of Christ.

3. Mourning and Repentance: The verse also predicts a reaction of mourning among those who rejected Christ, including those responsible for His crucifixion. This mourning may symbolize repentance or regret in the face of Christ's majesty and judgment.

4. Amen: The affirmation of "Amen" underscores the certainty of this future event. It is a solemn declaration of agreement and acceptance.

Verse 8: "I am the Alpha and the Omega," says the Lord God, "who is, and who was, and who is to come, the Almighty."

• This verse contains a declaration by the Lord God, identifying Himself as the Alpha and the Omega, the eternal and Almighty God.

Interpretation and Commentary:

1. Divine Identity: The titles "Alpha and Omega" represent the beginning and end of the Greek alphabet, signifying God's eternality and all-encompassing nature. God, in this declaration, asserts His divinity and sovereignty.

2. "Who is, and who was, and who is to come": This phrase reinforces God's eternal existence and active presence throughout history. He is the God of the past, present, and future, emphasizing His unchanging nature.

3. "The Almighty": The title "the Almighty" underscores God's omnipotence and absolute power over all creation. It assures believers of His ability to accomplish His purposes and fulfill His promises.

Verse 9: "I, John, your brother and companion in the suffering and kingdom and patient endurance that are ours in Jesus, was on the island of Patmos because of the word of God and the testimony of Jesus."

• In this verse, John introduces himself as the author, addressing the recipients as fellow believers, sharing in their suffering and participation in the kingdom of Christ. He mentions his exile on the island of Patmos due to his commitment to the word of God and the testimony of Jesus.

Interpretation and Commentary:

1. John's Humility: John identifies himself not as an authoritative figure but as a fellow brother in Christ, emphasizing his solidarity with the recipients of this letter. This fosters a sense of unity among believers.

2. Suffering and Kingdom: John acknowledges the reality of suffering for the sake of Christ but also underscores the glorious hope of the kingdom that believers share in. This reflects the paradox of the Christian experience.

3. Exile on Patmos: John's exile on Patmos was a result of his unwavering commitment to proclaiming the word of God and bearing witness to Jesus Christ. It highlights the cost of faithful discipleship.

Verse 10: "On the Lord's Day I was in the Spirit, and I heard behind me a loud voice like a trumpet,"

• John describes his experience on the Lord's Day when he was "in the Spirit" and heard a loud voice behind him resembling a trumpet.

Interpretation and Commentary:

1. The Lord's Day: This phrase likely refers to Sunday, the day of the resurrection, which early Christians often set aside for worship and remembrance of Christ's victory over death.

2. "In the Spirit": John was in a state of spiritual receptivity or trance, possibly indicating a vision or divine encounter. This is reminiscent of similar experiences by Old Testament prophets.

3. "Loud Voice like a Trumpet": The use of a loud voice resembling a trumpet emphasizes the significance and authority of the message John was about to receive. Trumpet imagery is frequent in prophetic contexts, signaling divine announcements.

Verse 11: "which said: 'Write on a scroll what you see and send it to the seven churches: to Ephesus, Smyrna, Pergamum, Thyatira, Sardis, Philadelphia, and Laodicea.'"

• The voice instructs John to write down what he sees and send it to the seven specific churches in Asia: Ephesus, Smyrna, Pergamum, Thyatira, Sardis, Philadelphia, and Laodicea.

Interpretation and Commentary:

1. Divine Commission: John is commissioned to record the visions and messages he receives. The message is intended not only for his personal understanding but also for the benefit of the seven churches.

2. Symbolic Significance: The number seven often symbolizes completeness or fullness in the Bible. These seven churches represent not only the specific historical congregations but also the broader Church, encompassing various spiritual conditions and challenges.

Verse 12: "I turned around to see the voice that was speaking to me. And when I turned, I saw seven golden lampstands,"

• John responds to the voice by turning around to see its source and observes seven golden lampstands.

Interpretation and Commentary:

1. Turning to See: John's response reflects his curiosity and eagerness to comprehend the source of the voice. It signifies his readiness to receive the revelation.

2. Seven Golden Lampstands: Later in Revelation (verse 20), it's explained that these lampstands represent the seven churches. They symbolize the churches as bearers of Christ's light and truth in their respective communities.

Verse 13: "And among the lampstands was someone like a son of man, dressed in a robe reaching down to his feet and with a golden sash around his chest."

• John sees a figure resembling a "son of man" among the lampstands, clothed in a robe that reaches his feet and wearing a golden sash.

Interpretation and Commentary:

1. Son of Man: The term "son of man" is a significant title used by Jesus to refer to Himself throughout the Gospels (e.g., Daniel 7:13-

14). In this context, it emphasizes Christ's humanity and His role as the divine-human mediator.

2. Robe and Golden Sash: The attire of this figure is reminiscent of the clothing of a priest or a king. It signifies Christ's roles as both our High Priest and King, symbolizing His authority, righteousness, and priestly intercession.

Verse 14: "The hair on his head was white like wool, as white as snow, and his eyes were like blazing fire."

• John describes the appearance of the figure, noting white hair like wool and eyes like blazing fire.

Interpretation and Commentary:

1. White Hair: The white hair symbolizes wisdom, purity, and eternity.

It portrays Christ as the Ancient of Days, who possesses timeless wisdom and righteousness (Daniel 7:9).

2. Eyes like Blazing Fire: The fiery eyes symbolize Christ's penetrating gaze and discernment. They represent His knowledge, judgment, and the refining work He performs.

Verse 15: "His feet were like bronze glowing in a furnace, and his voice was like the sound of rushing waters."

• John continues to describe the figure, noting feet like glowing bronze and a voice like rushing waters.

Interpretation and Commentary:

1. Feet like Bronze: The bronze feet suggest strength, stability, and the refining work of judgment. They symbolize Christ's authority and firmness in executing divine justice.

2. Voice like Rushing Waters: The voice resembling rushing waters signifies the power and authority of Christ's words. It echoes the imagery of God's majestic voice in the Old Testament (Ezekiel 43:2).

Verse 16: "In his right hand he held seven stars, and coming out of his mouth was a sharp, double-edged sword. His face was like the sun shining in all its brilliance."

• In this verse, John provides additional details about the figure he sees among the lampstands.

Interpretation and Commentary:

1. Seven Stars: Later explained in verse 20, these seven stars represent the angels or messengers of the seven churches. Christ holds

them in His right hand, signifying His authority and protection over the leadership and guidance of these churches.

2. Sharp, Double-Edged Sword: This is a symbolic representation of the Word of God, which is described as "living and active, sharper than any double-edged sword" in Hebrews 4:12. It signifies the power of Christ's spoken word and its ability to discern and judge with precision.

3. Face like the Sun: The radiance of Christ's face, like the sun in its full brilliance, symbolizes His divine glory and majesty. It emphasizes His divine nature and the overwhelming splendor of His presence.

Verse 17: "When I saw him, I fell at his feet as though dead. Then he placed his right hand on me and said: 'Do not be afraid. I am the First and the Last.'"

• John's reaction to the sight of the glorified Christ is to fall at His feet in reverence and fear. Christ reassures John and identifies Himself as the "First and the Last."

Interpretation and Commentary:

1. Profound Awe: John's response, falling at Christ's feet as though dead, illustrates the overwhelming sense of awe and reverence in the presence of divine glory. It's a common reaction in the Bible when encountering God or heavenly beings.

2. Comforting Words: Christ's response, placing His right hand on John and comforting him with the words "Do not be afraid," reflects His compassion and understanding toward John's fear and weakness.

3. The First and the Last: This title underscores Christ's eternal nature and preeminence. He is the beginning and the end of all things, signifying His sovereign authority over the entire timeline of history.

Verse 18: "I am the Living One; I was dead, and now look, I am alive forever and ever! And I hold the keys of death and Hades."

• Christ declares His eternal life, His resurrection from the dead, and His authority over death and Hades (the realm of the dead). Interpretation and Commentary:

1. The Living One: Christ emphasizes His resurrection and eternal life.

He conquered death, and His resurrection is a central theme of Christian faith, offering hope and assurance of eternal life for believers.

2. Authority over Death and Hades: Christ's possession of the keys signifies His authority over life and death, including the realm of the departed souls. Believers need not fear death because Jesus holds the keys, determining the destiny of every soul.

Verse 19: "Write, therefore, what you have seen, what is now and what will take place later."

• Christ instructs John to write down what he has seen, what is presently occurring, and what will transpire in the future.

Interpretation and Commentary:

1. Divine Commission to Write: This command reaffirms John's role as the recorder of the prophetic visions he experiences. It emphasizes the importance of preserving and conveying this divine revelation.

2. Threefold Timeframe: The instruction to write about the past, present, and future events suggests that the content of Revelation encompasses various aspects of history and eschatology (the study of end times).

Verse 20: "The mystery of the seven stars that you saw in my right hand and of the seven golden lampstands is this: The seven stars are the angels of the seven churches, and the seven lampstands are the seven churches."

• In this verse, Christ provides an interpretation of the symbolism of the seven stars and seven golden lampstands.

Interpretation and Commentary:

1. Seven Stars: The seven stars represent the angels or messengers of the seven churches mentioned earlier in verse 16. These angels likely symbolize the leadership or divine representatives of each church.

2. Seven Golden Lampstands: The seven golden lampstands represent the seven churches themselves. They symbolize the role of the churches in shining forth the light of Christ's truth and presence in their communities.

Revelation Chapter 1 introduces us to the vision of the glorified Christ, emphasizing His divinity, authority, and eternal nature. It sets the stage for the prophetic revelations and messages to the seven churches in the subsequent chapters. The rich symbolism and imagery convey important theological truths and serve as a call to faithfulness, readiness, and reverence in the worship of our risen Lord, Jesus Christ.

Prophetic Commentary:

From its very inception to its conclusion, the Bible intricately weaves a narrative of both blessings and curses.

The book of Genesis commences by depicting God's benevolence in bestowing blessings upon the animals and the first human beings (Genesis 1:22, 28). However, this era of blessings takes a swift turn when humanity's disobedience ushers in a cascade of curses (Genesis 3:17-19).

As we reach the book of Revelation, it symbolizes the culmination of humanity's defiance, wherein the resultant curses manifest as end-time plagues, strategically designed to catalyze humanity's repentance and reunion with God and His blessings.

Amidst the tumultuous backdrop of the plagues in Revelation, seven distinct blessings serve as guiding beacons toward a future where the curse shall cease to exist (Revelation 22:3). These blessings are occasionally referred to as the seven beatitudes of Revelation.

Blessings and Curses in the Biblical Context

Within the Bible, blessings carry the essence of God's love, serving as the fruits of a life aligned with His divine will and pleasing to His heart.

Conversely, curses emerge as consequences of disobedience to God's commands—occasions when we breach the protective boundaries that God, in His love, has set to safeguard our well-being and joy. Remarkably, even these curses can serve as wake-up calls, prompting us to recognize the necessity for transformation. They possess the potential to yield a positive outcome, leading us toward repentance and spiritual conversion.

12

Understanding the Meaning of Beatitudes

The term "beatitudes" is an elegant expression denoting blessings, rooted in its Latin origins. The most renowned set of beatitudes are those spoken by Jesus during the Sermon on the Mount, commencing with the statement, "Blessed are the poor in spirit, for theirs is the kingdom of heaven" (Matthew 5:3).

In Greek, the word "makarios," which translates to "blessed," carries profound implications. It signifies being blessed, possessing the favor of God, and experiencing a state of fullness emanating from God. This term denotes the condition of believers in Christ, as exemplified in passages such as Matthew 5:3-11, where it is stated, "Blessed... for my sake," or Luke 6:20-22, which reads, "Blessed... for the Son of man's sake." It is used to describe those who partake in God's nature through faith in Christ, as articulated in 2 Peter 1:4. "Makarios" is a multifaceted term that encompasses a sense of prosperity and good fortune. It extends beyond mere emotional happiness, encompassing a profound sense of contentment and fulfillment.

It's vital to recognize that God's blessings do not hinge on chance or luck. They encompass a joy that remains unshaken, impervious to external circumstances or influences, as affirmed in John 16:22.

The Seven Beatitudes Unveiled in Revelation

Revelation, often remembered for its sobering prophecies of end-time tribulations and divine judgments upon a wayward world, also holds within its pages a collection of seven blessings. These blessings serve as beacons of hope, reinforcing the notion that God's path is one of profound blessing, and ultimately, His triumph prevails.

The recurrent appearance of the number seven in the book of Revelation symbolizes completeness, a theme that extends to the unnumbered beatitudes scattered throughout the text. It appears as though God, in His divine inspiration, chose this precise number of blessings to convey the totality of His intention to bestow blessings upon His people.

These seven beatitudes are discreetly woven into the fabric of Revelation, surfacing in key verses such as Revelation 1:3, 14:13, 16:15, 19:9, 20:6, and 22:7 and 14, extending from the book's initial chapters to its conclusion. Thus, they contribute significantly to the overarching structure of this profound book.

In the words of The Expositor's Bible Commentary, Abridged Edition, which notes the deliberate literary pattern maintained by John throughout Revelation, "A comparison of the Prologue (1:1-3) with the Epilogue (22:7-21) shows that John has followed throughout Revelation a deliberate literary pattern" (Revelation 1:3).

The Initial Beatitude: Revelation 1:3

Revelation 1:3 opens with a profound declaration: "Blessed is the one who reads aloud the words of this prophecy, and blessed are those who hear it and take to heart what is written in it, because the time is near."

This verse underscores the manifold blessings that accompany the study of God's divinely inspired words. It emphasizes that those who engage in reading and listening to these sacred teachings should go beyond mere comprehension—they should also embrace them, responding obediently to God's directives.

The book of Revelation places a compelling emphasis on the imminence of the prophetic events it unveils—an urgency that permeates its message. While humans may perceive the nearly 2,000 years since John penned these words as a lengthy span, it's crucial to acknowledge that in the divine perspective, these prophetic occurrences are indeed drawing near, and God's timing is unfailingly precise.

The Second Beatitude: Revelation 14:13

Revelation 14:13 presents the second beatitude, declaring, "Then I heard a voice from heaven saying to me, 'Write: "Blessed are the dead who die in the Lord from now on."' 'Yes,' says the Spirit, 'that they may rest from their labors, and their works follow them.'"

This passage within Revelation draws a clear distinction between the destinies of those who worship the malevolent beast and bear its mark (verse 9) and God's loving design for those who "keep the commandments of God and the faith of Jesus" (verse 12).

For those who choose to worship the beast, they will ultimately face the righteous wrath of God. In stark contrast, those who faithfully obey God's commandments, even if they meet death, will receive a profound blessing.

This timeless truth finds resonance in the words of the psalmist, who penned, "Precious in the sight of the LORD is the death of His saints" (Psalm 116:15). Whether death comes naturally or through persecution, the promise of God to resurrect the "dead in Christ" serves as a source of solace and hope for all His faithful people (1 Thessalonians 4:16-18).

Contemplating martyrdom may evoke discomfort, yet God offers a perspective that reframes it as a welcome respite from troubles and persecution. The saints—comprising all Christians who have been sanctified through baptism and the indwelling of the Holy Spirit—are assured a unique blessing and a rest that transcends the ordinary.

The Third Beatitude: Revelation 16:15

Revelation 16:15 unveils the third beatitude, where it is stated, "Behold, I am coming as a thief. Blessed is he who watches, and keeps his garments, lest he walk naked and they see his shame."

In the climactic moment when the world's armies converge at Armageddon to confront the returning Jesus Christ, the Lord Himself imparts a timely reminder and blessing. He emphasizes that His return will catch many by surprise unless they maintain a vigilant watch.

Collectively, the seven beatitudes within Revelation encapsulate numerous paramount promises and recurring themes from the Bible, serving as a source of hope and guidance for those who steadfastly worship God throughout the challenging days of the end times. This echoes the teachings of Jesus in the Olivet Prophecy, where He cautioned against becoming ensnared by worldly distractions, emphasizing the importance of remaining watchful and prayerful to avoid being caught unprepared when the appointed time arrives (Luke 21:34-36). Further insights on this subject can be explored in our article titled "Watch and Pray."

The metaphor of putting on spiritual garments and guarding against spiritual nakedness is a recurring motif in the book of Revelation. This theme is also addressed in the message to the church in Laodicea (Revelation 3:17-18), highlighting its significance in the context of spiritual readiness and preparedness.

The Fourth Beatitude: Revelation 19:9

Revelation 19:9 introduces the fourth beatitude, proclaiming, "Then he said to me, 'Write: "Blessed are those who are called to the marriage supper of the Lamb!'" And he said to me, 'These are the true sayings of God.'"

Revelation 19 ushers in a momentous series of events associated with the triumphant return of Jesus Christ. Just prior to this fourth blessing, John bore witness to the resounding thunderous acclamations, heralding:

'Alleluia! For the Lord God Omnipotent reigns! Let us be glad and rejoice and give Him glory, for the marriage of the Lamb has come, and His wife has made herself ready.'

"And to her it was granted to be arrayed in fine linen, clean and bright, for the fine linen is the righteous acts of the saints" (Revelation 19:6-8).

In this grand narrative, the Bride of Christ is symbolized by the Church of God, adorned in the "fine linen" of righteous deeds that align with God's divine will. The call to partake in the marriage supper of the Lamb represents a profound blessing, illustrating the union between Christ and His faithful followers. This imagery underscores the sanctity of living in accordance with God's righteousness.

The Fifth Beatitude: Revelation 20:6

Revelation 20:6 presents the fifth beatitude, declaring, "Blessed and holy is he who has part in the first resurrection. Over such, the second death has no power, but they shall be priests of God and of Christ, and shall reign with Him a thousand years."

Upon the glorious return of Christ, those who have passed away in the faith will experience a resurrection to eternal life, destined to serve alongside Christ in His Kingdom. This remarkable resurrection, occurring prior to the commencement of the Millennium, is termed the "first resurrection." It earns this distinction because the remaining individuals among "the rest of the dead" will not experience a resurrection to physical life for judgment until the conclusion of the 1,000-year reign (as indicated in verse 5).

Those fortunate enough to partake in the first resurrection are shielded from the grasp of the second death—an eternal demise from which there is no possibility of revival. This beatitude underscores the unparalleled blessings and holiness of those who share in this initial resurrection, as they are designated as priests of God and Christ, appointed to reign with Him for a period spanning one thousand years.

The Sixth Beatitude: Revelation 22:7

Revelation 22:7 unveils the sixth beatitude, with Jesus Christ proclaiming, "Behold, I am coming quickly! Blessed is he who keeps the words of the prophecy of this book."

In this concluding chapter of Revelation, Jesus Christ revisits the essence of the first beatitude. Coupled with a renewed sense of urgency is a poignant reminder to steadfastly uphold the teachings contained within these prophecies. It underscores the imperative for Christians to heed the admonitions and find strength in the promises embedded within this transformative message.

Revelation 22:14 presents the seventh beatitude, proclaiming, "Blessed are those who do His commandments, that they may have the right to the tree of life, and may enter through the gates into the city."

From the very beginning, God has been in pursuit of those who choose obedience, thereby avoiding the forbidden fruit that leads to eternal death, and instead, seeking the tree of life that grants the profound blessing of eternal existence. As we journey through the conclusion of this book, it not only harkens us back to the Garden of Eden but propels us forward, unveiling the awe-inspiring vision of the resplendent New Jerusalem (further explored in our article titled "New Jerusalem").

Collectively, the seven beatitudes within Revelation encapsulate numerous paramount promises and recurring themes from the Bible. They stand as a beacon of hope and guidance for those who remain steadfast in their worship of God, even amid the challenging days of the end times.

CHAPTER TWO

The Loveless, the Persecuted, the Compromising, and the Corrupt Church

Introduction:

Chapter 2 of the Book of Revelation contains the beginning of a series of letters addressed to the seven churches in Asia Minor. Each of these letters follows a similar structure, beginning with an introduction of Christ, followed by commendations, criticisms, exhortations, and promises. These letters serve both as messages to the specific historical churches and as symbolic representations of the various spiritual conditions and challenges that the Church may face throughout history.

In Chapter 2, the first letter is addressed to the church in Ephesus. The letter commends the Ephesian believers for their hard work, perseverance, and refusal to tolerate false apostles. However, it also criticizes them for losing their initial love and passion for Christ. They are called to remember their first love and repent, with the promise of eating from the tree of life in paradise if they do so. This letter sets the pattern for the subsequent letters to the other six churches, emphasizing both commendation for faithfulness and correction for areas of spiritual decline. It underscores the importance of maintaining a fervent and sincere love for Christ amidst the challenges of life and ministry.

Verse 1: "To the angel of the church in Ephesus write: These are the words of him who holds the seven stars in his right hand and walks among the seven golden lampstands."

• In this verse, John is instructed to write a message to the church in Ephesus, introducing the imagery of Christ holding the seven stars and walking among the seven golden lampstands.

Interpretation and Commentary:

1. Ephesus: Ephesus was an ancient city in Asia Minor and the location of one of the seven churches mentioned in Revelation. It was a significant center of early Christianity.

2. Seven Stars and Lampstands: As explained in Revelation 1:20, the seven stars represent the angels or messengers of the seven churches, while the seven golden lampstands represent the churches themselves.

Christ's presence among them signifies His intimate care, oversight, and authority over the church.

Verse 2: "I know your deeds, your hard work and your perseverance. I know that you cannot tolerate wicked people, that you have tested those who claim to be apostles but are not, and have found them false."

• Christ commends the church in Ephesus for their diligent work, perseverance, discernment, and their rejection of false apostles.

Interpretation and Commentary:

1. Deeds and Hard Work: The church's commitment to good deeds and hard work reflects their dedication to living out the Christian faith and serving their community.

2. Perseverance: The church's ability to endure challenges and remain steadfast in their faith is acknowledged and praised.

3. Discernment: Their discernment in testing those who claimed to be apostles but were false demonstrates their commitment to sound doctrine and protecting the purity of their faith community.

Verse 3: "You have persevered and have endured hardships for my name, and have not grown weary."

• The church in Ephesus is further commended for their endurance in the face of hardships and their unwavering commitment to Christ's name.

Interpretation and Commentary:

1. Endurance in Persecution: The church in Ephesus faced various trials and persecutions for their faith in Jesus Christ. Their unwavering commitment, despite these difficulties, is a testament to their faithfulness.

2. Not Growing Weary: Their perseverance and resilience in the face of challenges reveal their determination to continue living out their faith and mission without faltering.

Verse 4: "Yet I hold this against you: You have forsaken the love you had at first."

• Despite their commendable qualities, the church is rebuked for having abandoned their initial love for Christ.

Interpretation and Commentary:

1. Loss of First Love: The church in Ephesus had allowed their fervent love and passion for Christ to diminish over time. This warning highlights the danger of becoming mechanical or ritualistic in one's faith and losing the deep, heartfelt love for Jesus.

2. Prioritizing Relationship: Christ values not only the church's deeds and endurance but also the depth of their relationship with Him. The call to return to their first love is a call to prioritize an intimate, affectionate relationship with Christ.

Verse 5: "Consider how far you have fallen! Repent and do the things you did at first. If you do not repent, I will come to you and remove your lampstand from its place."

• Christ urges the church to recognize their decline, repent, and return to their initial works of love. He warns of consequences if they do not repent.

Interpretation and Commentary:

1. Recognition and Repentance: Christ's call to "consider how far you have fallen" emphasizes the need for self-examination and acknowledgment of spiritual decline. Repentance involves turning away from this decline and returning to the practices of genuine love and devotion to Christ.

2. Consequences of Unrepentance: The warning that Christ will "remove your lampstand" implies that if the church does not repent and rekindle their love for Him, they may lose their status as a faithful church, indicating a withdrawal of His presence and blessing.

Verse 6: "But you have this in your favor: You hate the practices of the Nicolaitans, which I also hate."

• Despite their shortcomings, the church is commended for their righteous stance against the practices of the Nicolaitans, which Christ also condemns.

Interpretation and Commentary:

1. Nicolaitans: The Nicolaitans were a group or sect within early Christianity, and their practices are not fully described in the New Testament. However, they seem to have promoted compromising behaviors or beliefs. The church in Ephesus is praised for rejecting these ungodly practices.

2. Shared Disapproval: Christ affirms His shared disapproval of the Nicolaitans' practices with the church. This aligns with His expectation of purity and holiness within the church.

Verse 7: "Whoever has ears, let them hear what the Spirit says to the churches. To the one who is victorious, I will give the right to eat from the tree of life, which is in the paradise of God."

• Christ concludes His message to the church in Ephesus by emphasizing the importance of spiritual understanding and promising a reward for those who overcome.

Interpretation and Commentary:

1. Spiritual Hearing: The call to "hear what the Spirit says to the churches" underscores the need for spiritual discernment and attentiveness to God's message. It's a call to listen and respond to the Holy Spirit's guidance.

2. Promise of Eternal Life: The promise of eating from the tree of life in the paradise of God is a significant reward for those who remain faithful. It symbolizes eternal life and restoration to God's presence, reminiscent of the Garden of Eden.

The message to the church in Ephesus serves as a reminder that while commendable actions and discernment are vital, maintaining a fervent love for Christ is equally important. The call to repentance and a return to their first love emphasizes the centrality of a deep and intimate relationship with Jesus. Christ encourages perseverance, discernment, and a passion for Him while warning against spiritual decline and its potential consequences.

Verse 8: "To the angel of the church in Smyrna write: These are the words of him who is the First and the Last, who died and came to life again."

• John is instructed to write a message to the church in Smyrna, introducing the imagery of Christ as the First and the Last, emphasizing His death and resurrection.

Interpretation and Commentary:

1. Smyrna: Smyrna was another of the seven churches in Asia Minor, and it was known for its steadfast Christian community.

2. First and the Last: Similar to Revelation 1:17-18, this title highlights Christ's eternal nature and authority over all things. His resurrection is mentioned, emphasizing His triumph over death.

Verse 9: "I know your afflictions and your poverty—yet you are rich! I know about the slander of those who say they are Jews and are not but are a synagogue of Satan."

• Christ acknowledges the church in Smyrna's suffering, poverty, and the slander they endure from those falsely claiming to be Jews.

Interpretation and Commentary:

1. Afflictions and Poverty: The church in Smyrna was facing significant hardships and material poverty. However, Christ reassures them that despite their external circumstances, they are spiritually rich. This echoes Jesus' teachings about the value of spiritual wealth (Matthew 6:19-21).

2. Slander and False Jews: The church is dealing with false accusers who claim to be Jews but are, in reality, opponents of the true faith. This reference to a "synagogue of Satan" likely pertains to those opposing Christianity.

Verse 10: "Do not be afraid of what you are about to suffer. I tell you, the devil will put some of you in prison to test you, and you will suffer persecution for ten days. Be faithful, even to the point of death, and I will give you life as your victor's crown."

• Christ forewarns the church in Smyrna of impending suffering and persecution but encourages them to remain faithful, promising eternal life as a victor's crown for those who endure.

Interpretation and Commentary:

1. Suffering and Persecution: The church is told that some of its members will face imprisonment and persecution as a test of their faith. This aligns with Jesus' teachings that believers may face trials and persecution for their faith (Matthew 24:9-13).

2. Faithfulness: Christ emphasizes the importance of remaining faithful, even in the face of extreme adversity. The promise of a victor's crown underscores the eternal reward for those who endure faithfully.

Verse 11: "Whoever has ears, let them hear what the Spirit says to the churches. The one who is victorious will not be hurt at all by the second death."

• Christ concludes His message to Smyrna by urging spiritual attentiveness and promising that those who overcome will be spared from the second death.

Interpretation and Commentary:

1. Spiritual Hearing: As in previous messages, Christ emphasizes the need to heed the Spirit's message. Spiritual understanding and obedience are crucial.

2. The Second Death: The second death refers to eternal separation from God in the lake of fire, as mentioned in Revelation 20:14-15. The promise that the victorious will not be hurt by the second death assures believers of their eternal security in Christ.

Verse 12: "To the angel of the church in Pergamum write: These are the words of him who has the sharp, double-edged sword."

• John is instructed to write a message to the church in Pergamum, introducing the imagery of Christ holding a sharp, double-edged sword.

Interpretation and Commentary:

1. Pergamum: Pergamum was another of the seven churches, known for its historical significance as a prominent center of culture and religion.

2. Sharp, Double-Edged Sword: This imagery, as previously mentioned in Revelation 1:16, represents the Word of God and the authority of Christ in judgment and discernment.

Verse 13: "I know where you live—where Satan has his throne. Yet you remain true to my name. You did not renounce your faith in me, not even in the days of Antipas, my faithful witness, who was put to death in your city—where Satan lives."

• Christ acknowledges the church in Pergamum's challenging environment, where Satan's influence is strong. Despite this, they have remained faithful, even in the face of martyrdom.

Interpretation and Commentary:

1. Satan's Influence: Pergamum was known for its pagan religious practices and temples, which may have contributed to its association with Satan's throne. The church had to contend with significant spiritual opposition.

2. Faithfulness and Martyrdom: The church's commitment to Christ is commendable, especially in light of the martyrdom of Antipas, who is referred to as Christ's faithful witness. This underscores the high cost of discipleship.

Verse 14: "Nevertheless, I have a few things against you: There are some among you who hold to the teaching of Balaam, who taught Balak to entice the Israelites to sin so that they ate food sacrificed to idols and committed sexual immorality."

• Christ reproves the church in Pergamum for tolerating individuals who adhere to the teachings of Balaam, which led to idolatry and sexual immorality.

Interpretation and Commentary:

1. Teaching of Balaam: The reference to Balaam points to a spiritual compromise within the church, allowing false teaching and immoral behavior to infiltrate their community. Balaam's actions in the Old Testament involved leading the Israelites into sin (Numbers 31:16).

2. Idolatry and Immorality: The specific sins mentioned here likely symbolize spiritual compromise and unfaithfulness to God's commands. Idolatry represents the worship of false gods, and sexual immorality signifies moral unfaithfulness.

Verse 15: "Likewise, you also have those who hold to the teaching of the Nicolaitans."

• Similar to the church in Ephesus (Revelation 2:6), the church in Pergamum is rebuked for tolerating the teachings of the Nicolaitans.

Interpretation and Commentary:

1. Continued Tolerance: The reference to the Nicolaitans suggests that this issue was not unique to one church. The Nicolaitan teachings likely promoted compromise with pagan practices and immorality within the Christian community.

Verse 16: "Repent therefore! Otherwise, I will soon come to you and will fight against them with the sword of my mouth."

• Christ continues His message to the church in Pergamum, urging them to repent and warning of His impending judgment. Interpretation and Commentary:

1. Call to Repentance: The call to repentance remains a central theme. Christ desires the church to turn away from false teachings and compromise, emphasizing the urgency of this call.

2. Sword of My Mouth: This phrase echoes the earlier imagery of the sharp, double-edged sword (Revelation 1:16). It symbolizes the power of Christ's spoken word in judgment and discernment. He will confront and judge those who persist in error.

Verse 17: "Whoever has ears, let them hear what the Spirit says to the churches. To the one who is victorious, I will give some of the hidden manna. I will also give that person a white stone with a new name written on it, known only to the one who receives it."

• Christ concludes His message to Pergamum by emphasizing the importance of spiritual understanding and offering promises to the victorious.

Interpretation and Commentary:

1. Spiritual Hearing: As in previous messages, Christ emphasizes the need to heed the Spirit's message. Spiritual understanding and obedience are crucial.

2. Hidden Manna: This reference to hidden manna likely symbolizes the spiritual nourishment and sustenance that believers receive from Christ. It may allude to the provision of God in the wilderness, as in the case of manna provided to the Israelites (Exodus 16:15).

3. White Stone with a New Name: In biblical times, a white stone was often used as a token of acquittal or admission to a banquet. The new name, known only to the recipient, may symbolize a unique and personal relationship with Christ, reflecting His intimate knowledge of each believer.

Verse 18: "To the angel of the church in Thyatira write: These are the words of the Son of God, whose eyes are like blazing fire and whose feet are like burnished bronze."

• John is instructed to write a message to the church in Thyatira, introducing the imagery of Christ as the Son of God with fiery eyes and feet like burnished bronze.

Interpretation and Commentary:

1. Thyatira: Thyatira was another of the seven churches in Asia Minor, known for its trade guilds and associations.

2. Son of God: Christ is introduced with the title "Son of God," emphasizing His divine nature and authority.

3. Eyes like Blazing Fire: This imagery represents Christ's penetrating gaze and judgment, signifying His knowledge of all things and His ability to discern truth from falsehood.

4. Feet like Burnished Bronze: Burnished bronze is often associated with strength and durability. Christ's feet being like burnished bronze may symbolize His unwavering and firm stance against sin and unrighteousness.

Verse 19: "I know your deeds, your love and faith, your service and perseverance, and that you are now doing more than you did at first."

• Christ commends the church in Thyatira for their good deeds, love, faith, service, perseverance, and growth in their works. Interpretation and Commentary:

1. Good Deeds and Love: The church's positive qualities include their acts of love and their faith in Christ, which is demonstrated through their service to others.

2. Service and Perseverance: Their commitment to serving and their endurance in the face of challenges are acknowledged.

3. Growth in Works: The mention that they are doing "more than you did at first" suggests that the church in Thyatira had been growing in their good works and service to God.

Verse 20: "Nevertheless, I have this against you: You tolerate that woman Jezebel, who calls herself a prophet. By her teaching she misleads my servants into sexual immorality and the eating of food sacrificed to idols."

• Christ rebukes the church in Thyatira for tolerating the influence of a woman referred to as Jezebel, who leads His servants into sexual immorality and idolatry through her false teachings.

Interpretation and Commentary:

1. Jezebel: The reference to Jezebel is symbolic and does not necessarily denote a specific individual. It evokes the image of the wicked Queen Jezebel in the Old Testament (1 Kings 16-21), known for promoting idolatry and immorality.

2. False Teaching: Jezebel's teaching in Thyatira involves leading believers into sexual immorality and participation in idolatrous practices, which is clearly condemned in Christian ethics. Verse 21: "I have given her time to repent of her immorality, but she is unwilling."

• Christ has allowed time for Jezebel to repent of her immoral teachings and actions, but she remains unrepentant. Interpretation and Commentary:

1. Grace and Patience: Christ's patience and grace are evident in giving Jezebel an opportunity to turn away from her sinful ways. This reflects God's desire for repentance and restoration.

2. Unwillingness to Repent: Jezebel's refusal to repent highlights the seriousness of her sin and the importance of genuine repentance in Christian life.

Verse 22: "So I will cast her on a bed of suffering, and I will make those who commit adultery with her suffer intensely, unless they repent of her ways."

• Christ announces His judgment on Jezebel and those who follow her teachings, warning of suffering unless they repent.

Interpretation and Commentary:

1. Divine Judgment: Christ's declaration of casting Jezebel on a bed of suffering indicates His judgment upon her. Those who engage in her sinful practices will also experience intense suffering unless they repent.

Verse 23: "I will strike her children dead. Then all the churches will know that I am he who searches hearts and minds, and I will repay each of you according to your deeds."

• Christ proclaims judgment not only on Jezebel but also on her followers. His omniscience is emphasized, as He searches hearts and minds, and He promises to reward individuals according to their deeds.

Interpretation and Commentary:

1. Divine Omniscience: Christ's ability to search hearts and minds underscores His complete knowledge and discernment of the inner motives and thoughts of individuals.

2. Justice and Judgment: Christ's promise to repay each person according to their deeds highlights the principle of divine justice. This aligns with biblical teachings about God being the righteous Judge (Psalm 7:11) who rewards and punishes based on actions.

Verse 24: "Now I say to the rest of you in Thyatira, to you who do not hold to her teaching and have not learned Satan's so-called deep secrets, 'I will not impose any other burden on you.'"

• Christ addresses the faithful in Thyatira who have not embraced Jezebel's false teachings, assuring them that He will not burden them further.

Interpretation and Commentary:

1. Faithful Remnant: In contrast to those who followed Jezebel's false teachings, there is a faithful remnant within the church who have remained steadfast in their commitment to sound doctrine and moral purity.

2. No Additional Burden: Christ's promise not to impose any other burden on them signifies that these believers will not face further trials or judgment beyond what they have already endured. He recognizes their faithfulness.

Verse 25: "Only hold on to what you have until I come."

• Christ encourages the faithful in Thyatira to continue steadfastly in their faith and adherence to sound doctrine until His return.

Interpretation and Commentary:

1. Endurance and Perseverance: This exhortation emphasizes the importance of remaining faithful and unwavering in their commitment to Christ and His teachings until His second coming. It echoes Jesus' teachings about enduring to the end (Matthew 24:13).

Verse 26: "To the one who is victorious and does my will to the end, I will give authority over the nations."

• Christ promises authority over the nations to those who are victorious and faithfully follow His will until the end.

Interpretation and Commentary:

1. Victorious and Obedient: The promise of authority is extended to those who not only overcome trials and tribulations but also remain obedient to Christ's will throughout their lives.

2. Authority Over the Nations: This promise may signify a future role in Christ's kingdom where believers will have a role in ruling and reigning with Him (Revelation 20:4). It reflects Jesus' promise to His disciples of authority in the coming kingdom (Matthew 19:28).

Verse 27: "That one will rule them with an iron scepter and will dash them to pieces like pottery—just as I have received authority from my Father."

• Christ elaborates on the authority given to the victorious, emphasizing that they will rule the nations with His authority, much like He has received authority from God the Father.

Interpretation and Commentary:

1. Rule with an Iron Scepter: The image of ruling with an iron scepter denotes firm and unyielding authority. It reflects the power and dominion that Christ exercises over the nations, including judgment and justice (Psalm 2:9).

2. Received Authority from the Father: Christ's authority is not self-derived but comes from God the Father. This reaffirms His divine nature and the hierarchical relationship within the Trinity.

Verse 28: "I will also give that one the morning star."

• Christ promises the morning star to the victorious.

Interpretation and Commentary:

1. The Morning Star: In the context of Revelation, the "morning star" likely symbolizes Christ Himself. Jesus refers to Himself as the "bright morning star" in Revelation 22:16. Therefore, this promise signifies a deep and intimate union with Christ, sharing in His glory and radiance.

Verse 29: "Whoever has ears, let them hear what the Spirit says to the churches."

• Christ concludes His message to Thyatira with a call for spiritual attentiveness, highlighting the importance of heeding the Spirit's message.

Interpretation and Commentary:

1. Spiritual Hearing: As in previous messages to the churches, Christ emphasizes the need for spiritual discernment and attentiveness to God's message. It's a call to listen and respond to the Holy Spirit's guidance.

The message to the church in Thyatira serves as a reminder of Christ's unwavering commitment to righteousness and justice. While commending the faithful remnant for their endurance and perseverance, He issues a stern warning against tolerating false teachings and immorality. The promises to the victorious underscore the eternal rewards for those who remain faithful and obedient to Christ until His return.

Prophetic Commentary:

The History of the Church in Smyrna and Its Timeless Lessons from Revelation 2

The church in Smyrna, mentioned in Revelation 2, was an ancient Christian community located in the city of Smyrna (modern-day Izmir, Turkey). It holds a significant place in Christian history, not only due to its biblical mention but also because of its endurance in the face of persecution.

The church in Smyrna faced intense opposition and persecution from both the Roman authorities and local Jewish communities. This hostility often resulted in the suffering and martyrdom of its members. Despite these challenges, the church remained steadfast in its faith and commitment to Christ.

In Revelation 2:8-11, Jesus Christ delivers a message specifically to the church in Smyrna. He commends them for their faithfulness in the midst of tribulation and poverty, acknowledging their enduring patience. Christ also warns them of impending persecution and imprisonment but encourages them to remain faithful, even to the point of death, promising them the crown of life.

Timeless Lessons from Christ's Message to Smyrna:

1. Endurance in Persecution: The church in Smyrna serves as a timeless example of perseverance in the face of adversity. Their unwavering commitment to Christ, even under the threat of persecution and death, teaches us the importance of standing firm in our faith when confronted with challenges.

2. Faithfulness: Christ commends the Smyrnan Christians for their faithfulness. Their dedication to the Lord despite hardships reminds us of the importance of remaining faithful to God's teachings and commands, no matter the circumstances.

3. Trust in God's Promises: Christ's promise of the crown of life to those who remain faithful, even unto death, underscores the trustworthiness of God's promises. It encourages us to place our confidence in God's assurances and look forward to the eternal rewards that await the faithful.

4. Persecution and Suffering: The experience of the Smyrnan church reminds us that persecution and suffering are not uncommon for believers. It challenges us to prepare spiritually for times of trial and tribulation, relying on our faith to sustain us.

5. Staying True to Christ: Despite external pressures, the Smyrnan Christians held fast to their faith in Christ. This serves as a reminder that our loyalty to Jesus should be unwavering, regardless of the challenges we may encounter.

The history and message of the church in Smyrna remind us of the enduring nature of the Christian faith and the importance of remaining steadfast in our devotion to Christ, even when facing trials and persecution. These timeless lessons continue to inspire and guide believers today as they navigate their own journeys of faith.

When John received the visionary messages intended for the seven congregations of the Church of God in Asia Minor, he transcribed Jesus' words: "'I am the Alpha and the Omega, the First and the Last,' and 'What you see, write in a book and send it to the seven churches which are in Asia: to Ephesus, to Smyrna, to Pergamos, to Thyatira, to Sardis, to Philadelphia, and to Laodicea'" (Revelation 1:11).

The sequence of these seven cities, signifying congregations of the Church of God, corresponds to an ancient postal route that interlinked these urban centers. For more context on these messages, you can refer to the article titled "Seven Churches of Revelation." In this discussion, our primary focus centers on the city of Smyrna during the initial and subsequent centuries, the essence of the message it received, and the relevance of Christ's directives to this assembly for our contemporary understanding.

Much like Ephesus, situated just 40 miles to the south, Smyrna welcomed a steady stream of visitors. Benefiting from a superb harbor and the starting point of a well-traveled route into the hinterlands, Smyrna was a frequent stopover for travelers. Founded by the renowned Alexander the Great, this bustling trade hub endures to this day as the modern Turkish city of Izmir, boasting a populace of approximately 2.8 million.

Smyrna in the First Century

During Roman times, Smyrna held the distinction of being the most illustrious city in Asia Minor, successfully competing with Pergamos and Ephesus for preeminence. Its thoroughfares were broad and meticulously paved, bearing witness to its prosperity. The city's history is etched in its currency, with coins from various eras discovered throughout its environs. Smyrna was renowned for its distinguished centers of learning in the fields of science and medicine, as well as for its elegant architectural achievements. Among these structures was the Homerium, a site associated with the claim that Smyrna was one of several places vying for the honor of being the birthplace of the revered poet.

Perched on the slopes of Mt. Pagus, Smyrna boasted a grand theater with seating for an impressive 20,000 spectators. In 23 AD, a temple dedicated to Tiberius and his mother Julia was erected, further enhancing the city's architectural splendor. Notably, the Golden Street, which linked the temples of Zeus and Cybele, was reputed to be the finest of its kind in any ancient city (International Standard Bible Encyclopedia, 1939, "Smyrna").

The Smyrna Christian Congregation

Our knowledge of the first-century congregation in Smyrna is limited. Apart from the mentions of this church in Revelation 1:11 and Revelation 2:8, the Bible provides no further details. However, historians have shed some light on this period, particularly regarding figures like Polycarp and Polycrates, who played significant roles during the second century in Smyrna and Ephesus.

Polycarp, a prominent individual in early Christian history, was a disciple of the apostle John and later assumed the role of bishop in Smyrna. While the biblical record is silent about this connection, the historical accounts underscore his close association with the apostolic era. Notably, Polycarp's relationship with the apostle John is reflected in the divergence between the practices of the Christians in Asia and those in Rome concerning the observance of Passover, one of God's annual festivals. This variance demonstrates the direct link between Polycarp and the teachings of the apostles.

Additionally, noteworthy historians such as Ignatius and Irenaeus corroborate the claim that Polycarp received instruction from the apostle John. These historical insights provide valuable context for understanding the early Christian community in Smyrna and its connection to the apostolic age.

The Pressure to Abandon Passover

Amidst the evolving practices of early Christian congregations, a notable distinction emerged regarding the observance of Passover. While the churches in Rome had transitioned to celebrating Easter as a replacement for Passover, Polycarp and the congregations in Asia adhered to the biblical requirement of observing Passover on the 14th day of Nisan, the first month (as stipulated in Leviticus 23:5). This divergence became evident because Easter consistently fell on a Sunday, whereas Passover could fall on various days of the week, contingent upon the annual calendar.

This distinction between the Roman churches and those in Asia persisted throughout the lifetimes of Polycarp and Pope Anicetus. Subsequently, Pope Victor of Rome embarked on an effort to standardize practices across Christian congregations by pressuring the Asian churches to relinquish their observance of Passover in favor of adopting Easter.

Upholding the Observance of Passover

The leaders of the Asian congregations, under the guidance of Polycrates, made a resolute decision to remain steadfast in their adherence to the practice they had received from the apostles of the first century. In conveying their determination, Polycrates penned a letter to Pope Victor, outlining their rationale:

"We steadfastly adhere to the exact day, making no alterations. Moreover, in Asia, numerous luminaries in the faith have fallen asleep, destined to rise on the day of the Lord's glorious return. On that day, He shall come from heaven in His resplendent glory to gather all His saints. Among these luminaries are Philip, one of the twelve apostles, who rested in Hierapolis, along with his two venerable virgin daughters, and another daughter who lived in the Holy Spirit and now rests in Ephesus. Also, John, the beloved disciple, who bore witness and imparted teachings, reclining on the Lord's bosom. He, a priest, bore the sacerdotal plate and passed away in Ephesus.

Additionally, Polycarp, the bishop and martyr of Smyrna, and Thraseas, the bishop and martyr from Eumeneia, who rested in Smyrna, must be mentioned. Why not recount Bishop and Martyr Sagaris, who passed away in Laodicea, or the revered Papirius, or Melito the Eunuch, who lived wholly in the Holy Spirit and now rests in Sardis, awaiting his heavenly episcopate upon resurrection? All these faithfully observed the fourteenth day of Passover in accordance with the Gospel, making no deviations but adhering to the rule of faith.

As for myself, Polycrates, the least among you, I follow the tradition of my forebears, some of whom I have closely followed. Seven of my forebears served as bishops, and I am the eighth. My forebears consistently observed the day when the people put away leaven.

The Message to the Church in Smyrna

The message directed to the church in Smyrna reads as follows:

"To the angel of the church in Smyrna, write: 'These words are spoken by the First and the Last, who was once dead and has come back to life: I know about your deeds, your tribulation, and your financial struggles (though you are rich). I am also aware of the slander from those who claim to be Jews but are not; they are, in fact, a congregation of Satan.

Do not fear what you are about to suffer. The devil is planning to throw some of you into prison, putting you to the test for ten days. Remain faithful, even if it means facing death, and I will grant you the crown of life. Whoever possesses ears, let them hear the message the Spirit conveys to the churches. Those who conquer will not be harmed by the second death.'" (Revelation 2:8-11)

Meaning of the Message

The message to the church in Smyrna carries several significant points. Firstly, it emphasizes that God is fully aware of their deeds, just as He possesses knowledge of our actions and even our thoughts (Psalm 94:11).

Furthermore, God acknowledges the tribulations and financial struggles endured by the Smyrna congregation. He is also cognizant of the presence of individuals falsely claiming to be Jews. Concerning these individuals, it remains somewhat unclear why Christ identified them as blasphemers and a congregation of Satan, but it appears that they contributed to the hardships faced by the Smyrna church.

While the first-century apostles and Church of God members interacted with numerous Jews, the exact reasons for Christ's strong language against these individuals in Smyrna remain uncertain. However, in subsequent centuries, this hostility toward Christians in Smyrna persisted. Notably, during the martyrdom of Polycarp, the Jews of Smyrna played a particularly fervent role in demanding his execution.

Some interpret the condemnation of those claiming to be Jewish in a literal sense, implying that these individuals were descendants of the tribe of Judah. Nevertheless, another interpretation exists. In his letter to the Romans, the apostle Paul asserted that true Jews are those of the heart, not merely by outward appearance (Romans 2:28-29). In this spiritual sense, all Christians, regardless of their ethnic backgrounds, are considered Jews.

If we understand the reference to Jews in Smyrna in this spiritual context, it aligns with certain historical developments within the Christian church. Some who identified as Christians began to deviate from the foundational principles of the Church of God, such as the observance of the Passover. They retained the label "Christian" while abandoning the core teachings established by Jesus and the apostles in the first century.

The statement about their "poverty (but you are rich)" underscores that, despite their financial hardships, the members of the church in Smyrna were spiritually wealthy in their relationship with God. This concept, as articulated by the apostle Paul, highlights that the Lord is rich in blessings for all who call upon Him (Romans 10:12; see also 2 Corinthians 8:9).

In the face of trials, the message to the Smyrna church encourages them to remain faithful even unto death, despite tribulations and poverty. History offers examples of individuals like Polycarp who heeded this call to faithfulness.

Relevance for Today

In His concluding words to the church in Smyrna, Jesus delivered a vital message: "He who has an ear, let him hear what the Spirit says to the churches. He who overcomes shall not be hurt by the second death" (Revelation 2:11). Similar to His closing remarks to the Ephesian church, Jesus reiterates the importance of heeding all the messages imparted to the various churches to secure eternal life.

The counsel given to Smyrna holds enduring relevance for us today. We, too, must exhibit unwavering faith in the face of tribulation or poverty. To maintain our faithfulness to God, we must follow in the footsteps of the early Christians in Smyrna and resist the pressures that seek to lead us away from "the faith which was once for all delivered to the saints" (Jude 3-4).

Throughout the years, many practices established by Jesus, the apostles, and the first-century Church have been set aside in favor of human reasoning. A pertinent example is the disregard some have for the biblical holy days. Often, individuals falsely rationalize that it is acceptable to worship God through humanly devised celebrations rather than on the days He specifically ordained.

God holds a promising future for those who are willing to heed His instructions. The timeless lessons contained in Christ's message to Smyrna urge us to maintain our faithfulness, regardless of external influences. Let us remain steadfast and resolute, undeterred by detractors, as we journey forward in faith!

CHAPTER THREE

The Dead, the Faithful, and the Lukewarm Church

Introduction:

Chapter 3 of the Book of Revelation continues with the letters to the seven churches in Asia Minor. In this chapter, John records messages from Jesus to the churches in Sardis, Philadelphia, and Laodicea. Each of these letters follows a similar format, providing commendations, criticisms, exhortations, and promises tailored to the unique spiritual condition of each church. These letters serve as both historical messages to the specific congregations in John's time and timeless lessons for the broader Church.

The letter to the church in Sardis begins with commendations for having a reputation for being alive but is followed by a stern criticism that they are actually spiritually dead. The church is called to wake up, strengthen what remains, and repent. The promise for those who overcome is that their names will not be blotted out from the Book of Life. The letter to the church in Philadelphia, in contrast, offers no criticisms. Instead, it commends the believers for their faithfulness and endurance, emphasizing an open door that no one can shut. Jesus promises to keep them from the hour of trial that is coming upon the world. Lastly, the letter to the church in Laodicea presents a strong rebuke for being lukewarm, neither hot nor cold. The church is encouraged to buy refined gold, white garments, and eye salve as symbols of spiritual wealth and healing. Jesus stands at the door, knocking, and those who open the door to Him will enjoy fellowship and victory. These letters highlight the importance of genuine faith, spiritual vigilance, and wholehearted devotion to Christ within the Church.

Verse 1: "To the angel of the church in Sardis write: These are the words of him who holds the seven spirits of God and the seven stars. I know your deeds; you have a reputation of being alive, but you are dead."

- Christ addresses the church in Sardis and identifies Himself as the one who holds the seven spirits of God and the seven stars. He acknowledges their reputation but reveals that they are spiritually dead.

Interpretation and Commentary:

1. Sardis: Sardis was one of the seven churches in Asia Minor. Historically, it was known for its wealth and prominence.

2. Seven Spirits and Stars: The reference to the seven spirits of God and the seven stars echoes previous imagery in Revelation (Revelation 1:4, 1:16). The seven spirits represent the fullness and perfection of the Holy Spirit, while the stars signify the angels or messengers of the churches.

3. Spiritual Deadness: Despite their outward appearance and reputation, the church in Sardis is spiritually lifeless. This serves as a solemn warning against complacency and hypocrisy within the church.

Verse 2: "Wake up! Strengthen what remains and is about to die, for I have found your deeds unfinished in the sight of my God."

- Christ admonishes the church in Sardis to awaken from their spiritual lethargy, strengthen what little spiritual vitality remains, and complete the unfinished work in God's sight.

Interpretation and Commentary:

1. Call to Repentance: The call to "wake up" emphasizes the need for spiritual revival and renewal. Christ desires the church to recognize their spiritual condition and take action to correct it.

2. Unfinished Deeds: The church's deeds, while visible, are incomplete in the eyes of God. This implies a lack of genuine faithfulness and dedication to God's purposes.

Verse 3: "Remember, therefore, what you have received and heard; hold it fast, and repent. But if you do not wake up, I will come like a thief, and you will not know at what time I will come to you."

- Christ urges the church in Sardis to remember and hold fast to the teachings they have received, to repent, and warns of His sudden and unexpected return if they fail to do so.

Interpretation and Commentary:

1. Remember and Hold Fast: The call to remember and hold fast to God's Word and teachings is a common theme throughout the Bible, emphasizing the importance of faithfulness and obedience (Hebrews 2:1).
2. Repentance: Christ's call to repentance is a recurring theme in Revelation, highlighting the necessity of turning away from sin and returning to faithful obedience.
3. Thief in the Night: The reference to Christ coming like a thief underscores the element of surprise and the need for readiness. It echoes Jesus' own teachings about His unexpected return (Matthew 24:43-44).

Verse 4: "Yet you have a few people in Sardis who have not soiled their clothes. They will walk with me, dressed in white, for they are worthy."

- Christ acknowledges that there are a few individuals in Sardis who have remained spiritually pure. He promises them white garments and the privilege of walking with Him.

Interpretation and Commentary:

1. Faithful Remnant: Despite the overall spiritual condition of the church, there is a faithful remnant who have maintained their spiritual purity and righteousness.
2. White Garments: White garments symbolize purity and righteousness in the Bible (Revelation 19:8). Those who remain faithful will be clothed in these garments, signifying their worthiness and acceptance.

Verse 5: "The one who is victorious will, like them, be dressed in white. I will never blot out the name of that person from the book of life, but will acknowledge that name before my Father and his angels."

- Christ promises that those who overcome will also be clothed in white garments and assures that their names will never be removed from the book of life. He will acknowledge them before the Father and His angels.

Interpretation and Commentary:

1. Victorious and White Garments: The promise of white garments and eternal acceptance is extended to all who overcome through faith in Christ. It signifies their righteousness and eternal security.
2. Book of Life: The book of life contains the names of those who belong to God and have eternal life. Christ's assurance that names will not be blotted out reinforces the concept of eternal security for believers (Revelation 20:15).
3. Acknowledgment Before the Father: This indicates that Christ will publicly declare the faithful before God the Father and His angels, affirming their status as His own.

Verse 6: "Whoever has ears, let them hear what the Spirit says to the churches."

- Christ concludes His message to the church in Sardis with a reminder of the importance of spiritual attentiveness and heeding the Spirit's message.

Interpretation and Commentary:

1. Spiritual Hearing: This recurring phrase emphasizes the need for spiritual discernment and attentiveness to God's message. It serves as an invitation to listen and respond to the Holy Spirit's guidance.

Verse 7: "To the angel of the church in Philadelphia write: These are the words of him who is holy and true, who holds the key of David. What he opens no one can shut, and what he shuts no one can open."

- Christ addresses the church in Philadelphia and introduces Himself as the holy and true one who holds the key of David, signifying His authority.

Interpretation and Commentary:

1. Philadelphia: Philadelphia was another of the seven churches in Asia Minor. It was situated in a strategic location and was known for its loyalty to Rome.
2. Holy and True: Christ's description as holy and true underscores His moral purity and absolute truthfulness. This title emphasizes His divine attributes.
3. Key of David: The reference to the key of David alludes to Isaiah 22:22 and signifies Christ's authority and control over

access to God's kingdom. What He opens or shuts, no one can alter.

Verse 8: "I know your deeds. See, I have placed before you an open door that no one can shut. I know that you have little strength, yet you have kept my word and have not denied my name."

- Christ acknowledges the deeds of the church in Philadelphia and mentions that He has opened a door for them that cannot be closed. Despite their limited strength, they have remained faithful to His word and name.

Interpretation and Commentary:

1. Open Door: The open door symbolizes opportunities and blessings that Christ has provided for the church in Philadelphia. It signifies divine favor and access to God's purposes.

2. Little Strength: The church may have been small or faced challenges, but Christ commends their faithfulness despite their limitations. It underscores the principle that God's strength is made perfect in weakness (2 Corinthians 12:9).

3. Faithfulness to Christ's Word: Their commitment to keeping Christ's word and not denying His name demonstrates their unwavering faith in Him, even when faced with difficulties.

Verse 9: "I will make those who are of the synagogue of Satan, who claim to be Jews though they are not, but are liars—I will make them come and fall down at your feet and acknowledge that I have loved you."

- Christ promises to deal with those who falsely claim to be Jews but are not, likely referring to opponents or false teachers. He will make them acknowledge His love for the faithful in Philadelphia.

Interpretation and Commentary:

1. Synagogue of Satan: This phrase implies a group opposing the Christian faith. Christ will expose their falsehood and hypocrisy.

2. Acknowledgment of Love: Christ's promise reflects the ultimate vindication of His faithful followers. Those who falsely opposed them will recognize that God's love is with the believers.

Verse 10: "Since you have kept my command to endure patiently, I will also keep you from the hour of trial that is going to come on the whole world to test the inhabitants of the earth."

- Christ commends the church in Philadelphia for patiently enduring and promises to protect them from a coming global trial intended to test the world's inhabitants.

Interpretation and Commentary:

1. Endurance and Patience: The church's patient endurance in the face of trials is highly praised. This promise echoes Jesus' teachings about the need for endurance during tribulations (Matthew 24:13).

2. Protection from the Hour of Trial: Christ assures believers in Philadelphia that they will be spared from a future, worldwide trial. The exact nature of this trial is a matter of interpretation, but it emphasizes God's providential care for His faithful.

Verse 11: "I am coming soon. Hold on to what you have, so that no one will take your crown."

- Christ reaffirms His imminent return and urges the church to hold fast to their faith and rewards, warning against losing their crowns.

Interpretation and Commentary:

1. Imminent Return: Christ's declaration of coming soon underscores the expectation of His second coming throughout the New Testament (Revelation 22:20).

2. Hold On to What You Have: The exhortation to "hold on" emphasizes the importance of remaining faithful and not letting go of their spiritual blessings or rewards.

3. Preservation of Crowns: Believers are encouraged to persevere to ensure they do not forfeit the rewards and blessings promised to them. Crowns often represent various aspects of heavenly rewards (2 Timothy 4:8).

Verse 12: "The one who is victorious I will make a pillar in the temple of my God. Never again will they leave it. I will write on them the name of my God and the name of the city of my God, the new Jerusalem, which is coming down out of heaven from my God; and I will also write on them my new name."

- Christ promises special honors and blessings to those who are victorious, including becoming a permanent fixture in the temple of God, bearing the names of God, the new Jerusalem, and Christ's new name.

Interpretation and Commentary:

1. Pillar in the Temple: Being made a pillar in the temple symbolizes stability, permanence, and honor within God's dwelling place. It signifies the eternal presence and standing of the victorious believers.
2. Names of God and the New Jerusalem: Having the names of God and the new Jerusalem written on them signifies a deep and eternal connection with God's heavenly city and His divine nature.
3. Christ's New Name: The mention of Christ's new name suggests a unique and intimate relationship with Him in His glorified state.

Verse 13: "Whoever has ears, let them hear what the Spirit says to the churches."

- Christ concludes His message to the church in Philadelphia with a reminder of the importance of spiritual attentiveness and heeding the Spirit's message.

Interpretation and Commentary:

1. Spiritual Hearing: This recurring phrase emphasizes the need for spiritual discernment and attentiveness to God's message. It serves as an invitation to listen and respond to the Holy Spirit's guidance.

Verse 14: "To the angel of the church in Laodicea write: These are the words of the Amen, the faithful and true witness, the ruler of God's creation."

- Christ addresses the church in Laodicea and introduces Himself as the "Amen," the faithful and true witness, and the ruler of God's creation.

Interpretation and Commentary:

1. Laodicea: Laodicea was another of the seven churches in Asia Minor. It was known for its wealth and self-sufficiency.
2. The Amen: "Amen" signifies truth and certainty. Christ, as the "Amen," is the embodiment of truth and the final authority.

3. Faithful and True Witness: Christ's faithfulness and truthfulness are emphasized, highlighting His reliability and accuracy as a witness.

4. Ruler of God's Creation: This title underscores Christ's sovereignty and authority over all of God's creation, emphasizing His divine nature.

Verse 15: "I know your deeds, that you are neither cold nor hot. I wish you were either one or the other!"

- Christ acknowledges the deeds of the church in Laodicea but criticizes their spiritual lukewarmness, expressing a desire for either hot or cold faith.

Interpretation and Commentary:

1. Lukewarmness: The term "lukewarm" symbolizes a lack of spiritual fervor and commitment. Christ finds their spiritual condition displeasing.

2. Hot or Cold: Christ expresses a preference for either passionate devotion (hot) or a clear stance against Him (cold) over spiritual indifference.

Revelation 3:16 (ESV) states:

"So, because you are lukewarm, and neither hot nor cold, I will spit you out of my mouth."

Interpretation and Commentary:

This verse is part of the message to the church in Laodicea, one of the seven churches addressed in Revelation 2-3. Jesus uses the metaphor of being "lukewarm" to convey a powerful spiritual message:

1. Lukewarmness: Being "lukewarm" suggests a state of spiritual indifference or complacency. The people in Laodicea were neither passionately committed to their faith (symbolized by being "hot") nor openly rejecting it (symbolized by being "cold"). Instead, they seemed apathetic and self-satisfied.

2. Warning of Rejection: Jesus' statement, "I will spit you out of my mouth," conveys a strong sense of displeasure and rejection. It indicates that a lukewarm faith is unacceptable to Him. It's a call to genuine devotion and commitment rather than mere lip service.

Bible References:
- The idea of being "hot" or "cold" has historical and regional significance in Laodicea. Nearby Hierapolis had hot springs, known for their healing properties, and Colossae had cold, refreshing mountain waters. Laodicea had neither; its water source was lukewarm and mineral-rich, which serves as the backdrop for this metaphor.

Spiritual Application:

This verse challenges believers to examine the depth of their faith and commitment to Christ. It warns against complacency and half-hearted devotion. Instead, it calls for fervent and genuine love for God. It's a reminder that God desires a passionate and wholehearted relationship with His followers, not a lukewarm or apathetic one.

It's important to note that this message is not about works-based salvation but about the sincerity and depth of one's relationship with God. Jesus invites those in Laodicea, and all believers, to repent, turn from their lukewarmness, and embrace a fervent and authentic faith in Him.

In summary, Revelation 3:16 serves as a warning against spiritual indifference and complacency. It encourages believers to be passionately committed to their faith and relationship with Christ, rather than settling for a lukewarm or apathetic attitude.

Verse 17: "You say, 'I am rich; I have acquired wealth and do not need a thing.' But you do not realize that you are wretched, pitiful, poor, blind, and naked."
- Christ rebukes the Laodicean church for their spiritual complacency, despite their material wealth and self-sufficiency.

Interpretation and Commentary:
1. Spiritual Blindness: The Laodicean church's self-sufficiency has led to spiritual blindness. They are unable to see their true spiritual condition, which is characterized by poverty and need.
2. Spiritual Poverty: Despite their material wealth, they are spiritually impoverished and in need of the riches found in Christ (Matthew 5:3).

Verse 18: "I counsel you to buy from me gold refined in the fire so you can become rich and white clothes to wear so you can cover your shameful nakedness and salve to put on your eyes so you can see."

- Christ counsels the Laodicean church to seek true spiritual wealth, righteousness, and vision through Him.

Interpretation and Commentary:

1. Gold Refined in Fire: This symbolizes genuine faith and spiritual riches obtained through trials and purification (1 Peter 1:7).
2. White Clothes: These represent spiritual purity and righteousness. Believers need Christ's righteousness to cover their spiritual nakedness (Revelation 19:8).
3. Salve for the Eyes: This signifies the need for spiritual insight and discernment, which can only come through a deeper relationship with Christ (Ephesians 1:18).

Verse 19: "Those whom I love I rebuke and discipline. So be earnest and repent."

- Christ emphasizes His love for the Laodicean church and admonishes them to take His rebuke and discipline seriously by repenting.

Interpretation and Commentary:

1. Divine Love: Christ's rebuke and discipline are rooted in His love for His people. Discipline is a sign of His desire for their spiritual well-being (Hebrews 12:6).
2. Call to Repentance: The Laodicean church is called to respond to Christ's correction with earnest repentance, turning away from their spiritual indifference.

Verse 20: "Here I am! I stand at the door and knock. If anyone hears my voice and opens the door, I will come in and eat with that person, and they with me."

- Christ offers a gracious invitation to anyone who will open the door of their heart to Him. He desires a close and intimate relationship with them.

Interpretation and Commentary:

1. Door of the Heart: Christ's knocking at the door symbolizes His desire to enter into a personal and intimate relationship with individuals. It is an invitation to salvation and fellowship (John 10:9).
2. Shared Fellowship: The imagery of eating together signifies communion and close fellowship with Christ. It reflects His

desire for a deep and meaningful relationship with believers (Revelation 19:9).

Verse 21: "To the one who is victorious, I will give the right to sit with me on my throne, just as I was victorious and sat down with my Father on his throne."

- Christ promises those who are victorious that they will share in His victory and have the privilege of reigning with Him.

Interpretation and Commentary:

1. Victory and Throne Sharing: Believers who overcome will share in Christ's victory and authority, symbolized by sitting with Him on His throne. This echoes the promise of reigning with Christ in His kingdom (Revelation 20:4).

Verse 22: "Whoever has ears, let them hear what the Spirit says to the churches."

- Christ concludes His message to the Laodicean church with a reminder of the importance of spiritual attentiveness and heeding the Spirit's message.

Interpretation and Commentary:

1. Spiritual Hearing: This recurring phrase emphasizes the need for spiritual discernment and attentiveness to God's message. It serves as an invitation to listen and respond to the Holy Spirit's guidance.

In this message to the church in Laodicea, Christ's rebuke is balanced with His love and invitation to fellowship. He calls them to recognize their spiritual condition, repent, and open their hearts to Him. The promise of sharing in His victory and throne underscores the gracious offer of eternal rewards and a close relationship with Him.

Prophetic Commentary:

The History of Philadelphia

Situated in modern-day Turkey along the Cogamus River, approximately 105 miles east of Smyrna and 25 miles southeast of Sardis, Philadelphia had a relatively later founding compared to many other cities in Asia Minor. It was established sometime after 189 B.C. along one of the highways leading to the region's interior.

Philadelphia, which means "brotherly love," received its name in honor of Attalus II, as a tribute to his loyalty to his elder brother, Eumenes II, who was the king of Lydia. The city also went by other names, including Decapolis, denoting its status as one of the ten cities on the plain. During the 1st century AD, it was known as Neo-kaisaria, as evidenced by coins minted during that era. Additionally, it was referred to as Flavia during the reign of Vespasian.

Its present-day name, Ala-shehir, is thought by some to be derived from the Turkish words "Allah-shehir," meaning "the city of God," although it is more likely linked to the reddish color of the local soil. Philadelphia also earned the epithet "Little Athens" due to the grandeur of its temples and other public structures.

Philadelphia rapidly grew into a significant and prosperous trading center. As coastal cities declined, it gained in prominence and maintained its importance, even into the late Byzantine period. However, like other cities in Asia Minor, Philadelphia frequently faced the need for reconstruction due to earthquakes. Roman emperors often provided assistance in rebuilding these cities. In the early 1st century, the renowned historian Strabo, who hailed from the region, noted the damage to the city's houses caused by earthquakes.

Today, a few remnants of Philadelphia's past can still be observed, including architectural elements, sections of walls, and the foundations of churches spanning various centuries.

The Message

"To the angel of the church in Philadelphia, write: 'These words are spoken by the Holy One, the True One, He who possesses the key of David, who opens and no one can shut, who shuts and no one can open: I know your deeds. Look, I have set before you an open door, and no one can shut it; for you have little strength, yet you have kept My word and have not denied My name.

'Indeed, I will make those from the synagogue of Satan, who claim to be Jews yet are not, but are lying—indeed, I will make them come and bow before your feet and acknowledge that I have loved you. Because you have kept My command to endure, I will also keep you from the hour of trial that is going to come upon the whole world to test those who dwell on the earth.

'Look, I am coming quickly! Hold fast to what you have, so that no one may take your crown. The one who conquers, I will make him a pillar in the temple of My God, and he will never leave it. I will inscribe on him the name of My God and the name of the city of My God, the New Jerusalem, which descends from heaven, from My God. I will also write on him My new name. Let the one who has an ear, hear what the Spirit says to the churches.'" (Revelation 3:7-13, emphasis added throughout)

The Explanation

The message to the church in Philadelphia commences with Christ's declaration that He possesses "the key of David," emphasizing His exclusive authority. He asserts that what He opens, no one can close, and what He shuts, no one can open (Revelation 3:7).

This statement echoes a similar passage in Isaiah 22:20-22, where Eliakim is entrusted with the key of the house of David, symbolizing his authority to regulate access to David's house. Eliakim had the power to determine who could enter and exit.

Christ's proclamation of having "the key of David" carries significant implications:

First, in fulfillment of prophecy, Christ has inherited "the throne of His father David" (Luke 1:32).

Second, He wields the authority to open and close doors for the benefit of the congregation in Philadelphia. His decisions in this regard are irreversible.

Regarding how Christ exercised this authority to open or close doors, He proceeds to convey to the Philadelphia church that He is well aware of their deeds. He assures them that He has opened "an open door" for them, and no one can obstruct it. This assurance is granted to them because, despite their limited strength, they have remained faithful to His teachings and have not renounced His name (verse 8).

The Synagogue of Satan

Moving forward, Jesus declares that He will compel "those of the synagogue of Satan, who say they are Jews and are not," to worship before the members in Philadelphia and acknowledge His love for them (Revelation 3:9). Although it is evident that Jesus is making these individuals, part of the "synagogue of Satan," aware of His love and respect for the Philadelphia church, it remains somewhat unclear who these individuals claiming to be Jews within this synagogue of Satan truly are.

This reference to people falsely professing to be Jews mirrors Christ's words to Smyrna: "I know the blasphemy of those who say they are Jews and are not, but are a synagogue of Satan" (Revelation 2:9). As discussed in the article on Smyrna, the implication of individuals falsely claiming to be Jews might extend to those falsely asserting themselves as Christians.

As elucidated by Paul, all Christians, regardless of their ethnic background, are regarded as spiritual Jews: "For he is not a Jew who is one outwardly, nor is circumcision that which is outward in the flesh; but he is a Jew who is one inwardly; and circumcision is that of the heart, in the Spirit, not in the letter; whose praise is not from men but from God" (Romans 2:28-29).

The underlying message behind Christ's actions toward those labeled as the "synagogue of Satan" is to demonstrate His love and respect for them and for others to witness. As established in previous articles within this series on the seven churches of Revelation, the Church of God, founded by Jesus and the apostles, encountered substantial persecution over the centuries.

This persecution emanated from the Roman government, Jewish adherents of Judaism, and individuals who professed to be Christians but did not steadfastly adhere to the teachings of Christ and the apostles. (The Smyrna article elucidates the challenges devout Christians faced in the second century with others who claimed to be Christians but had mistakenly abandoned the observance of Passover in favor of Easter.)

The Hour of Testing

Because the members in Philadelphia persevered in keeping Christ's command, He assures them that they will be shielded from "the hour of trial which shall come upon the whole world" (Revelation 3:10). While some have sought a historical fulfillment of this period of trial, such as a particularly severe persecution by a Roman emperor, the central interpretation of this phrase pertains to the challenging circumstances that will prevail at the end of this age, just prior to Christ's return.

When explaining to His disciples the conditions that would confront His faithful followers upon His return, Jesus stated, "Then they will deliver you up to tribulation and kill you, and you will be hated by all nations for My name's sake. And then many will be offended, will betray one another, and will hate one another" (Matthew 24:9-10).

In a subsequent section of the same chapter, He elaborated: "For then there will be great tribulation, such as has not been since the beginning of the world until this time, no, nor ever shall be. And unless those days were shortened, no flesh would be saved; but for the elect's sake those days will be shortened" (verses 21-22).

Considering that the chronological progression of the Church is one of the methods to comprehend the messages directed to the seven churches, it becomes evident that "the hour of trial" signifies the Great Tribulation, which will unfold immediately before Christ's second coming. As the world approaches the brink of self-destruction and devout Christians face hatred and even martyrdom, Christ pledges protection for those residing in Philadelphia during this particularly tumultuous period in human history that will "test those who dwell on the earth" (Revelation 3:10).

While these harrowing events transpire, Jesus urges the Philadelphians to steadfastly adhere to God's way of life to ensure that no one seizes their "crown" (verse 11)—their opportunity to attain eternal life and rule alongside Christ over the nations (Revelation 1:6; 2:26; 5:10).

Promises for Victors

The message to the Philadelphia congregation concludes with significant pledges that Christ promises to bestow upon those who prevail. These include the privilege of becoming "a pillar in the temple of My God" and bearing God's "new name" (Revelation 3:12).

The allusion to becoming a pillar in God's temple and the added explanation, "he shall go out no more" (verse 12), would have been profoundly comforting for the Philadelphians. They frequently witnessed the collapse of city buildings, including pillars, due to earthquakes, necessitating inhabitants to exit structures for safety. The prospect of possessing a new name that signifies their belonging to God was undeniably more appealing than the numerous name changes the city of Philadelphia had undergone over time.

Lessons for Us to Embrace

While Christ did not provide any corrective guidance to the church in Philadelphia, there are still valuable insights in this message that are pertinent to us. What pleased Christ about this church was their unwavering commitment in the face of pressure to forsake God's instructions. Instead of renouncing God's name, they remained loyal and seemingly spread the gospel as opportunities arose.

Christ encouraged these devoted members to "hold fast what you have" (verse 11), emphasizing the importance of staying on this righteous path. He also reminded them of His promise to reward those who overcome (verse 12, as seen in Revelation 2:7, 11, 17, 26; 3:5, 21). A significant lesson for us is that once we embark on obeying God and living according to His commands, we must remain steadfast in our commitment.

CHAPTER FOUR

The Throne Room of Heaven

Introduction:

Chapter 4 of the Book of Revelation marks a pivotal moment in John's visionary journey. In this chapter, John is transported into the heavenly realm, and he describes a breathtaking scene of heavenly worship. The chapter begins with the words "After this I looked, and behold, a door standing open in heaven!" This open door symbolizes John's access to a divine revelation, an invitation into God's presence. As he enters heaven, John sees a magnificent throne at the center, and the One seated on it, who is described in terms of divine brilliance. The throne is surrounded by twenty-four elders, dressed in white and wearing crowns, representing the redeemed and glorified saints. There are also flashes of lightning and peals of thunder, emphasizing the majesty and power of God. Seven fiery torches, symbolizing the Holy Spirit's presence and completeness, are before the throne. This chapter sets the stage for the unfolding of the prophetic events that follow in the Book of Revelation, emphasizing God's sovereignty and the heavenly perspective on earthly affairs.

The heavenly worship portrayed in Revelation 4 is a grand and awe-inspiring spectacle. The four living creatures, each with unique faces representing creation (lion, ox, human, eagle), join in ceaseless worship, declaring God's holiness and eternal nature. They cry out, "Holy, holy, holy, is the Lord God Almighty, who was and is and is to come!" This Trisagion (threefold "holy") emphasizes the infinite holiness of God. In response, the twenty-four elders fall down before the throne, casting their crowns and worshiping the One who lives forever. They acknowledge God as the Creator of all things, and their worship underscores the central theme of God's sovereignty and His worthiness to receive glory, honor, and power. Revelation 4 paints a vivid picture of the heavenly throne room and serves as a reminder of the eternal worship that takes place in God's presence, encouraging believers to acknowledge and honor His majesty in their lives.

Verse 1: "After this I looked, and there before me was a door standing open in heaven. And the voice I had first heard speaking to me like a trumpet said, 'Come up here, and I will show you what must take place after this.'"

- John sees a door standing open in heaven, and a voice invites him to come and witness future events.

Interpretation and Commentary:

1. Heavenly Revelation: The open door in heaven symbolizes access to divine revelation. John is given a glimpse of what is to come, indicating that these are heavenly visions.
2. Voice Like a Trumpet: The powerful voice's resemblance to a trumpet signifies its authoritative and commanding nature, highlighting the significance of the message.
3. Events Yet to Occur: John is told that he will witness future events, emphasizing the prophetic nature of the visions he is about to receive.

Verse 2: "At once I was in the Spirit, and there before me was a throne in heaven with someone sitting on it."

- John is immediately in the Spirit and sees a throne in heaven with a divine figure seated on it.

Interpretation and Commentary:

1. In the Spirit: John is granted a spiritual vision, transported into a state of heightened spiritual awareness to perceive heavenly realities.
2. Throne in Heaven: The throne symbolizes God's sovereignty, majesty, and authority over all creation. It is a central image in Revelation, representing divine rule and judgment.
3. Someone Sitting on It: The identity of the One seated on the throne is not explicitly mentioned here, but it is often understood to be God the Father, the ultimate ruler of the universe.

Verse 3: "And the one who sat there had the appearance of jasper and ruby. A rainbow that shone like an emerald encircled the throne."

- The One on the throne has a radiant appearance like jasper and ruby, and a rainbow resembling an emerald encircles the throne.

Interpretation and Commentary:
1. Radiant Appearance: The description of jasper and ruby suggests a dazzling, multicolored brilliance, signifying the splendor and majesty of the One on the throne.
2. Rainbow as a Covenant Sign: The rainbow is a symbol of God's covenant and faithfulness (Genesis 9:12-16). In this context, it underscores God's enduring commitment to His creation and His promises.
3. Emerald Green: The emerald green color of the rainbow might represent renewal and life, reminding us of God's role as the source of life and renewal.

Verse 4: "Surrounding the throne were twenty-four other thrones, and seated on them were twenty-four elders. They were dressed in white and had crowns of gold on their heads."

- Around the central throne, John sees twenty-four other thrones, each with an elder dressed in white and wearing a golden crown.

Interpretation and Commentary:
1. Twenty-Four Elders: The identity of these elders has been interpreted in various ways, including as representatives of the redeemed saints or as angelic beings. Their white garments and crowns suggest a position of honor and authority.
2. White Garments: White is a symbol of purity and righteousness. The elders' attire signifies their holiness and worthiness to stand in God's presence.
3. Golden Crowns: The golden crowns represent victory and honor, possibly indicating that these elders have triumphed and are rewarded for their faithfulness.

Verse 5: "From the throne came flashes of lightning, rumblings, and peals of thunder. In front of the throne, seven lamps were blazing. These are the seven spirits of God."

- Various dramatic phenomena emanate from the throne: lightning, thunder, and seven blazing lamps symbolizing the seven spirits of God.

Interpretation and Commentary:

1. Divine Majesty: The lightning, thunder, and rumblings are symbolic of God's majesty, power, and authority, reminiscent of the awe-inspiring encounter with God on Mount Sinai (Exodus 19:16-18).
2. Seven Lamps: The seven lamps represent the seven spirits of God, symbolizing the fullness and perfection of the Holy Spirit's presence and work (Isaiah 11:2).

Verse 6: "Also in front of the throne there was what looked like a sea of glass, clear as crystal."

- Before the throne, John sees a sea of glass as clear as crystal.

Interpretation and Commentary:

1. Sea of Glass: The sea of glass is often seen as a symbol of purity and tranquility, contrasting with the chaotic and turbulent seas often mentioned in biblical imagery. It represents the peace and order in God's presence.

Verse 7: "In the center, around the throne, were four living creatures, and they were covered with eyes, in front and in back."

- Four living creatures, each covered with eyes on all sides, are positioned around the central throne.

Interpretation and Commentary:

1. Four Living Creatures: These beings are often identified as cherubim or seraphim and are associated with God's divine presence and holiness (Ezekiel 1:5-14; Isaiah 6:2-3).
2. Eyes Everywhere: The multitude of eyes symbolizes their watchfulness, knowledge, and insight into the depths of God's wisdom and creation.

Verse 8: "Each of the four living creatures had six wings and was covered with eyes all around, even under its wings. Day and night they never stop saying: 'Holy, holy, holy is the Lord God Almighty, who was, and is, and is to come.'"

- The four living creatures, covered in eyes and with six wings each, continually proclaim the holiness and eternal nature of the Lord God Almighty.

Interpretation and Commentary:
1. Symbolic Creatures: These four living creatures are highly symbolic and are often associated with heavenly beings who worship and serve God (Isaiah 6:2-3; Ezekiel 1:4-10).
2. Six Wings and Eyes: The six wings indicate their readiness to serve and move swiftly in worship. The eyes symbolize their profound awareness of God's glory and providence in all directions.
3. Trisagion: Their ceaseless declaration of "Holy, holy, holy" emphasizes the holiness and uniqueness of God. The triple repetition is a common biblical way of expressing superlative attributes.
4. Eternal God: The declaration that God is "who was, and is, and is to come" underscores His eternal existence and unchanging nature. This echoes God's self-revelation in Exodus 3:14 (I AM WHO I AM).

Verse 9: "Whenever the living creatures give glory, honor, and thanks to him who sits on the throne and who lives forever and ever,"

- The four living creatures offer continual praise, honor, and gratitude to the One on the throne, emphasizing His eternal nature.

Interpretation and Commentary:
1. Praise and Worship: These heavenly beings engage in an unceasing act of worship, acknowledging God's glory, honor, and eternal life. Their worship sets an example of adoration for all believers.
2. God's Eternal Life: The phrase "who lives forever and ever" reiterates God's unending existence and reign. It contrasts His eternal nature with the transient nature of the created world.

Verse 10: "the twenty-four elders fall down before him who sits on the throne and worship him who lives forever and ever. They lay their crowns before the throne and say:"

- The twenty-four elders, in response to the worship of the living creatures, bow down before the One on the throne, offering their own worship and laying their crowns before Him.

Interpretation and Commentary:

1. Elderly Worship: The twenty-four elders represent a group of honored and redeemed beings. Their act of bowing down and casting their crowns symbolizes their recognition of God's ultimate authority and worthiness.

2. Crown Surrender: By laying their crowns before the throne, the elders express their acknowledgment that all honor and glory belong to God alone, reflecting humility and devotion.

Verse 11: "'You are worthy, our Lord and God, to receive glory and honor and power, for you created all things, and by your will they were created and have their being.'"

- The elders continue their worship by proclaiming the worthiness of the Lord God Almighty, acknowledging His role as the Creator of all things and the sustainer of existence.

Interpretation and Commentary:

1. Worthiness of God: The declaration of God's worthiness to receive glory, honor, and power echoes the eternal praise offered to Him. It emphasizes His inherent greatness and majesty.

2. Creator and Sustainer: The acknowledgment of God as the Creator of all things affirms His role in bringing the universe into existence. Furthermore, recognizing that all things exist by His will underscores His sovereignty and providence over creation (Colossians 1:16-17).

In Revelation 4:1-11, John's vision unveils a heavenly scene of worship and adoration centered around God's throne. The vivid imagery, symbolic creatures, and ceaseless praise highlight the holiness, eternity, and sovereignty of God. The heavenly beings, including the four living creatures and twenty-four elders, serve as models of worship and reverence for believers. This vision sets the stage for the unfolding events and judgments in the book of

Revelation, emphasizing God's central role in the course of human history.

Prophetic Commentary:

In Revelation 4, the apostle John describes a profound vision of God's heavenly throne room. The angelic beings encircling God's throne offer praise and worship to their Creator. In verse 11, John records the words spoken by the 24 elders.

The Creator, God Himself, possesses supreme power and is deserving of all adoration and honor from the very beings He has brought into existence. When even mighty angels recognize this truth, how much more should frail and mortal human beings, uniquely created in the image of God! It is by His divine will that we are granted existence, and it is through His gracious will that He extends to us the extraordinary opportunity to become His own children (1 John 3:1-2).

CHAPTER FIVE

The Lamb Takes the Scroll

Introduction:

Chapter 5 of the Book of Revelation continues John's vision in the heavenly throne room. In this chapter, John sees a scroll in the right hand of the One seated on the throne, which is often referred to as the "title deed to the universe." This scroll represents God's divine plan for history and the unfolding of His redemptive purposes. However, the scroll is sealed with seven seals, signifying that its contents are hidden and that only the One who is worthy can open it. John is deeply distressed because no one in heaven or on earth is found worthy to open the scroll. But then, one of the elders tells John that the Lion of the tribe of Judah, the Root of David, has triumphed and is worthy to open the scroll. John expects to see a mighty lion, but instead, he sees a Lamb, appearing as if it had been slain, standing before the throne. This Lamb, symbolizing Jesus Christ, takes the scroll from the hand of the One on the throne, signifying His authority to carry out God's plan of redemption. This pivotal moment in Revelation underscores Jesus' role as both the conquering Lion and the sacrificial Lamb, the only One worthy to reveal and execute God's divine plan.

The heavenly beings and elders burst into a magnificent song of worship, praising the Lamb for His worthiness. They declare that He was slain and by His blood, He has ransomed people from every tribe and language, making them a kingdom and priests to God. This heavenly worship reflects the profound truth of Christ's sacrificial death and redemption, which is central to the Christian faith. The chapter emphasizes that it is through Jesus, the Lamb, that God's ultimate plan of salvation will be revealed and executed. It sets the stage for the opening of the seals in the subsequent chapters, unveiling the events leading to the consummation of God's kingdom and the ultimate victory of Christ. Chapter 5 serves as a powerful reminder of

Jesus' central role in God's divine plan and His worthiness to receive worship and honor.

Verse 1: "Then I saw in the right hand of him who sat on the throne a scroll with writing on both sides and sealed with seven seals."

- John's vision reveals a scroll in the right hand of the One seated on the throne. This scroll is written on both sides and sealed with seven seals.

Interpretation and Commentary:

1. The Scroll: The scroll represents God's divine plan for the future, which includes both judgments and redemption. It's significant that it is sealed, signifying the secrecy of its contents until the appointed time (Isaiah 29:11).

2. Seven Seals: The seven seals suggest that the scroll contains seven sections or events, each with specific significance. These seals will be opened progressively, unveiling God's plan step by step (Revelation 6-8).

Verse 2: "And I saw a mighty angel proclaiming in a loud voice, 'Who is worthy to break the seals and open the scroll?'"

- A powerful angel makes a proclamation, asking who is worthy to open the sealed scroll.

Interpretation and Commentary:

1. The Angel's Proclamation: This angel's question highlights the importance of finding someone worthy to open the scroll and execute God's divine plan. It reflects the significance of God's unfolding purpose in human history.

Verse 3: "But no one in heaven or on earth or under the earth could open the scroll or even look inside it."

- Initially, no one is found in heaven, on earth, or under the earth who is worthy to open the scroll.

Interpretation and Commentary:

1. Universal Search: The fact that no one in these realms is initially found worthy underscores the gravity of the situation. It demonstrates the need for a uniquely qualified redeemer.

Verse 4: "I wept and wept because no one was found who was worthy to open the scroll or look inside."

- John is overcome with grief because no one is found worthy to open the scroll.

Interpretation and Commentary:

1. John's Grief: John's deep sorrow reflects his awareness of the importance of the scroll and the urgency of its contents. He understands that the fulfillment of God's plan hinges on finding the worthy one.

Verse 5: "Then one of the elders said to me, 'Do not weep! See, the Lion of the tribe of Judah, the Root of David, has triumphed. He is able to open the scroll and its seven seals.'"

- One of the elders comforts John, declaring that the Lion of the tribe of Judah, the Root of David, has triumphed and is worthy to open the scroll.

Interpretation and Commentary:

1. The Lion of the Tribe of Judah: This title identifies the worthy one as Jesus Christ, who is often associated with the tribe of Judah (Genesis 49:10) and the promised Messiah (Isaiah 11:1-10).
2. The Root of David: This title emphasizes Christ's royal lineage and messianic identity as the descendant of King David (Isaiah 11:1, 10). It affirms His authority and right to rule.
3. Triumph Overcame: The declaration that Christ has triumphed signifies His victory over sin and death through His sacrificial death and resurrection (1 Corinthians 15:55-57).

Verse 6: "Then I saw a Lamb, looking as if it had been slain, standing at the center of the throne, encircled by the four living creatures and the elders. The Lamb had seven horns and seven eyes, which are the seven spirits of God sent out into all the earth."

- John sees a Lamb, symbolizing Jesus Christ, at the center of the throne. The Lamb, though bearing the marks of having been slain, has seven horns and seven eyes, representing the fullness of His power and divine knowledge.

Interpretation and Commentary:

1. The Lamb of God: The imagery of a slain Lamb points to Jesus Christ's sacrificial death for the forgiveness of sins (John 1:29). He is the Passover Lamb who redeems humanity.

2. Seven Horns: Horns represent power and authority. The Lamb's seven horns symbolize His complete and absolute sovereignty and strength.

3. Seven Eyes: The seven eyes symbolize the fullness of the Holy Spirit's presence and wisdom, representing Christ's perfect knowledge and discernment (Isaiah 11:2).

4. Encircled by Heavenly Beings: The presence of the Lamb at the center of the throne, surrounded by the four living creatures and the elders, highlights His central role in heaven's worship and administration.

Verse 7: "He went and took the scroll from the right hand of him who sat on the throne."

- The Lamb, Jesus Christ, approaches the throne and takes the scroll from the right hand of God.

Interpretation and Commentary:

1. Authority and Dominion: By taking the scroll, Christ asserts His authority and sovereignty over God's divine plan for the future. This act signifies His role as the executor of God's will.

Verse 8: "And when he had taken it, the four living creatures and the twenty-four elders fell down before the Lamb. Each one had a harp and they were holding golden bowls full of incense, which are the prayers of God's people."

- In response to the Lamb taking the scroll, the four living creatures and the twenty-four elders fall down before Him, holding harps and golden bowls filled with incense, symbolizing the prayers of God's people.

Interpretation and Commentary:

1. Adoration and Worship: The worshipful response of the heavenly beings acknowledges the Lamb's worthiness and His role in God's divine plan. The use of harps and incense

underscores the praise and intercessory role of these heavenly beings.

2. Golden Bowls of Incense: The incense represents the prayers of God's people. This imagery highlights the connection between the heavenly and earthly realms, indicating that the prayers of believers have a significant place in God's unfolding plan.

Verse 9: "And they sang a new song, saying: 'You are worthy to take the scroll and to open its seals, because you were slain, and with your blood, you purchased for God persons from every tribe and language and people and nation.'"

- The heavenly beings continue their song, affirming the Lamb's worthiness to open the scroll because of His sacrificial death, which redeemed people from every corner of the earth.

Interpretation and Commentary:

1. A New Song: The new song reflects the ongoing revelation of God's plan and emphasizes the redemptive work of the Lamb. It praises His worthiness to execute God's plan.

2. Worthiness through Redemption: The Lamb's worthiness is attributed to His sacrificial death on the cross. Through His blood, He purchased people from every corner of the world, highlighting the universality of His salvation (Ephesians 1:7).

3. Universal Redemption: The phrase "persons from every tribe and language and people and nation" underscores the inclusivity of God's redemptive work. It points to the fulfillment of God's promise to bless all nations through Abraham's offspring (Genesis 12:3).

Verse 10: "You have made them to be a kingdom and priests to serve our God, and they will reign on the earth."

- The heavenly beings declare that those redeemed by the Lamb have been made a kingdom of priests to serve God, and they will reign on the earth.

Interpretation and Commentary:

1. A Kingdom of Priests: This echoes God's original plan for Israel (Exodus 19:6). Believers are not only redeemed but also set apart as priests, implying a special relationship with God and the privilege of intercession and worship.

2. Reigning on the Earth: This suggests that believers will share in Christ's future reign on the earth during His millennial kingdom (Revelation 20:4). It signifies their participation in God's ultimate purpose for His creation.

Verse 11: "Then I looked and heard the voice of many angels, numbering thousands upon thousands, and ten thousand times ten thousand. They encircled the throne and the living creatures and the elders."

- John sees and hears a vast multitude of angels surrounding the throne, the living creatures, and the elders.

Interpretation and Commentary:

1. Multitude of Angels: The enormous number of angels emphasizes the grandeur and importance of the moment. It signifies the universal recognition of the Lamb's worthiness and the significance of His role.

Verse 12: "In a loud voice they were saying: 'Worthy is the Lamb, who was slain, to receive power and wealth and wisdom and strength and honor and glory and praise!'"

- The countless angels declare the Lamb's worthiness to receive various attributes, including power, wealth, wisdom, strength, honor, glory, and praise.

Interpretation and Commentary:

1. Attributes of Praise: Each attribute ascribed to the Lamb underscores His supreme worthiness and majesty. The angels acknowledge His complete and unparalleled perfection.

Verse 13: "Then I heard every creature in heaven and on earth and under the earth and on the sea, and all that is in them, saying: 'To him who sits on the throne and to the Lamb be praise and honor and glory and power, forever and ever!'"

- John hears every creature, including those in heaven, on earth, under the earth, and in the sea, offering praise, honor, glory, and power to both the One on the throne and the Lamb.

Interpretation and Commentary:

1. Universal Worship: The worship described here is universal, involving every created being. This echoes passages like Philippians 2:10-11, where every knee will bow and every tongue confess the lordship of Jesus Christ.

2. Eternal Praise: The phrase "forever and ever" emphasizes the eternal nature of this worship. It signifies that God's praise will continue throughout eternity.

Verse 14: "The four living creatures said, 'Amen,' and the elders fell down and worshiped."

- The four living creatures respond with "Amen," and the elders bow down and worship in affirmation of the worship and praise offered to the Lamb.

Interpretation and Commentary:

1. Amen and Worship: The response of the living creatures and the elders confirms their agreement with the worship and praise given to the Lamb. It symbolizes their submission and reverence before God's plan and the Lamb's redemptive work.

Revelation Chapter 5 presents a profound scene of worship and adoration centered around the Lamb, Jesus Christ. The Lamb's worthiness to open the sealed scroll is attributed to His sacrificial death and redemptive work, which extends to people from every corner of the world. The heavenly beings, angels, and all created beings unite in acknowledging the Lamb's worthiness, attributing to Him praise, honor, glory, power, and eternal worship. This chapter underscores the central role of Jesus Christ in God's divine plan for redemption and the culmination of history.

Prophetic Commentary:

Revelation chapter 5 shows a scroll being presented to Jesus Christ in heaven. This scroll is closed by seven seals that are opened one by one to indicate events that will occur before and during Christ's second coming.

What awaits the faithful saints, those who steadfastly "keep the commandments of God and the faith of Jesus Christ" (Revelation 14:12)? God's calling for His people is to a life that transcends time—an eternal existence of service (Matthew 20:25-28).

This newly composed hymn, sung by the four living creatures and the 24 elders, provides insight into the roles designated for human beings who have been "redeemed ... to God" through the sacrifice of Christ's blood (Revelation 5:9).

Devout Christians will be appointed as both kings and priests within the Kingdom of God, collaborating with Jesus Christ to disseminate and administer God's way of life here on Earth following His second coming.

Revelation 1:6 underscores this point, as John affirms that Jesus Christ "has appointed us as kings and priests to His God and Father, to whom be glory and dominion forever and ever. Amen."

The opening of the seven seals in Revelation is a significant moment where Jesus Christ is honored as the only one worthy to reveal these profound events. While this passage indeed portrays events preceding the unsealing of the seals, it also provides a broader perspective on future occurrences.

For instance, Revelation 5:9-10 discusses redeemed humans who will serve as kings and priests on Earth. Additionally, verse 13 depicts the worship of "every creature in heaven and on Earth and under the Earth and in the sea" praising God the Father and the Lamb, an alternate name for Jesus Christ.

Rather than implying a pre-seal rapture of the saints, these verses offer insights into what will transpire once the seals are opened, unveiling God's ultimate plan. Subsequent chapters, starting with Revelation 6, delve into the detailed unfolding of these events, including the emergence of a righteous populace who will wholeheartedly worship God.

In alignment with the culmination of God's plan, we observe that when the "new heaven" and "new earth" are introduced in Revelation 21:1, only faithful overcomers will remain.

"Those who conquer will inherit all these blessings, and I will be their God, and they will be my children. But cowards, unbelievers, the corrupt, murderers, the immoral, those who practice witchcraft, idol worshipers, and all liars—their fate is in the fiery lake of burning sulfur. This is the second death" (verses 7-8).

Subsequently, there will be a time when "every creature," as mentioned in Revelation 5:13, will exalt God the Father and Jesus.

First four seals are the four horsemen of the Apocalypse

The first four seals in the book of Revelation are symbolically represented as messengers riding differently colored horses and are collectively known as the four horsemen of the Apocalypse. The term "apocalypse" is derived from the Greek word "apokálypsis," which means "disclosure" or "revelation." Hence, when we refer to "the four horsemen of the Apocalypse," we are talking about the four horsemen described in the book of Revelation.

In this article, we will briefly touch upon the meanings of the first four seals, as they serve as the foundation for the discussion of the latter three seals.

First seal: a white horse

When the first seal was opened, the apostle John recorded the following: "And I looked, and behold, a white horse. He who sat on it had a bow; and a crown was given to him, and he went out conquering and to conquer" (Revelation 6:2).

In the context of comparing the seals to the events foretold by Jesus Christ in His renowned Olivet Discourse or Prophecy, this first seal symbolizes religious deception, as indicated in Matthew 24:5.

It's essential to note how our comprehension of this seal is enriched when we align it with Jesus' earlier teachings. This comparison helps prevent any erroneous assumption that this horseman represents Christ, who is also depicted in Revelation 19:11 as returning on "a white horse."

Religious deception has been an ongoing challenge, dating back to the first century (Galatians 1:6; Jude 1:3-4), and it is destined to escalate prior to Christ's return, driven by the actions of an individual identified in Scripture as "the man of sin," "the Antichrist," and "a beast" (2 Thessalonians 2:3; 1 John 2:18; Revelation 13:11).

Second seal: a red horse

As the second seal was broken, John observed: "Another horse, fiery red, went out. And it was granted to the one who sat on it to take peace from the earth, and that people should kill one another; and there was given to him a great sword" (Revelation 6:4).

This aligns with Christ's prediction that there would be "wars and rumors of wars" and that "nation will rise against nation" (Matthew 24:6-7).

Third seal: a black horse

Regarding the third seal, John described, "So I looked, and behold, a black horse, and he who sat on it had a pair of scales in his hand. And I heard a voice in the midst of the four living creatures saying, 'A quart of wheat for a denarius, and three quarts of barley for a denarius; and do not harm the oil and the wine'" (Revelation 6:5-6).

This vividly illustrates Christ's prophecy about the occurrence of "famines" before His return (Matthew 24:7).

Fourth seal: a pale horse

Describing the fourth horse, John wrote, "So I looked, and behold, a pale horse. And the name of him who sat on it was Death, and Hades followed with him. And power was given to them over a fourth of the earth, to kill with sword, with hunger, with death, and by the beasts of the earth" (Revelation 6:8).

This depiction symbolizes the "pestilences" or disease epidemics foretold by Jesus as events that would afflict the people of the earth before His return (Matthew 24:7).

The events symbolized by the first four seals—religious deception, war, famine, and pestilences—have already been occurring. These are listed as signs of Christ's second coming and referred to as "the beginning of sorrows" (Matthew 24:8). As we approach the end times, these distressing events will escalate in intensity.

CHAPTER SIX

The First to the Sixth Seals

Introduction:

Chapter 6 of the Book of Revelation introduces the opening of the first six seals, which signify a series of cataclysmic events that will occur on Earth in the lead-up to the end times. As each seal is broken by the Lamb (Jesus Christ), various judgments and calamities are unleashed upon the world. The opening of the first seal reveals a white horse, and its rider is given a crown, symbolizing a conquering force or perhaps false peace. The second seal reveals a fiery red horse, symbolizing conflict and bloodshed. The third seal introduces a black horse, symbolizing famine and economic hardship. The fourth seal reveals a pale horse, representing death, and Hades follows closely behind, signifying a significant loss of life. The fifth seal unveils the souls of martyrs under the altar in heaven, crying out for justice and vindication. Finally, the sixth seal is opened, resulting in cosmic disturbances, such as earthquakes and the darkening of the sun, moon, and stars. This chapter sets the stage for the unfolding of God's divine judgment and signals the escalating intensity of the events leading up to the end times.

Chapter 6 also underscores the sovereignty of God and the Lamb in orchestrating these events. The chapter begins with the Lamb opening the seals, indicating Jesus' central role in the unfolding of God's plan. As the seals are opened, the imagery and symbolism convey a sense of foreboding and impending judgment, emphasizing the seriousness of these events. The chapter also hints at the cries of the persecuted and the desire for justice among the martyrs, which will be addressed in subsequent chapters. Chapter 6 serves as a dramatic and sobering introduction to the judgments that will come upon the world and highlights the importance of recognizing the Lamb's authority and responding to the call for repentance and faith in light of these prophetic events.

Verse 1: "I watched as the Lamb opened the first of the seven seals. Then I heard one of the four living creatures say in a voice like thunder, 'Come!'"

- John observes the Lamb opening the first of the seven seals, and one of the four living creatures summons someone with a voice resembling thunder.

Interpretation and Commentary:

1. The Seals: The seven seals represent God's plan for revealing and unfolding significant events in human history, especially during the period leading to the end times.

2. The Lamb: The Lamb, as established in Revelation 5, is Jesus Christ, who is the only one found worthy to open the seals, signifying His authority over God's plan.

3. The Living Creature's Voice: The thunderous voice of the living creature emphasizes the solemnity and importance of what is about to occur. It is as if creation itself echoes the significance of these events.

Verse 2: "I looked, and there before me was a white horse! Its rider held a bow, and he was given a crown, and he rode out as a conqueror bent on conquest."

- John sees a white horse, and its rider holds a bow and is given a crown, riding out as a conqueror.

Interpretation and Commentary:

1. The White Horse: In biblical symbolism, a white horse often represents conquest, purity, and righteousness. However, the context matters, and here it signifies a form of conquest that may initially appear positive but is not.

2. The Rider: This rider is commonly interpreted as representing false teachings, deceptive ideologies, or even an anti-Christ

figure. The bow without arrows suggests a bloodless or ideological conquest.

3. The Crown: The crown given to the rider may indicate a form of authority, but it is not the royal diadem of Christ. Instead, it might symbolize deceptive authority or a false claim to power.

Verse 3: "When the Lamb opened the second seal, I heard the second living creature say, 'Come!'"

- The Lamb opens the second seal, and the second living creature calls for another action.

Interpretation and Commentary:

1. Sequential Unveiling: The sequential opening of the seals introduces a series of events, each building upon the previous one, as God's plan unfolds in stages.

Verse 4: "Then another horse came out, a fiery red one. Its rider was given the power to take peace from the earth and to make people kill each other. To him was given a large sword."

- A red horse follows, and its rider is granted the authority to take peace from the earth, causing people to engage in violence and conflict. He wields a large sword.

Interpretation and Commentary:

1. The Red Horse: The red horse signifies bloodshed, conflict, and war. Its rider's actions result in widespread violence and turmoil on the earth.

2. Loss of Peace: This horseman's mission is to remove peace from the world, and the large sword represents the destructive nature of the conflicts that will arise.

Verse 5: "When the Lamb opened the third seal, I heard the third living creature say, 'Come!' I looked, and there before me was a black horse! Its rider was holding a pair of scales in his hand."

- The third seal is opened by the Lamb, and the third living creature calls for another action. John sees a black horse, and its rider holds a pair of scales.

Interpretation and Commentary:

1. The Black Horse: The black horse symbolizes famine and scarcity. Its appearance follows the red horse of war, often indicative of the consequences of conflict on resources.

2. The Pair of Scales: The scales suggest economic hardships and inequalities, as resources are measured and controlled. This period may be characterized by food shortages and economic instability.

Verse 6: "Then I heard what sounded like a voice among the four living creatures, saying, 'Two pounds of wheat for a day's wages, and six pounds of barley for a day's wages, and do not damage the oil and the wine!'"

- A voice among the four living creatures provides a declaration regarding the cost of basic food items, indicating high prices and scarcity.

Interpretation and Commentary:

1. Economic Struggles: The high prices for wheat and barley in relation to daily wages suggest economic difficulties, scarcity, and inflation during this period.
2. Preservation of Luxuries: The command not to damage the oil and wine implies that while basic necessities are scarce and expensive, luxury items are still available. This highlights economic inequality and the persistence of affluence for some.

Verse 7: "When the Lamb opened the fourth seal, I heard the voice of the fourth living creature say, 'Come!'"

- The Lamb opens the fourth seal, and the fourth living creature calls for another action.

Interpretation and Commentary:

1. Sequential Revelation: The sequence of the seals being opened continues, revealing further events and judgments in God's unfolding plan.

Verse 8: "I looked, and there before me was a pale horse! Its rider was named Death, and Hades was following close behind him. They were given power over a fourth of the earth to kill by sword, famine, and plague, and by the wild beasts of the earth."

- John sees a pale horse, and its rider is named Death, with Hades following closely. They are given power to cause death through various means, affecting a significant portion of the earth.

Interpretation and Commentary:

1. The Pale Horse: The pale horse represents death and destruction. Its rider, Death, is accompanied by Hades, symbolizing the realm of the dead.
2. Various Means of Death: The methods of death mentioned—sword, famine, plague, and wild beasts—highlight the widespread and multifaceted nature of the judgments during this period. A quarter of the earth's population is affected.

Verse 9: "When he opened the fifth seal, I saw under the altar the souls of those who had been slain because of the word of God and the testimony they had maintained."

- As the Lamb opens the fifth seal, John sees under the altar the souls of those who were martyred for their faith in God's Word and their testimony.

Interpretation and Commentary:
1. The Fifth Seal: The opening of the fifth seal reveals a significant aspect of God's plan during this period, focusing on the suffering and martyrdom of believers.
2. Souls Under the Altar: This imagery symbolizes the souls of the martyrs in the presence of God. The altar is associated with sacrifice and represents the ultimate sacrifice these believers made for their faith.
3. Martyrs for the Word of God: The martyrs' deaths were a result of their unwavering commitment to God's Word and their proclamation of the Gospel. This reflects the ongoing spiritual battle between the forces of evil and the faithful.

Verse 10: "They called out in a loud voice, 'How long, Sovereign Lord, holy and true, until you judge the inhabitants of the earth and avenge our blood?'"

- The souls of the martyrs cry out to God, asking how long it will be until He judges the people of the earth and avenges their deaths.

Interpretation and Commentary:
1. Cry for Justice: The souls' cry reveals their longing for justice and God's righteous judgment upon those who persecuted and killed them. They acknowledge God's holiness and truth.
2. The Timing of Judgment: Their question reflects a common theme in the Bible, where the faithful often wonder about the

timing of God's judgment and the resolution of suffering (Psalm 13:1-2; Habakkuk 1:2-4).

Verse 11: "Then each of them was given a white robe, and they were told to wait a little longer, until the full number of their fellow servants, their brothers and sisters, were killed just as they had been."

- The martyrs are given white robes and are instructed to wait until the full number of their fellow believers is martyred as they were.

Interpretation and Commentary:

1. White Robes: The white robes symbolize righteousness, purity, and victory. These martyrs are honored and vindicated for their faithfulness to the end.

2. Waiting for God's Plan: They are asked to be patient as God's plan unfolds. The idea is that more persecution and martyrdom will occur until a predetermined number of believers have been martyred for their faith.

3. The Full Number: God has a predetermined number of martyrs in mind, and this number must be reached before the final judgment. This concept underscores God's sovereignty and His perfect plan.

Verse 12: "I watched as he opened the sixth seal. There was a great earthquake. The sun turned black like sackcloth made of goat hair, the whole moon turned blood red,"

- John observes the opening of the sixth seal, resulting in a series of dramatic events, including a great earthquake, a darkened sun, and a blood-red moon.

Interpretation and Commentary:

1. Dramatic Cosmic Signs: These events are apocalyptic in nature, signifying significant upheaval and cosmic disturbance. They are not only physical but also symbolic of God's judgment and the nearing climax of His plan.

2. Great Earthquake: Earthquakes in the Bible often signify God's power and the shaking of worldly foundations. This earthquake is a monumental event signaling divine intervention.

3. Symbolic Sun and Moon: The darkened sun and blood-red moon are symbolic of disruptions in the natural order and may signify judgment and chaos (Joel 2:31; Matthew 24:29).

Verse 13: "and the stars in the sky fell to earth, as figs drop from a fig tree when shaken by a strong wind."

- John describes stars falling from the sky, likening it to figs dropping from a tree during a strong wind.

Interpretation and Commentary:

1. Symbolic Stars: In prophetic and apocalyptic literature, falling stars often represent the fall of rulers or powers. This imagery suggests a significant upheaval in earthly authority and power structures.

Verse 14: "The heavens receded like a scroll being rolled up, and every mountain and island was removed from its place."

- John witnesses the heavens rolling up like a scroll, and mountains and islands are displaced.

Interpretation and Commentary:

1. Cosmic Unraveling: The imagery of the heavens rolling up like a scroll signifies a profound transformation in the cosmos, suggesting that the very fabric of creation is undergoing a radical change.

2. Physical and Spiritual Displacement: The shifting of mountains and islands represents unprecedented geological and geopolitical upheaval, possibly symbolizing the collapse of earthly systems and nations.

Verse 15: "Then the kings of the earth, the princes, the generals, the rich, the mighty, and everyone else, both slave and free, hid in caves and among the rocks of the mountains."

- In response to the cosmic upheaval and dramatic events, people from all societal strata, including rulers, military leaders, the wealthy, and all others, seek refuge in caves and among the mountains.

Interpretation and Commentary:

1. Universal Terror: The magnitude of the unfolding events terrifies people without distinction. This highlights the all-encompassing nature of God's judgment and the recognition of His sovereignty over all humanity (Isaiah 2:10-22).

2. Cries for Safety: People instinctively seek shelter from the perceived wrath of God. Their actions reflect the human response of fear and a desire to escape divine judgment.

Verse 16: "They called to the mountains and the rocks, 'Fall on us and hide us from the face of him who sits on the throne and from the wrath of the Lamb!'"

- In their distress, people cry out to the mountains and rocks, pleading for them to fall and hide them from the presence of the One who sits on the throne and from the wrath of the Lamb.

Interpretation and Commentary:

1. Recognition of Divine Authority: The people's plea acknowledges the ultimate authority and power of God, who sits on the throne, and the Lamb, Jesus Christ. They understand that these events are divine judgments.

2. Wrath of the Lamb: The Lamb, who represents Jesus Christ, is associated with wrath in this context. This underscores the biblical truth that Jesus will ultimately execute judgment as well as extend salvation (Revelation 19:11-16).

Verse 17: "For the great day of their wrath has come, and who can withstand it?"

- The people express that the great day of God's wrath has arrived, and they question who can endure or withstand it.

Interpretation and Commentary:

1. The Day of Wrath: This phrase emphasizes the eschatological understanding that there will be a culmination of God's judgment. It signifies a period of intense divine intervention in the world's affairs.

2. A Call for Reflection: The question posed underscores the severity of God's judgment and the inability of humanity to escape it by their own strength. It invites contemplation on humanity's need for salvation and reliance on God's mercy.

3. Hope in God's Grace: While these verses emphasize God's judgment, it's important to remember that Revelation also presents the hope of redemption and the ultimate victory of Christ over evil. Believers are encouraged to place their trust in God's grace and seek refuge in Him.

Revelation Chapter 6 paints a vivid picture of cosmic disturbances, upheaval, and human response in the face of divine judgment. The people's cries for the mountains and rocks to hide them from God's wrath underscore the recognition of His authority and the need for salvation. These verses serve as a powerful reminder of the importance of faith, repentance, and trust in God's mercy in the face of impending judgment.

Prophetic Commentary:

First seal: a white horse

When the first seal was opened, the apostle John recorded the following: "And I looked, and behold, a white horse. He who sat on it had a bow; and a crown was given to him, and he went out conquering and to conquer" (Revelation 6:2).

In the context of comparing the seals to the events foretold by Jesus Christ in His renowned Olivet Discourse or Prophecy, this first seal symbolizes religious deception, as indicated in Matthew 24:5.

It's essential to note how our comprehension of this seal is enriched when we align it with Jesus' earlier teachings. This comparison helps prevent any erroneous assumption that this horseman represents Christ, who is also depicted in Revelation 19:11 as returning on "a white horse."

Religious deception has been an ongoing challenge, dating back to the first century (Galatians 1:6; Jude 1:3-4), and it is destined to escalate prior to Christ's return, driven by the actions of an individual identified in Scripture as "the man of sin," "the Antichrist," and "a beast" (2 Thessalonians 2:3; 1 John 2:18; Revelation 13:11).

Second seal: a red horse

As the second seal was broken, John observed: "Another horse, fiery red, went out. And it was granted to the one who sat on it to take peace from the earth, and that people should kill one another; and there was given to him a great sword" (Revelation 6:4).

This aligns with Christ's prediction that there would be "wars and rumors of wars" and that "nation will rise against nation" (Matthew 24:6-7).

Third seal: a black horse

Regarding the third seal, John described, "So I looked, and behold, a black horse, and he who sat on it had a pair of scales in his hand. And I heard a voice in the midst of the four living creatures saying, 'A quart of wheat for a denarius, and three quarts of barley for a denarius; and do not harm the oil and the wine'" (Revelation 6:5-6).

This vividly illustrates Christ's prophecy about the occurrence of "famines" before His return (Matthew 24:7).

Fourth seal: a pale horse

Describing the fourth horse, John wrote, "So I looked, and behold, a pale horse. And the name of him who sat on it was Death, and Hades followed with him. And power was given to them over a fourth of the earth, to kill with sword, with hunger, with death, and by the beasts of the earth" (Revelation 6:8).

This depiction symbolizes the "pestilences" or disease epidemics foretold by Jesus as events that would afflict the people of the earth before His return (Matthew 24:7).

The events symbolized by the first four seals—religious deception, war, famine, and pestilences—have already been occurring. These are listed as signs of Christ's second coming and referred to as "the beginning of sorrows" (Matthew 24:8). As we approach the end times, these distressing events will escalate in intensity.

Fifth seal: tribulation

"When He opened the fifth seal, I saw under the altar the souls of those who had been slain for the word of God and for the testimony which they held. And they cried with a loud voice, saying, 'How long, O Lord, holy and true, until You judge and avenge our blood on those who dwell on the earth?' Then a white robe was given to each of them; and it was said to them that they should rest a little while longer, until both the number of their fellow servants and their brethren, who would be killed as they were, was completed" (Revelation 6:9-11).

Context of the fifth seal Before delving into the significance of this seal, it's important to consider the broader context of this vision.

In this vision, John is witnessing faithful martyrs from various times in history and is inquiring of God how long it will be before their unjust deaths are avenged. Some have mistakenly interpreted this as these saints being alive in heaven, awaiting God's judgment on their killers. However, we must remember that this is a symbolic vision meant to illustrate future events and not necessarily a depiction of reality.

The Bible frequently employs metaphors to symbolize past, present, or future events, and these metaphors should not be taken literally. For instance, in Genesis, after Cain murdered his brother Abel, God declared, "The voice of your brother's blood cries out to me from the ground" (Genesis 4:10). Clearly, this is a metaphorical expression.

The vision of the fifth seal, wherein faithful martyrs from different eras await God's judgment, symbolically represents God's overarching purpose for humanity and the world. This vision underscores God's intention to bring "many sons to glory" (Hebrews 2:10).

The apostle Paul also used metaphorical language to describe this process, stating, "For we know that the whole creation groans and labors with birth pangs together until now" (Romans 8:22). The purpose of the book of Revelation and its seals is to unveil future events and demonstrate that God's plan of salvation will ultimately be fulfilled.

Meaning of the fifth seal The vision that John witnessed to represent the fifth seal signifies the Great Tribulation that will target the physical descendants of Jacob and faithful believers before Christ's return.

In reference to this time, Jesus foretold, "Then they will deliver you up to tribulation and kill you, and you will be hated by all nations for My name's sake. And then many will be offended, will betray one another, and will hate one another" (Matthew 24:9-10).

Continuing to describe this period of unprecedented trial, Jesus proclaimed, "For then shall be great tribulation, such as has not been since the beginning of the world until this time, no, nor ever shall be. And unless those days were shortened, no flesh would be saved [alive]; but for the elect's sake those days will be shortened" (Matthew 24:21-22).

The fifth seal symbolizes Satan's wrath, which will be directed against humanity, particularly God's people.

Revelation 12:12 serves as a warning about Satan's actions during this end-time period: "Woe to the inhabitants of the earth and the sea! For the devil has come down to you, having great wrath, because he knows that he has a short time."

During this time of tribulation, faithful believers will face severe persecution, and this vision in Revelation represents their suffering and endurance as they await God's justice and the eventual fulfillment of His plan.

Sixth seal: cosmic disturbances

When the sixth seal was opened, John recorded his vision of remarkable cosmic disturbances: "And behold, there was a great earthquake; and the sun became black as sackcloth of hair, and the moon became like blood. And the stars of heaven fell to the earth, as a fig tree drops its late figs when it is shaken by a mighty wind. Then the sky receded as a scroll when it is rolled up, and every mountain and island was moved out of its place" (Revelation 6:12-14).

These extraordinary occurrences had been prophesied long before as indicators of the day of the Lord, signifying the time of Christ's return to Earth.

The prophet Joel had foretold it as "a day of darkness and gloominess, a day of clouds and thick darkness," during which "the sun and moon will grow dark, and the stars will diminish their brightness. ... The heavens and earth will shake" (Joel 2:2; Joel 3:15-16).

As these awe-inspiring events unfold, humanity will recognize that God is about to enact His judgment upon the world due to disobedience to His laws.

"Then the kings of the earth, the great men, the rich men, the commanders, the mighty men, every slave and every free man, hid themselves in the caves and in the rocks of the mountains, and said to the mountains and rocks, 'Fall on us and hide us from the face of Him who sits on the throne and from the wrath of the Lamb! For the great day of His wrath has come, and who is able to stand?'" (Revelation 6:15-17).

The seventh seal: the wrath and mercy of God

The seventh seal, which introduces the seven trumpets, is a pivotal moment in the book of Revelation. It embodies the central theme of Revelation—the Day of the Lord. This seal signifies both "the wrath of the Lamb" (Revelation 6:16), the judgment that Christ will bring upon humanity due to their disobedience to God's laws, and the mercy of God, which will ultimately be manifested through Jesus Christ's return to establish the Kingdom of God on Earth.

Before the commencement of the seventh seal, God will seal two distinct groups of people: the 144,000 individuals, symbolically representing the 12 tribes of Israel (Revelation 7:3-4, 9), and a vast multitude from all nations (verse 9).

The 144,000 will include descendants from 12 of the tribes of the ancient Israelites, not solely Jews who primarily descend from the tribe of Judah. It's essential to recognize that a separate, substantial group of people—"a great multitude that no one could number"—from diverse nations will also be sealed (verse 9).

The Greek term "sphragizo," translated as "sealed," conveys the idea of marking or stamping for security. This same word is employed by the apostle Paul in Ephesians 1:13 to describe Christians who were "sealed with that holy Spirit of promise" and in Ephesians 4:30 to refer to Christians who were "sealed for the day of redemption."

God's faithful followers will be divinely protected from the impending judgments that will befall the rest of humanity, those who have rebelled against God.

As the seventh seal is initiated, a sequence of seven trumpets, each representing a series of divine judgments, is set to sound (Revelation 8:6). By the time of the fifth trumpet, the judgments will be so severe that "men will seek death and will not find it; they will desire to die, and death will flee from them [temporarily]" (Revelation 9:6). During the sixth trumpet, one-third of humanity will perish (verse 18).

For a more comprehensive understanding of why God's anger is kindled against humanity, please refer to the article titled "Wrath of God."

Following these judgments, the mercy of God is displayed as the seventh trumpet resounds, heralding the proclamation that "the kingdoms of this world have become the kingdoms of our Lord and of His Christ" (Revelation 11:15).

Although there will still be "seven last plagues," also known as "bowls full of the wrath of God," until "the wrath of God is complete" (Revelation 15:1, 7), conditions on Earth will significantly improve. With the return of Christ as the King of Kings and Lord of Lords, the Kingdom of God will be established, ushering in a thousand years of peace and prosperity.

CHAPTER SEVEN

The Sealed of Israel

Introduction:

Chapter 7 of the Book of Revelation offers a pause in the sequence of the seal judgments, providing a glimpse into a significant interlude in the prophetic narrative. John sees four angels stationed at the four corners of the earth, holding back the four winds of destruction. Another angel ascends from the east, carrying the seal of the living God, and he instructs the four angels not to harm the earth, sea, or trees until the servants of God are sealed on their foreheads. The sealing of these servants totals 144,000, representing a symbolic and complete number, and they are described as being from the twelve tribes of Israel. This vision conveys the idea that God is both protecting and designating a specific group of His people for preservation during the tumultuous events to come. Additionally, John sees a multitude of people from every nation, tribe, people, and language standing before the throne and the Lamb, clothed in white robes and holding palm branches. These are the ones who have come out of the great tribulation and have washed their robes in the blood of the Lamb. They serve God day and night and are sheltered from hunger, thirst, and the scorching sun. The chapter presents a contrast between the sealing of God's servants and the countless multitude of redeemed believers, highlighting God's faithfulness and His ultimate purpose of salvation for people from all nations.

Chapter 7 is significant for several reasons. First, it offers reassurance to believers that God knows and protects His own during times of trial and judgment. The sealing of the 144,000 represents divine protection and consecration, ensuring their preservation during the tribulation. Second, the vision of the redeemed multitude from all nations emphasizes the inclusivity of God's salvation. It underscores the universal scope of the Gospel and the promise that people from every background can find redemption through faith in Christ. This chapter provides a message of hope amidst the impending judgment, reminding believers of God's sovereignty, faithfulness, and the ultimate victory of His redeemed people.

Verse 1: "After this, I saw four angels standing at the four corners of the earth, holding back the four winds of the earth to prevent any wind from blowing on the land or on the sea or on any tree."

- John witnesses four angels stationed at the four corners of the earth, restraining the winds to prevent them from affecting the land, sea, or trees.

Interpretation and Commentary:

1. Angelic Restraint: These angels are tasked with controlling natural forces, symbolized by the winds. The winds often represent divine judgment or chaos in the Bible (Jeremiah 49:36-37; Daniel 7:2). Their restraint signifies a pause in God's judgment.

2. Geographical Symbolism: The "four corners of the earth" is a symbolic expression representing the entirety of the earth. This scene signifies a moment of divine restraint and preparation.

Verse 2: "Then I saw another angel coming up from the east, having the seal of the living God. He called out in a loud voice to the four angels who had been given power to harm the land and the sea."

- Another angel, bearing the seal of the living God, emerges from the east and instructs the four angels with the power to harm the land and sea.

Interpretation and Commentary:

1. The Seal of God: This seal signifies protection and ownership by God. In biblical times, seals were used to mark ownership or secure something precious (Ephesians 1:13; 2 Timothy 2:19).

2. Divine Authority: The angel with the seal asserts God's authority over the natural elements and the ability to restrain or unleash them as part of His divine plan.

Verse 3: "Do not harm the land or the sea or the trees until we put a seal on the foreheads of the servants of our God."

- The angel with the seal commands the four angels to refrain from harming the earth, sea, or trees until God's servants are sealed on their foreheads.

Interpretation and Commentary:

1. Protection of God's Servants: The sealing of God's servants on their foreheads signifies divine protection and ownership (Revelation 9:4). Before any judgments unfold, God ensures the safety of His faithful followers.

Verse 4: "Then I heard the number of those who were sealed: 144,000 from all the tribes of Israel."

- John hears the specific number of those sealed: 144,000 individuals from the twelve tribes of Israel.

Interpretation and Commentary:

1. Symbolic or Literal: Interpretations of the 144,000 vary. Some view them symbolically, representing the entirety of God's redeemed people, while others take it more literally, believing these are a specific group of Jewish believers.

2. Symbolism of 12: The number twelve symbolizes completeness and is associated with the twelve tribes of Israel. This suggests that those sealed represent a complete and chosen group of God's people.

Verses 5-8: The following verses provide a list of the twelve tribes and the number sealed from each tribe, totaling 144,000.

- It's important to note that this list deviates from the standard tribal listings in the Old Testament, possibly indicating a symbolic or representative nature rather than a literal census.

Verse 9: "After this I looked, and there before me was a great multitude that no one could count, from every nation, tribe, people and language, standing before the throne and before the Lamb. They were wearing white robes and were holding palm branches in their hands."

- John observes a vast, innumerable multitude from every corner of the world, standing before the throne and the Lamb. They are dressed in white robes and hold palm branches.

Interpretation and Commentary:

1. The Great Multitude: This multitude, unlike the 144,000, is composed of people from all nations and languages, emphasizing the universality of salvation through Jesus Christ.

2. White Robes: The white robes symbolize purity and righteousness, signifying the redeemed's washed and forgiven state (Revelation 7:14; Revelation 19:8).
3. Palm Branches: Palm branches are symbols of victory and celebration. They reflect the triumphant nature of their salvation through Christ (John 12:13).

Verse 10: "And they cried out in a loud voice: 'Salvation belongs to our God, who sits on the throne, and to the Lamb.'"

- The multitude raises a joyful cry, acknowledging that salvation belongs to God, who is seated on the throne, and to the Lamb.

Interpretation and Commentary:

1. Worship and Acknowledgment: The cry of the multitude reflects their gratitude and worship. They attribute salvation to God and the Lamb, recognizing Jesus' role in their redemption.

Verse 11: "All the angels were standing around the throne and around the elders and the four living creatures. They fell down on their faces before the throne and worshiped God,"

- The angels are gathered around the throne, the elders, and the four living creatures, falling on their faces before the throne in worship of God.

Interpretation and Commentary:

1. Angelic Worship: The angels' posture of worship emphasizes the majesty and holiness of God. They join in adoration of the One on the throne.

Verse 12: "saying: 'Amen! Praise and glory and wisdom and thanks and honor and power and strength be to our God forever and ever. Amen!'"

- The angels declare "Amen!" and ascribe praise, glory, wisdom, thanks, honor, power, and strength to God for all eternity.

Interpretation and Commentary:

1. Amen and Worship: The response of the angels confirms and affirms the worship and praise offered to God. Their declaration emphasizes the completeness and eternal nature of God's attributes.

Verse 13: "Then one of the elders asked me, 'These in white robes—who are they, and where did they come from?'"

- One of the elders asks John about the identity and origin of those in white robes.

Interpretation and Commentary:

1. Clarification Sought: The elder's question suggests that the identity and significance of this multitude are not immediately apparent, prompting John to inquire further.

mmentary)

Revelation 7:14-17 (ESV) contains a powerful message of hope and assurance within the context of the great multitude standing before the throne of God:

Verse 14: "I said to him, 'Sir, you know.' And he said to me, 'These are the ones coming out of the great tribulation. They have washed their robes and made them white in the blood of the Lamb.'"

Interpretation and Commentary:

1. The Great Multitude: John is conversing with one of the elders in this passage. The elder explains that the great multitude John sees are those who have come out of the "great tribulation." This tribulation refers to the intense suffering and persecution faced by believers during a time of unprecedented turmoil and spiritual conflict.

2. Washed in the Blood of the Lamb: The key to the multitude's standing before God's throne is their redemption through faith in Jesus Christ. Their robes have been washed and made white in the blood of the Lamb, which is a powerful symbol of Jesus' sacrificial death on the cross. This emphasizes that salvation is obtained through faith in Christ's atoning work.

Bible References:

- The imagery of robes made white in the blood of the Lamb alludes to passages like Isaiah 1:18 and Psalm 51:7, where cleansing and forgiveness are associated with God's gracious provision.

Verse 15: "Therefore, they are before the throne of God, and serve him day and night in his temple; and he who sits on the throne will shelter them with his presence."

Interpretation and Commentary:

1. Access to God's Presence: Those who have come out of the great tribulation are now in the presence of God. They have

the privilege of serving Him continually in His temple, signifying unbroken communion and worship.

2. Divine Protection: God Himself, the One who sits on the throne, provides protection and shelter for them. His presence is a source of comfort, security, and assurance, especially in contrast to the trials they endured on earth.

Bible References:

- The concept of serving God in His temple is reminiscent of Old Testament imagery, where priests served in the tabernacle or temple as an act of worship and devotion (Exodus 29:1-9, 1 Chronicles 9:33).

Verse 16: "They shall hunger no more, neither thirst anymore; the sun shall not strike them, nor any scorching heat."

Interpretation and Commentary:

1. Relief from Suffering: In the presence of God, the multitude will experience a cessation of suffering. They will no longer hunger, thirst, or endure physical discomfort. This imagery reflects the idea of divine provision and care.

2. Spiritual and Physical Comfort: Beyond physical relief, this verse signifies the fulfillment of spiritual needs as well. It portrays God's care for His people on every level, providing nourishment for both body and soul.

Bible References:

- This passage echoes the promises of comfort and provision found in passages like Psalm 23:1-3 and Isaiah 49:10.

Verse 17: "For the Lamb in the midst of the throne will be their shepherd, and he will guide them to springs of living water, and God will wipe away every tear from their eyes."

Interpretation and Commentary:

1. The Lamb as Shepherd: Jesus, symbolized as the Lamb, takes on the role of Shepherd for this redeemed multitude. He guides them, cares for their needs, and leads them to the source of spiritual refreshment and sustenance.

2. Wiping Away Tears: The promise that God will wipe away every tear from their eyes signifies the complete removal of sorrow, suffering, and pain. It represents the ultimate comfort and healing that God provides to His people.

Bible References:
- The imagery of Jesus as the Shepherd is in line with the biblical portrayal of Him as the Good Shepherd (John 10:11) who cares for His flock.

Revelation 7:14-17 is a message of profound hope, assuring believers of the ultimate victory and reward that awaits them. It conveys the idea that, through faith in Christ, believers will find eternal relief from suffering, unbroken communion with God, and complete healing of their wounds and sorrows. This passage serves as a source of encouragement and comfort to those facing trials and tribulations, reminding them of the ultimate destination and reward for their faithfulness.

Prophetic Commentary:

Who are the 144,000 mentioned in Revelation 7 and 14? When are they chosen? Do they represent the Church today? Is salvation limited to this special group?

The 144,000 mentioned in the book of Revelation, specifically in Revelation 7 and 14, are a group of individuals who are chosen by God for a special role during the end times. Here's what we can understand about them:

1. Identity of the 144,000: In Revelation 7:4-8, the 144,000 are described as being "sealed" from the twelve tribes of Israel. The list of tribes mentioned includes some variations from the traditional list of Israelite tribes, which has led to various interpretations. It's important to note that this description is highly symbolic and may not refer to a literal 144,000 people from these tribes.

2. When they are chosen: Revelation 7 portrays the sealing of the 144,000 before the great tribulation begins. They are sealed for protection during a time of intense trials and tribulations on Earth.

3. Their role: Revelation 7:3-4 indicates that they are sealed "servants of our God on their foreheads." While the exact nature of their service is not explicitly stated, they are associated with proclaiming the message of God during a time of great turmoil.

96

4. Relation to the Church: There are various interpretations regarding the relationship between the 144,000 and the Church. Some believe that they represent a distinct group with a unique calling during the end times, while others see them symbolically representing the Church or a subset of believers who remain faithful.

5. Salvation: The Bible does not indicate that salvation is limited to the 144,000. The message of salvation is universal, and countless passages in the Bible emphasize that God desires the salvation of all people. The 144,000, like other believers, are recipients of God's grace and salvation.

The book of Revelation makes three distinct references to a group consisting of 144,000 individuals.

In Revelation 7:4, it is written, "One hundred and forty-four thousand of all the tribes of the children of Israel were sealed." Among this assembly, there were 12,000 individuals chosen from each tribe, with the exception of the tribe of Dan (as outlined in verses 5-8). The reason for Dan's exclusion remains a subject of speculation.

Revelation 14:1 introduces the same "one hundred and forty-four thousand" who are depicted as standing alongside a Lamb on Mount Zion, bearing the name of God "written on their foreheads."

The third reference depicts this group singing praises before God and emphasizes that "no one could learn that song except the one hundred and forty-four thousand who were redeemed from the earth" (verse 3).

To discern the identity and significance of this group, several fundamental questions must be addressed.

The 144,000 are sealed at a specific point in the events described in the book of Revelation. This sealing takes place following the opening of six seals, each of which unleashes suffering and devastation upon the inhabitants of the earth. These calamities include symbolic representations such as the four horses (signifying false prophets, war, famine, and pestilence), followed by a religious inquisition resulting in the persecution and martyrdom of faithful Christians, as well as celestial signs.

These events, foretold by Christ in His Olivet Prophecy, are part of a future period known as the "great tribulation," a time characterized by unprecedented suffering and turmoil. Jesus described it as follows: "For then there will be great tribulation, such as has not been since the beginning of the world until this time, no, nor ever shall be. And unless those days were shortened, no flesh would be saved; but for the elect's sake those days will be shortened" (Matthew 24:21-22).

After this intense period of tribulation, which results from human misrule and Satan's destructive influence, God's judgment, referred to as "the wrath of the Lamb" and "the great day of His wrath," follows (Revelation 6:16-17).

The sealing of the 144,000 occurs after the great tribulation but before the outpouring of God's wrath. In the subsequent chapter, it is explained that the four angels tasked with bringing God's punishment upon the earth are instructed not to harm the earth until this group of individuals has been sealed (Revelation 7:1-3).

These passages make it clear that the 144,000 are individuals who survive the great tribulation, rather than being comprised of faithful saints who have lived and died throughout earlier ages.

What is the spiritual state of the 144,000?

The 144,000 will be people who have been faithful to God. They are called "the servants of our God" (Revelation 7:3), ones "who were not defiled with women, for they are virgins [meaning, they are spiritually pure]. These are the ones who follow the Lamb wherever He goes. These were redeemed from among men, being firstfruits to God and to the Lamb" (Revelation 14:4).

The book of Revelation identifies those faithful to God as people who "keep the commandments of God" (Revelation 12:17; Revelation 14:12). The last chapter notes: "Blessed are those who do His commandments, that they may have the right to the tree of life, and may enter through the gates into the city" (Revelation 22:14). Unfortunately, many who claim to be Christians today do not keep all of God's commandments.

Is it possible for members of the Church today to be part of the 144,000? Numerous churches and groups have made claims that their members, or a portion of their membership, constitute the 144,000 mentioned in the Bible. To gain insight into this matter, it is essential to examine what the Bible reveals regarding the timing of when members of God's Church are sealed in comparison to when the 144,000 will be sealed.

In Revelation 7:3, as previously discussed, it is noted that the angels were instructed not to harm the earth until the servants of God—the 144,000—had received the seal on their foreheads. A seal serves the purpose of closing or securely sealing something, like a letter or a book, and it also serves as an identifier or mark, signifying something as genuine or approved. An example from the Old Testament can be found in Ezekiel 9:4, where God commanded Ezekiel to place a mark on the foreheads of those who lamented and mourned over the abominations occurring within the city of Jerusalem. Whether this mark was literal or symbolic, it identified these individuals for God.

In the New Testament, there are instances of people being marked or identified by God as genuine or as future recipients of a special blessing. For instance, John 6:27 mentions Jesus, upon whom "God the Father has set His seal."

Members of the Church today are also recipients of a divine seal. The Apostle Paul provides insight into this sealing process. He described the believers in Ephesus as individuals who, having placed their faith in Christ, "were sealed with the Holy Spirit of promise" (Ephesians 1:13). Furthermore, he admonishes them not to grieve the Holy Spirit of God, who sealed them for the day of redemption (Ephesians 4:30). In his correspondence with the Corinthian brethren, Paul speaks of Jesus Christ as the one who has sealed them and granted them the Spirit in their hearts as a guarantee (2 Corinthians 1:22).

Those who are guided by God's Holy Spirit are thus sealed, marked, or identified as authentic Christians—children of God and heirs destined to attain eternal life (Romans 8:14-16). This sealing occurs at the time of baptism, when an individual, following repentance of their sins, receives the Holy Spirit and is immersed in water (Acts 2:38; Acts 19:6).

It is crucial to distinguish that members of God's true Church are sealed by God for the purpose of receiving eternal life when they accept the Holy Spirit and allow themselves to be led by it.

It appears that the 144,000 will be individuals who, amidst the turmoil of the Great Tribulation, will turn from their sins, committing themselves to God through faith and obedience, with the ultimate purpose of being sealed for salvation.

Additionally, it's important to emphasize that the vision of the 144,000 singing before God's throne, as described in Revelation 14:1-3, occurs subsequent to their passage through the Great Tribulation, which precedes the return of Christ. It is after they have been sealed and transformed into spiritual beings. This vision does not depict individuals currently residing in heaven, as some may mistakenly believe.

Is salvation restricted solely to the 144,000? Revelation 7 introduces the 144,000, specifying 12,000 individuals from each tribe of Israel, except for the tribe of Dan. Two crucial points to consider are that God still values the descendants of ancient Israel, and salvation is not confined to this specific group.

In addition to the 144,000, another countless multitude is described as standing before God in "white robes," symbolizing righteous living. This great multitude will comprise individuals from "all nations, tribes, peoples, and languages." The question arises regarding their identity and origin.

The response clarifies that they are individuals who have emerged from the great tribulation, cleansing their robes and making them white through the blood of the Lamb. Due to their response to God, they will serve in His presence.

What will motivate such a significant number of people to turn to God during the tribulation?

The Bible reveals that two witnesses, representing God, will prophesy for three and a half years during the tribulation. Despite the turmoil and hardships associated with this period, their ministry will lead to the addition of many individuals to God's eternal family. These people will come from both the 144,000 and the countless multitude.

CHAPTER EIGHT

Seventh Seal: Prelude to the Seven Trumpets

Introduction:

Chapter 8 of the Book of Revelation marks the beginning of a new series of judgments known as the trumpet judgments. As the Lamb (Jesus) opens the seventh and final seal from the scroll introduced in earlier chapters, there is a brief silence in heaven. This silence signifies a sense of awe and anticipation for the catastrophic events that are about to unfold. Then, seven angels are given seven trumpets, each symbolizing a divine judgment. The first four trumpet judgments bring destruction upon the earth, affecting the natural elements such as land, sea, rivers, and the sky. These judgments result in a series of ecological disasters, causing widespread devastation and loss. The imagery used in this chapter is highly symbolic and conveys the idea of God's sovereign authority over creation, as well as His ability to use natural forces to execute His judgments.

Chapter 8 serves as a continuation of the judgments that began with the seal judgments in earlier chapters, emphasizing the escalating severity of God's judgments as the end times progress. It underscores the consequences of human rebellion and sin, which lead to the disruption of the natural order and the suffering of creation. Additionally, the trumpet judgments carry an element of warning and a call to repentance, urging people to turn back to God before it's too late. The chapter highlights the importance of acknowledging God's sovereignty and the need for humanity to seek reconciliation with Him in the face of impending judgment.

Verse 1: "When he opened the seventh seal, there was silence in heaven for about half an hour."

- As the Lamb opens the seventh seal, a period of silence in heaven lasting about half an hour occurs.

Interpretation and Commentary:

1. The Seventh Seal: The opening of the seventh seal represents the culmination of God's plan and judgments, marking a significant moment in the unfolding of prophetic events.
2. Silence in Heaven: The silence in heaven is profound and unusual, signifying the gravity and awe of what is about to transpire. It can also be seen as a moment of anticipation before the final judgments are unleashed (Habakkuk 2:20).

Verse 2: "And I saw the seven angels who stand before God, and seven trumpets were given to them."

- John sees seven angels who are in the presence of God, and they are each given a trumpet.

Interpretation and Commentary:

1. Seven Angels: These angels are special attendants in the heavenly court, indicating their significant roles in executing God's will and judgments.
2. Seven Trumpets: The seven trumpets symbolize divine pronouncements and judgments. In the biblical context, trumpets were used to announce important events or commands (Numbers 10:1-10). Here, they announce God's actions.

Verse 3: "Another angel, who had a golden censer, came and stood at the altar. He was given much incense to offer, with the prayers of all God's people, on the golden altar in front of the throne."

- A different angel, holding a golden censer, approaches the altar and is given a significant amount of incense to offer, along with the prayers of God's people, on the golden altar before the throne.

Interpretation and Commentary:
1. Golden Censer: The golden censer represents the offering of prayers and intercession before God. It's a symbol of the acceptance of the saints' prayers (Psalm 141:2).
2. Incense and Prayers: The incense and prayers offered together symbolize the earnest cries and petitions of God's people. It shows that the prayers of the faithful are heard and are a fragrant offering to God (Psalm 141:2; Revelation 5:8).

Verse 4: "The smoke of the incense, together with the prayers of God's people, went up before God from the angel's hand."

- The smoke from the incense, combined with the prayers of God's people, ascends before God from the angel's hand.

Interpretation and Commentary:
1. Symbolic Worship: This imagery emphasizes the worshipful nature of prayer and the pleasing fragrance it carries before God. It signifies the spiritual connection between the prayers of the saints and the divine presence.

Verse 5: "Then the angel took the censer, filled it with fire from the altar, and hurled it on the earth; and there came peals of thunder, rumblings, flashes of lightning and an earthquake."

- The angel takes the censer, fills it with fire from the altar, and casts it down to the earth, resulting in thunder, rumblings, lightning, and an earthquake.

Interpretation and Commentary:
1. Symbolic Act: This dramatic act by the angel represents the divine response to the prayers and petitions of God's people. It signifies that the time for divine judgment is at hand and that God's responses to the cries of His people can involve both mercy and judgment.
2. Cataclysmic Events: The thunder, rumblings, lightning, and earthquake depict the intensity and awe of God's judgment. Such natural phenomena are often associated with divine intervention throughout the Bible (Exodus 19:16; Psalm 18:13; Psalm 77:18).

Verse 6: "Then the seven angels who had the seven trumpets prepared to sound them."

- The seven angels who possess the seven trumpets make preparations to sound them, signaling forthcoming divine judgments.

Interpretation and Commentary:

1. Trumpet Judgments: The sounding of the trumpets symbolizes God's sequential judgments upon the earth. Each trumpet blast brings about specific and increasingly severe calamities (Revelation 9:1).

Verses 7-12: These verses describe the first four trumpet judgments, each resulting in destructive natural phenomena affecting the earth, sea, rivers, and heavenly bodies.

- The first trumpet brings hail and fire mixed with blood, causing destruction on the earth.
- The second trumpet results in a burning mountain cast into the sea, turning a third of the sea into blood.
- The third trumpet sees a great star called Wormwood fall from the sky, poisoning a third of the rivers and waters.
- The fourth trumpet darkens a third of the sun, moon, and stars, causing a decrease in light.

Interpretation and Commentary:

1. Symbolic Nature: These trumpet judgments contain symbolic elements, and their precise interpretation has been a subject of debate among scholars. They convey the idea of God's judgment on creation, with each trumpet intensifying the severity of the consequences.
2. Nature's Response: These judgments demonstrate nature itself being affected, illustrating the interconnectedness of God's creation with His judgments.
3. Spiritual Significance: While the events described have natural elements, they also carry spiritual significance, portraying the impact of sin and divine retribution on the world.

Verse 13: "As I watched, I heard an eagle that was flying in midair call out in a loud voice: 'Woe! Woe! Woe to the inhabitants of the earth because of the trumpet blasts about to be sounded by the other three angels!'"

- John hears an eagle flying in midair proclaiming three-fold woes to the inhabitants of the earth due to the impending trumpet judgments by the remaining three angels.

Interpretation and Commentary:
1. Warning of Woes: The eagle's proclamation serves as a warning of intensified judgments yet to come. The three remaining trumpet judgments are described as "woes," signifying greater devastation and suffering.
2. Divine Announcements: Throughout Revelation, various heavenly beings and creatures serve as messengers to announce and emphasize the significance of God's actions and judgments (Revelation 5:2-5; Revelation 10:1-4).

Revelation Chapter 8 presents a series of trumpet judgments, marked by a period of silence in heaven and accompanied by the intercession of prayers and the casting of a censer with fire. These judgments have symbolic and literal elements, highlighting the consequences of sin and divine intervention. The eagle's cry warns of more intense judgments yet to come, underscoring the gravity of these prophetic events.

Prophetic Commentary:

The book of Revelation unfolds with the description of seven seals on a prophetic scroll. When we reach Revelation 8:1-2, the first four seals, commonly known as the Four Horsemen of the Apocalypse, along with the fifth and sixth seals, have already been opened. At this point, Jesus Christ opens the seventh and final seal, revealing seven angels and their trumpets. These seven angels proceed to sound their trumpets in succession, heralding seven dreadful end-time events:
1. First trumpet: Striking of trees and grass (Revelation 8:7).
2. Second trumpet: Striking of the seas (8:8-9).
3. Third trumpet: Striking of fresh waters (8:10-11).
4. Fourth trumpet: Striking of the sun, moon, and stars (8:12).
5. Fifth trumpet (first woe): Torment inflicted by symbolic locusts upon people for a duration of five months (9:1-11).
6. Sixth trumpet (second woe): A 200-million-man army causing the death of one-third of humanity (9:13-21).

7. Seventh trumpet (third woe): Announcing the return of Jesus Christ and the subsequent arrival of the seven last plagues (11:15-19; 16:1-21).

CHAPTER NINE

The Fifth and Sixth Trumpets: The Locusts from the Bottomless Pit and The Angels from the Euphrates

Introduction:

Chapter 9 of the Book of Revelation introduces the fifth and sixth trumpet judgments, which bring intensified tribulation upon the earth. As the fifth trumpet is sounded, a star falls from heaven and is given the key to the bottomless pit. When the pit is opened, a cloud of smoke arises, and from it emerges a horde of locust-like creatures that are granted the power to torment humanity for five months. These creatures are described in vivid, symbolic language, with human faces, hair like women's hair, teeth like lions, and the ability to inflict painful stings like scorpions. Despite the excruciating torment, humanity does not repent of their wickedness. The sixth trumpet judgment follows, with four angels released to kill a third of mankind. An army of two hundred million mounted troops, whose horses breathe out fire, smoke, and sulfur, inflicts death and destruction upon the earth. Yet, once again, those who survive do not turn from their sinful ways but persist in idolatry and sorcery.

Chapter 9 offers a sobering depiction of the consequences of human rebellion and refusal to repent in the face of divine judgment. The vivid symbolism of the locust-like creatures and the destructive army underscores the severity of God's judgments during the end times. It also serves as a reminder of the urgency of repentance and the need to turn to God for mercy and salvation. Despite the horrors described in this chapter, it is a call to consider the eternal consequences of our choices and to seek reconciliation with God before it's too late.

Verse 1: "The fifth angel sounded his trumpet, and I saw a star that had fallen from the sky to the earth. The star was given the key to the shaft of the Abyss."

- The fifth angel sounds his trumpet, and John sees a fallen star, given the key to the Abyss.

Interpretation and Commentary:

1. The Fallen Star: This fallen star represents an angelic being with a specific role in the unfolding of these trumpet judgments. The key to the Abyss signifies authority over a place of great significance.

2. The Abyss: The Abyss is often associated with a place of confinement for evil spirits or demonic forces (Luke 8:31; Romans 10:7). The opening of the Abyss will release these malevolent beings.

Verses 2-3: "When he opened the Abyss, smoke rose from it like the smoke from a gigantic furnace. The sun and sky were darkened by the smoke from the Abyss, and out of the smoke locusts came down on the earth and were given power like that of scorpions of the earth."

- As the Abyss is opened, smoke rises, darkening the sky, and locusts emerge, possessing power similar to that of scorpions.

Interpretation and Commentary:

1. Symbolic Imagery: The smoke and locusts are symbolic elements, portraying the consequences of the Abyss being opened. The darkness and locusts signify spiritual and moral degradation and turmoil.

2. Locusts as a Biblical Symbol: In the Bible, locusts are often used as symbols of destruction and judgment (Exodus 10:12-15; Joel 2:1-11). In this context, they represent a malevolent force of destruction.

Verse 4: "They were told not to harm the grass of the earth or any plant or tree, but only those people who did not have the seal of God on their foreheads."

- The locusts are instructed not to harm the vegetation but to target only those who do not have the seal of God on their foreheads.

Interpretation and Commentary:

1. Selective Judgment: This instruction highlights a selective aspect of the judgment. God's people, symbolically sealed on their foreheads, are protected from this specific affliction. It illustrates the divine distinction between the righteous and the unrighteous.

Verse 5: "They were not allowed to kill them but only to torture them for five months. And the agony they suffered was like that of the sting of a scorpion when it strikes."

- The locusts are prevented from killing their targets but are allowed to torment them for five months, inflicting pain similar to a scorpion's sting.

Interpretation and Commentary:

1. Limited Duration: The torment inflicted by these locusts is severe but temporary, lasting for a specified period. This might signify a period of intense tribulation or suffering, but not necessarily eternal damnation.

Verse 6: "During those days people will seek death but will not find it; they will long to die, but death will elude them."

- In the midst of this torment, people will desperately seek death but will be unable to find it.

Interpretation and Commentary:

1. Intense Suffering: The level of suffering caused by the torment of the locusts is depicted as so extreme that people would prefer death over enduring it. This emphasizes the severity of the judgment.

Verse 7: "The locusts looked like horses prepared for battle. On their heads, they wore something like crowns of gold, and their faces resembled human faces."

- The appearance of the locusts is described as resembling horses ready for battle, wearing crowns of gold on their heads and having human-like faces.

Interpretation and Commentary:

1. Symbolic Appearance: The description of the locusts is highly symbolic, representing a destructive force with characteristics that might be associated with conquest or dominion.

Verses 8-10: A further description of the locusts, including their hair like women's hair, teeth like lions' teeth, breastplates of iron, and the sound of their wings.

- These descriptions emphasize the ferocity and formidable nature of the locusts.

Interpretation and Commentary:

1. Symbolic and Frightening: These descriptions are intended to evoke a sense of terror and dread. The combined imagery portrays a relentless and destructive force.

Verse 11: "They had tails with stingers, like scorpions, and in their tails, they had the power to torment people for five months."

- The locusts are described as having tails with stingers like scorpions, enabling them to torment people for five months.

Interpretation and Commentary:

1. Symbolic Power: The stingers in their tails symbolize their ability to inflict torment and suffering. The five-month duration suggests a finite period of distress.

Verse 12: "They had as king over them the angel of the Abyss, whose name in Hebrew is Abaddon and in Greek is Apollyon (that is, Destroyer)."

- These locusts have an angelic leader over them, identified as Abaddon in Hebrew and Apollyon in Greek, both of which mean "Destroyer."

Interpretation and Commentary:

1. Leadership by an Angel: The mention of an angelic leader underscores the supernatural and orchestrated nature of these events. This angelic leader has authority over the destructive forces released from the Abyss.

Verse 13: "The sixth angel sounded his trumpet, and I heard a voice coming from the four horns of the golden altar that is before God."

- The sixth angel sounds his trumpet, and John hears a voice emanating from the four horns of the golden altar before God.

Interpretation and Commentary:

1. Altar of Incense: The mention of the golden altar is significant. In the Jewish Tabernacle and Temple, this altar was associated with the offering of incense and prayers (Exodus 30:1-10). The

voice from this altar underscores the connection between prayer and divine intervention.

Verse 14: "It said to the sixth angel who had the trumpet, 'Release the four angels who are bound at the great river Euphrates.'"

- The voice instructs the sixth angel to release the four bound angels located at the great river Euphrates.

Interpretation and Commentary:

1. Bound Angels: The existence of bound angels waiting for a specific moment highlights the sovereignty of God over angelic beings and their involvement in executing divine judgments (2 Peter 2:4; Jude 1:6).

2. Euphrates River: The Euphrates River holds biblical significance as a geographical boundary and is associated with historical events and prophecies in the Bible (Genesis 15:18; Revelation 16:12). Releasing angels from this location signals a significant event.

Verse 15: "And the four angels who had been kept ready for this very hour and day and month and year were released to kill a third of mankind."

- The four angels, prepared for a specific time, are released to execute judgment, resulting in the death of one-third of humanity.

Interpretation and Commentary:

1. Precise Timing: The mention of a specific hour, day, month, and year emphasizes that these events are meticulously planned by God. This precision underscores the sovereignty of God over time and history.

2. One-Third Judgment: The scale of judgment is significant. It indicates widespread devastation and loss of life. Similar fractions of judgment are seen in other parts of Revelation, highlighting the magnitude of these judgments (Revelation 8:7-12; Revelation 16:1-21).

Verse 16: "The number of the mounted troops was twice ten thousand times ten thousand. I heard their number."

- The verse describes an immense army of mounted troops, numbering twice ten thousand times ten thousand, with their number heard by John.

Interpretation and Commentary:

1. Vast Multitude: This vast army is symbolic of a multitude of destructive forces unleashed as a result of these angelic actions. The use of a large, symbolic number signifies an overwhelming and unstoppable force.

Verse 17: "The horses and riders I saw in my vision looked like this: Their breastplates were fiery red, dark blue, and yellow as sulfur. The heads of the horses resembled the heads of lions, and out of their mouths came fire, smoke, and sulfur."

- John describes the appearance of the horses and riders in his vision, highlighting their fiery-red breastplates, dark blue, sulfur-colored, and lion-like heads, from which fire, smoke, and sulfur emerge.

Interpretation and Commentary:

1. Symbolic Description: The detailed description of these horses and riders is symbolic in nature, depicting the fearsome and destructive nature of this judgment. Fire, smoke, and sulfur are often associated with divine judgment in the Bible (Genesis 19:24; Revelation 14:10).
2. Lion-Like Heads: The lion-like heads may symbolize the strength, ferocity, and royal authority of these forces.

Verse 18: "A third of mankind was killed by the three plagues of fire, smoke, and sulfur that came out of their mouths."

- The result of this judgment is that one-third of humanity is killed by the three plagues of fire, smoke, and sulfur emitted from the mouths of these riders.

Interpretation and Commentary:

1. Severe Judgment: The severity of this judgment is evident, with the combination of fire, smoke, and sulfur causing widespread death. This mirrors the biblical theme of divine judgment resulting from human rebellion and sin (Isaiah 30:33; Genesis 19:24).

Verse 19: "The power of the horses was in their mouths and in their tails; for their tails were like snakes, having heads with which they inflict injury."

- The power of these horses lies in their mouths and tails, with their tails resembling snakes that possess heads capable of inflicting harm.

Interpretation and Commentary:

1. Symbolic Warfare: This description symbolizes the destructive capabilities of these forces. The mention of snake-like tails with heads for inflicting harm emphasizes their deadly nature.

Verse 20: "The rest of mankind who were not killed by these plagues still did not repent of the work of their hands; they did not stop worshiping demons, and idols of gold, silver, bronze, stone and wood—idols that cannot see or hear or walk."

- Despite the devastating judgments, the remaining people do not repent of their idolatry and continue worshiping demons and lifeless idols.

Interpretation and Commentary:

1. Stubborn Rebellion: This verse highlights the stubbornness of those who refuse to turn to God even in the face of severe judgments. It underscores the persistence of idolatry and spiritual blindness.

2. Idolatry and Demonic Worship: The continued worship of demons and idols reflects the spiritual deception that has gripped these people, despite the evident consequences of their actions (1 Corinthians 10:20).

Verse 21: "Nor did they repent of their murders, their magic arts, their sexual immorality, or their thefts."

- The people also do not repent of their sins, including murder, sorcery, sexual immorality, and theft.

Interpretation and Commentary:

1. Unrepentant Hearts: This verse reveals the hardness of their hearts and their refusal to turn away from sinful practices, even in the face of divine judgment.

2. List of Sins: The sins mentioned are representative of a broader pattern of rebellion and ungodliness. They reflect a society deeply entrenched in moral decay and spiritual darkness.

Revelation Chapter 9 portrays the unfolding of the sixth trumpet judgment, marked by the release of bound angels, the emergence of a destructive force symbolized by mounted troops, and severe plagues of fire, smoke, and sulfur. Despite the gravity of these judgments, many people remain unrepentant, persisting in idolatry and sinful behaviors. This chapter underscores the importance of repentance and the consequences of spiritual rebellion.

Prophetic Commentary:

The prophecies of Revelation can seem complex and even surreal. But here are three practical things we need to know now about the three woes.

The Day of the Lord is a prominent theme in numerous biblical prophecies, signifying the moment when God intervenes to bring an end to the oppression, corruption, sin, and wickedness that have plagued humanity under human misrule. It will be a time marked by retribution, severe plagues, and arguably the darkest period in human history. However, it also heralds the onset of a new era—an age when God will assume authority, ushering in an era of peace and prosperity for our troubled world.

The events of the Day of the Lord, as depicted in the book of Revelation, transpire subsequent to the Great Tribulation and the celestial signs. This series of events includes the emergence of seven trumpet plagues. Seven angels, in sequence, blow their trumpets, unleashing devastating plagues upon the earth due to humanity's rejection of God and His benevolent laws, which were designed for our well-being.

Humanity will find itself perilously close to self-destruction, having strayed so far from God's path that the majority will neither repent nor obey. While some will choose to repent—such as the great multitude emerging from the Great Tribulation who will turn to God (Revelation 7:9-17)—most will remain unrepentant. It appears that, in order to capture their attention, God will employ plagues, akin to His dealings with Pharaoh during the time of the Exodus.

The final three trumpet plagues are commonly referred to as the three woes. But why are they termed as such?

In Revelation 8:13, following the first four trumpet plagues, the apostle John heard an angel issue a warning: "Woe, woe, woe to the inhabitants of the earth, because of the remaining blasts of the trumpet of the three angels who are about to sound!"

This is where the designation "the three woes" originates. The Greek Lexicon by Louw & Nida defines "woe" as "a state of intense hardship or distress—disaster or horror." To put it differently, as rendered by the New Living Translation, it could be described as "Terror, terror, terror." Hence, it might also be referred to as the three terrors or catastrophic events.

The first woe, as described in Revelation 9:3, presents a plague likened to locusts but possessing the stinging power of scorpions! Revelation 9:4 specifies, "They were commanded not to harm the grass of the earth, or any green thing, or any tree, but only those men who do not have the seal of God on their foreheads."

Hence, the first woe inflicts torment for a period of five months upon those lacking the seal of God (verse 5). A seal signifies ownership, and God seals those who belong to Him—those who have repented, diligently strive to obey Him, and possess the Holy Spirit.

What should we take away from this first woe? It underscores the importance of having the seal of God.

We must avoid quenching the Holy Spirit, and we must refuse to accept the mark of the beast—a symbol of compromise with God's commandments. Any willingness to compromise for the sake of success or survival will result in bearing that dreadful mark, whether it takes the form of a literal and visible mark, an implanted microchip, or the spiritual manifestation of compromise.

Therefore, the first woe represents a painful and intense torment that falls short of causing death. The second woe, announced by the sixth trumpet, presents a vastly different scenario.

The second woe introduces a catastrophic event involving a 200-million-man army and the death of one-third of humanity in a devastating global conflict (Revelation 9:15-16). It appears that the forces of the beast power originating from Europe will confront a massive army hailing from Asia.

Surprisingly, despite the staggering death toll, one might expect people to be inclined to repent. However, Revelation 9:21 delivers a grim verdict: "And they did not repent of their murders or their sorceries or their sexual immorality or their thefts." The term "sorceries" originates from the Greek word "pharmakeia," which encompasses the concept of the occult, sorcery, witchcraft, illicit pharmaceuticals, trance, and magical incantation involving drugs (Spiros Zodhiates, The Complete Word Study Dictionary, New Testament, 1992).

Even in the face of this harrowing world war, resulting in the deaths of billions, the remaining population remains obstinate and refuses to repent.

The lesson for us is clear: We must not succumb to the immoralities and drug culture prevalent in the world. Instead, we must always remain open to God's correction, consistently repent of our sins, and draw nearer to God.

The third woe encompasses the seven last plagues, as detailed in Revelation 16. Additionally, it involves those remnants of the world's armies who are deceived into engaging in battle against Jesus Christ upon His return. However, this seventh trumpet culminates with Christ's triumphant victory in that conflict, as He sets foot on the Mount of Olives. Revelation 11:15 vividly portrays the scene when the seventh angel sounds his trumpet:

"Then the seventh angel sounded: And there were loud voices in heaven, saying, 'The kingdoms of this world have become the kingdoms of our Lord and of His Christ, and He shall reign forever and ever!'"

Following a period of woes, terrors, and wars, Jesus Christ will return to put an end to all suffering, distress, and conflict. His coming will rescue humanity from the brink of self-destruction. Christ, alongside the resurrected saints, will offer assistance, healing, comfort, and guidance to all people—a much-needed support for those who survive these three woes.

As we consider the third woe, it is essential to prepare ourselves now to extend help, guidance, and service to the individuals who emerge from these challenging times.

CHAPTER TEN

The Mighty Angel with the Little Book

Introduction:

Chapter 10 of the Book of Revelation introduces a vision of a mighty angel who descends from heaven with a small open scroll in his hand. This angel is described as having a radiant appearance and a voice like roaring thunder. As he cries out, seven thunders utter their voices, but John is instructed not to write down what they say. The angel then raises his right hand to heaven and swears an oath that there will be no more delay in God's plan, and that the seventh trumpet—the final trumpet judgment—will be sounded at the appointed time. He also declares that when the seventh trumpet is sounded, the mystery of God will be fulfilled, as God has declared to His prophets. John is then instructed to take the scroll from the angel's hand and eat it. It is sweet in his mouth, but it turns bitter in his stomach. This symbolic act signifies the sweetness of God's Word and the bitterness of the judgments contained within it.

Chapter 10 serves as an interlude in the sequence of trumpet judgments, providing insight into God's timing and His divine plan. The angel's oath underscores the certainty of God's sovereign purposes and the imminence of the final judgment. The symbolism of eating the scroll highlights the importance of internalizing God's Word, experiencing both its sweetness as a source of spiritual nourishment and its bitterness as a reminder of the judgment that awaits the unrepentant. Overall, this chapter emphasizes God's unwavering commitment to His plan, the significance of prophecy in Revelation, and the call for believers to engage deeply with the Word of God in anticipation of the events yet to come.

Verse 1: "Then I saw another mighty angel coming down from heaven. He was robed in a cloud, with a rainbow above his head; his face was like the sun, and his legs were like fiery pillars."

- John sees a powerful angel descending from heaven, clothed in a cloud, with a rainbow above his head. The angel's countenance is radiant like the sun, and his legs are like pillars of fire.

Interpretation and Commentary:

1. Mighty Angel: This angel's appearance is awe-inspiring, indicating his significance in the unfolding of events. Angels often serve as messengers and agents of God's divine purposes.

2. Rainbow: The rainbow symbolizes God's covenant and faithfulness (Genesis 9:12-17). Its presence above the angel may signify that this message is within the context of God's covenant promises.

3. Radiant Appearance: The description of the angel's face as shining like the sun underscores his glory and heavenly origin (Matthew 17:2). His fiery legs symbolize his strength and purpose.

Verse 2: "He was holding a little scroll, which lay open in his hand. He planted his right foot on the sea and his left foot on the land."

- The angel holds an open, little scroll and stands with one foot on the sea and the other on the land.

Interpretation and Commentary:

1. The Little Scroll: The scroll symbolizes a message or revelation. Its "open" state suggests that its contents are accessible or about to be revealed.

2. Feet on Land and Sea: The angel's posture, with one foot on the sea and one on the land, signifies authority and dominion over both realms. This symbolizes that the message is intended for the entire world.

Verse 3: "And he gave a loud shout like the roar of a lion. When he shouted, the voices of the seven thunders spoke."

- The angel emits a powerful shout reminiscent of a lion's roar, and as he does so, the voices of the seven thunders speak.

Interpretation and Commentary:

1. The Lion's Roar: The lion's roar is often associated with strength and authority (Amos 3:8). The angel's shout signifies the importance and urgency of the message.

2. Seven Thunders: The voices of the seven thunders are not disclosed in the text, and their content remains a mystery. This emphasizes that some aspects of God's plan and revelation are sealed.

Verse 4: "And when the seven thunders spoke, I was about to write; but I heard a voice from heaven say, 'Seal up what the seven thunders have said and do not write it down.'"

- John intends to record the words spoken by the seven thunders, but he hears a voice from heaven instructing him to seal and not write down what they have said.

Interpretation and Commentary:

1. Sealing of the Thunders: The decision to seal the content of the seven thunders underscores the selective nature of revelation. Some aspects of God's plan and purposes remain hidden and are not revealed to human understanding (Deuteronomy 29:29).

Verse 5: "Then the angel I had seen standing on the sea and on the land raised his right hand to heaven."

- The angel previously seen standing on the sea and land raises his right hand to heaven.

Interpretation and Commentary:

1. Raising the Right Hand: This action is often associated with making solemn oaths or declarations (Genesis 14:22; Daniel 12:7). It signifies the seriousness and significance of what is about to be proclaimed.

Verse 6: "And he swore by him who lives forever and ever, who created the heavens and all that is in them, the earth and all that is in it, and the sea and all that is in it, and said, 'There will be no more delay!'"

- The angel swears by the eternal God, the Creator of the heavens, the earth, and the sea. He declares that there will be no more delay.

Interpretation and Commentary:

1. Solemn Oath: The angel's oath underscores the authority of the message he is about to deliver. By invoking the name of the eternal Creator, he emphasizes the trustworthiness of what he is about to declare.
2. No More Delay: The declaration that there will be no more delay suggests a sense of imminence and urgency regarding the events to come, as if a divine timetable is reaching its climax.

Verse 7: "But in the days when the seventh angel is about to sound his trumpet, the mystery of God will be accomplished, just as he announced to his servants the prophets."

- The angel declares that, as the seventh angel is about to sound his trumpet, the mystery of God will be fulfilled, in accordance with the prophecies announced to His servants, the prophets.

Interpretation and Commentary:

1. Fulfillment of Prophecy: This verse affirms that the events foretold by the prophets of old will come to pass as the seventh trumpet judgment approaches. It signifies the culmination of God's plan.
2. Mystery of God: The "mystery of God" refers to the unfolding of His divine plan and purposes, which were previously concealed but are now being revealed in accordance with His timetable (1 Corinthians 2:7; Ephesians 3:9).

Verse 8: "Then the voice that I had heard from heaven spoke to me once more: 'Go, take the scroll that lies open in the hand of the angel who is standing on the sea and on the land.'"

- The voice from heaven instructs John to take the open scroll from the angel standing on the sea and the land.

Interpretation and Commentary:

1. Commission to Proclaim: John is commissioned to take the open scroll, suggesting that he is tasked with proclaiming its contents, which likely pertain to the unfolding of God's divine plan.

Verse 9: "So I went to the angel and asked him to give me the little scroll. He said to me, 'Take it and eat it. It will turn your stomach sour, but 'in your mouth it will be as sweet as honey.'"

- John approaches the angel and requests the little scroll. The angel grants it to him and instructs him to eat it, explaining that it will taste sweet like honey in his mouth but will turn his stomach sour.

Interpretation and Commentary:

1. Eating the Scroll: This symbolic act of eating the scroll signifies John's reception and internalization of God's message, both its sweetness and its potential bitterness.
2. Sweet and Sour: The dual taste represents the contrasting nature of God's message. It may be sweet in the sense of containing promises and revelations, but it may also carry a sense of judgment and hardship, causing a bitter reaction in John.

Verse 10: "I took the little scroll from the angel's hand and ate it. It tasted as sweet as honey in my mouth, but when I had eaten it, my stomach turned sour."

- John takes the little scroll from the angel's hand, eats it, and experiences the scroll tasting sweet like honey in his mouth. However, after eating it, he feels his stomach turn sour.

Interpretation and Commentary:

1. Symbolic Act of Ingestion: John's act of eating the scroll is symbolic. It represents his acceptance and internalization of God's message and revelation, which initially seems sweet.
2. Sweetness and Sourness: The contrasting taste conveys a deeper message. The initial sweetness represents the joy and delight found in God's Word and His promises (Psalm 119:103). However, the subsequent sourness implies that the message contains elements of judgment and tribulation, which can be difficult to digest and accept (Ezekiel 3:1-3).

Verse 11: "Then I was told, 'You must prophesy again about many peoples, nations, languages and kings.'"

- John receives a directive to prophesy once more, this time concerning various peoples, nations, languages, and kings.

Interpretation and Commentary:

1. Continuation of John's Prophetic Role: Despite the initial sweetness and sourness of the message, John is instructed to continue his prophetic ministry. He is called to deliver God's messages to a wide and diverse audience, encompassing different cultures and rulers.

2. Global Impact: The scope of John's prophetic ministry extends to "many peoples, nations, languages, and kings," emphasizing the global reach and significance of God's message in the unfolding events of Revelation.

In Revelation Chapter 10, we witness a powerful symbolic act as John ingests the little scroll, signifying his reception of God's message. The contrast between sweetness and sourness in his experience reflects the dual nature of God's Word—containing promises of blessing and warnings of judgment. John is then commissioned to continue his prophetic ministry, proclaiming God's message to a diverse and extensive audience, underlining the far-reaching impact of the revelation.

Prophetic Commentary:

The Mighty Angel with the Little Book (verses 1-6)

Many biblical scholars, including Pettingill, DeHaan, Ironsides, Godet, Vincent, and Kemp, believe that this "Mighty Angel" is none other than Christ. This belief gains support from the reference to the two witnesses as "my" two witnesses in chapter 11:3. Here are seven key aspects of this mighty angel:

A. He descended from heaven — This signifies His authority, encompassing all authority in both Heaven and on earth.

B. Clothed with a cloud — This symbolizes His majestic presence, akin to the cloud that accompanied the Lord of Glory, as seen in Exodus 13:21.

C. A rainbow upon His head — This signifies the covenant, reminiscent of the rainbow in Genesis 9:13.

D. Face shining like the sun — This radiance mirrors what John observed in chapter 1:16 and Matthew 17:2.

E. Feet like pillars of fire — A symbol of judgment, as seen in Revelation 1:15.

F. Voice like a lion (verse 3) — A kingly symbol, this voice caused seven thunders to sound their voices, as noted in Revelation 1:15.

G. Feet on the earth — Indicating His taking possession of both land and sea, signifying triumph and dominion (Psalm 24:1; Leviticus 25:23; Psalm 8:6-8) as seen in Joshua 1:1-3.

Verse Two

The "little book" appears to be the same book originally in the Father's possession, often referred to as the "title deed to the earth." Within it lie the judgments of the tribulation, through which the Lord Jesus will assume His reign. This book serves as His authority for asserting dominion over both sea and land.

The term "little" characterizes this book because most of the judgments it contains have already transpired, with only a brief period remaining (Romans 9:28).

Verse Three

The seven thunders serve as God's affirmation of the Angel's claim, denoting the perfection of God's judgment intervention (Job 37:5).

Verse Four

The seven thunders bring forth further revelation, including specific content that John understood. However, for reasons unknown to us, God did not intend for the words heard from the seven thunders to be recorded in the Book of Revelation. It's essential to remember that God reveals to humanity only what He deems necessary.

Verses Five and Six

The angel swears that there will be no further delay, signifying that "time no longer" separates us from the remaining tribulation events (Daniel 12:7). The raising of the hand is a solemn gesture used in oath-taking, symbolizing a pledge rather than profanity. In this instance, it signifies Christ's commitment to the Father that there will be no more delay. It's crucial to understand that all judgment is entrusted to Christ.

The Mystery of God — Verse 7

In the New Testament, the term "mystery" doesn't refer to something entirely incomprehensible but rather to a truth that was kept hidden throughout the ages and is revealed in the final period. Let's explore some examples of these mysteries:

A. The mystery of faith — Mentioned in I Timothy 3:9.

B. The mystery of Israel's blindness — Discussed in Romans 11:25.

C. The mystery of the rapture — Explored in I Corinthians 15:51.

D. The mystery of the kingdom — Found in Matthew 13:1.

E. The mystery of godliness — Addressed in I Timothy 3:16.

F. The mystery of iniquity — Discussed in II Thessalonians 2:7.

G. The mystery of God — As referenced in Revelation 10:7.

When we encounter the phrase "the days of the Voice," it signifies a period of time. The seventh angel will continue to sound the seventh trumpet until the Mystery of God reaches its culmination. This commencement is noted in chapter 11:15, and the conclusion of the Mystery of God will coincide with the conclusion of the book of Revelation, marking the dawn of eternity.

The Mystery of God revolves around profound questions: Why did God permit sin to enter the world and consequently lead to the fall of humanity and creation? Why did He ordain that mankind would require a Savior, even knowing it would entail the sacrifice of His only begotten Son? Why was it necessary for one to die for the salvation of many when God could have preserved all as innocent beings? Furthermore, after mankind's fall, why didn't God provide an alternative to the death of His Son to ultimately restore humanity and creation to their Edenic state? And why the extended delay in removing the curse from nature and bestowing resurrected bodies upon the redeemed? Lastly, why has God permitted the righteous to suffer while the wicked prosper? These are complex questions that may be challenging to answer comprehensively, but God will ultimately provide answers that satisfy our understanding. We will come to realize that His divine plan was, indeed, the best course of action.

"As he hath declared to His prophets" — God has revealed the culmination of these matters through His prophets (Jude 14). Even Enoch, who lived during Adam's time, prophesied about them. Over the centuries, God's prophets have foretold the conclusion of the Mystery of God (Acts 3:21).

The Book Consumed by John (verses 8-11)

It appears that John has returned to Earth in a spiritual sense. He is given a Book, which serves as the title deed to the Earth. John proceeds to consume the Book, resulting in a bittersweet experience. To "eat" the Book symbolizes receiving the Word of God through faith, a concept affirmed by biblical passages (Jeremiah 15:16; Ezekiel 3:1-3; Proverbs 16:24; Psalms 119:103).

The Book devoured by John contained judgments that initially brought sweetness to his mouth but turned bitter as he internalized them. This bitterness signifies sorrow and anguish due to impending judgment (Ruth 1:20; Ezekiel 2:9,10; 3:14). John eagerly embraced the Book's contents, but upon realizing that it foretold judgment, he experienced deep inner turmoil and heartache. It was sweet to taste but brought spiritual indigestion (I John 3:3).

Many individuals begin their study of prophecy with enthusiasm, but when they recognize its personal relevance and the demands it places on their lives, their interest wanes, and it becomes a bitter experience.

Verse Eleven

The phrase "before many peoples" implies that what John is about to record regarding future judgments will not pertain to a single empire but to many. Thus, John is chosen as a vessel to reveal even more. It is essential to note that our ability to serve God is a privilege bestowed upon us by His grace.

Conclusion:

The study of prophecy should have a profound impact on students. It should inspire us to lead our friends to Christ and to emulate His character. His imminent return is a reality we must be prepared for. The next lesson will delve into God's two special witnesses on Earth, who will be broadcast via satellite television in Jerusalem. This is an event not to be missed.

CHAPTER ELEVEN

The Two Witnesses

Introduction:

Chapter 11 of the Book of Revelation is a significant chapter that introduces the measurement of the temple, the two witnesses, and the seventh trumpet judgment. John is given a measuring rod and is told to measure the temple of God, along with its altar and those who worship there. This act of measurement symbolizes God's ownership and protection of His people, while also highlighting the distinction between the faithful and those who reject Him. The measuring of the temple precedes the announcement of the two witnesses, who will prophesy for 1,260 days, clothed in sackcloth. These witnesses have the power to perform miraculous signs and can bring fire from their mouths to consume their enemies. They are symbolically represented as two olive trees and two lampstands, signifying their spiritual significance. When their testimony is complete, they are killed by the beast from the abyss, and their bodies are left in the streets of Jerusalem for three and a half days. Then, they are resurrected and taken up to heaven, causing great fear and amazement among those who witness it.

Chapter 11 is rich in symbolism and prophetic imagery. The temple measurement represents God's covenant relationship with His people and His protection of the faithful. The two witnesses symbolize the prophetic ministry and power of God's servants, while their deaths and resurrection signify the triumph of God's purposes even in the face of opposition. The chapter also introduces the seventh trumpet judgment, signaling the climax of God's judgments and the inauguration of His kingdom. Overall, Chapter 11 emphasizes God's sovereignty, the role of His faithful witnesses, and the ultimate victory of His divine plan despite the challenges and opposition faced by His people. It provides a glimpse into the unfolding events leading up to the culmination of history.

Verse 1: "I was given a reed like a measuring rod and was told, 'Go and measure the temple of God and the altar, with its worshipers.'"

- John receives a reed like a measuring rod and is instructed to measure the temple of God, the altar, and those who worship there.

Interpretation and Commentary:

1. Measuring Symbolism: Measuring is often used in the Bible to denote God's ownership, protection, and evaluation (Ezekiel 40:3; Zechariah 2:1-2). Here, it signifies God's special care and preservation of His people during a time of trial.

2. The Temple and Altar: The temple represents the dwelling place of God or His people, and the altar is a place of worship and sacrifice. Measuring them implies their consecration and protection during challenging times.

Verse 2: "But exclude the outer court; do not measure it because it has been given to the Gentiles. They will trample on the holy city for 42 months."

- John is instructed not to measure the outer court of the temple because it will be given to the Gentiles, who will trample the holy city for 42 months (3.5 years).

Interpretation and Commentary:

1. Outer Court Excluded: The exclusion of the outer court from measurement signifies its desolation and vulnerability to Gentile occupation. This may represent a period of trial and tribulation.

2. 42 Months: This time frame aligns with the "time, times, and half a time" or 3.5 years mentioned elsewhere in Revelation (Revelation 12:14) and reflects a period of intensified persecution and opposition to God's people.

Verse 3: "And I will appoint my two witnesses, and they will prophesy for 1,260 days, clothed in sackcloth."

- God will appoint two witnesses who will prophesy for 1,260 days (3.5 years) while clothed in sackcloth, a symbol of mourning and repentance.

Interpretation and Commentary:

1. Two Witnesses: The identity of the two witnesses is a matter of debate, with various interpretations, including symbolic representations of faithful witnesses or prophetic figures. They are appointed to bear witness to God's truth during a challenging period.
2. 1,260 Days: This period mirrors the 42 months, indicating a parallel duration of prophetic ministry and witness during the same time of tribulation.
3. Sackcloth Garments: The use of sackcloth signifies a message of repentance and lamentation. The witnesses' message likely includes a call for repentance and turning to God in the midst of turmoil.

Verse 4: "They are 'the two olive trees' and the two lampstands, and 'they stand before the Lord of the earth.'"

- The two witnesses are described as "the two olive trees" and "the two lampstands" and are said to stand before the Lord of the earth.

Interpretation and Commentary:

1. Olive Trees and Lampstands: This imagery alludes to Zechariah's vision (Zechariah 4:1-14), where two olive trees provide oil to the lampstand, symbolizing the anointing and empowerment of God's Spirit. The witnesses are empowered by God to bear witness in a dark time.
2. Standing Before the Lord: This phrase underscores their divine commission and proximity to God, emphasizing their spiritual authority.

Verse 5: "If anyone tries to harm them, fire comes from their mouths and devours their enemies. This is how anyone who wants to harm them must die."

- The witnesses have the ability to breathe fire from their mouths, which consumes their enemies, ensuring that anyone who tries to harm them will be killed in this manner.

Interpretation and Commentary:

1. Divine Protection: The supernatural ability to breathe fire is a sign of God's divine protection over the witnesses and His vindication of their mission. It reinforces that their message is from God.

Verse 6: "They have power to shut up the heavens so that it will not rain during the time they are prophesying; and they have power to turn the waters into blood and to strike the earth with every kind of plague as often as they want."

- The witnesses possess the power to control natural elements, including shutting up the heavens to prevent rain, turning waters into blood, and inflicting various plagues on the earth at will.

Interpretation and Commentary:

1. Mimicking Biblical Events: Their ability to control natural elements mirrors events from the Old Testament, particularly the plagues in Egypt during the time of Moses (Exodus 7-11). This emphasizes their role as agents of God's judgment and divine authority.

Verse 7: "Now when they have finished their testimony, the beast that comes up from the Abyss will attack them, and overpower and kill them."

- After the witnesses have completed their prophetic ministry, a beast from the Abyss will rise, attack, overpower, and kill them.

Interpretation and Commentary:

1. Beast from the Abyss: This "beast" is a symbol of evil and may be associated with the forces of darkness or a human leader opposed to God. Its rising from the Abyss indicates its diabolical origin.

Verse 8: "Their bodies will lie in the public square of the great city—which is figuratively called Sodom and Egypt—where also their Lord was crucified."

- The bodies of the slain witnesses will be displayed in the public square of a city described figuratively as Sodom and Egypt, which is also where their Lord (Jesus) was crucified.

Interpretation and Commentary:

1. Symbolic City: The description of the city as "Sodom and Egypt" suggests moral corruption and spiritual oppression. This could symbolize a place of extreme wickedness.
2. Where Their Lord Was Crucified: This phrase points to Jerusalem as the location where Jesus was crucified. The city's association with the crucifixion highlights its spiritual significance and the opposition faced by God's witnesses.

Verse 9: "For three and a half days some from every people, tribe, language and nation will gaze on their bodies and refuse them burial."

- After the witnesses are killed, their bodies will remain unburied in a public spectacle for three and a half days, and people from all over the world will witness this.

Interpretation and Commentary:
1. Global Attention: The worldwide witness to this event underscores its global significance and impact, suggesting that these witnesses had a global ministry.

Verse 10: "The inhabitants of the earth will gloat over them and will celebrate by sending each other gifts because these two prophets had tormented those who live on the earth."

- The people of the earth will rejoice over the witnesses' deaths, exchanging gifts to celebrate their removal, as they believed the witnesses had tormented them.

Interpretation and Commentary:
1. Hostility and Opposition: The reaction of celebration reveals the hostility and opposition faced by these witnesses, indicating that their message provoked strong resistance.

Verse 11: "But after the three and a half days the breath of life from God entered them, and they stood on their feet, and terror struck those who saw them."

- After three and a half days, the breath of life from God enters the slain witnesses, and they are resurrected, causing great fear among those who witness this.

Interpretation and Commentary:
1. Resurrection: The resurrection of the witnesses mirrors the resurrection of Christ and signifies God's power over life and death (Matthew 28:5-7). It also serves as a powerful confirmation of the witnesses' divine authority and message.

2. Terror: The reaction of terror among the observers reflects the profound impact of this supernatural event, leading some to acknowledge God's power and authority.

Verse 12: "Then they heard a loud voice from heaven saying to them, 'Come up here.' And they went up to heaven in a cloud, while their enemies looked on."

- A voice from heaven calls the witnesses to come up, and they ascend to heaven in a cloud, visible to their enemies.

Interpretation and Commentary:

1. Ascension to Heaven: The witnesses' ascension to heaven symbolizes their vindication by God and their triumph over earthly opposition (Acts 1:9). It also marks the end of their earthly ministry.

2. Visible Witness: The witnesses' ascent in full view of their enemies serves as a testimony to God's sovereignty and authority, making it clear that they were indeed sent by Him.

Verse 13: "At that very hour there was a severe earthquake and a tenth of the city collapsed. Seven thousand people were killed in the earthquake, and the survivors were terrified and gave glory to the God of heaven."

- Following the witnesses' ascension, a powerful earthquake strikes, causing significant destruction in the city. Seven thousand people are killed, and those who survive are filled with terror and give glory to God.

Interpretation and Commentary:

1. Divine Judgment: The earthquake symbolizes God's judgment upon the wicked and serves as a consequence for the mistreatment of His witnesses (Revelation 6:12). It is a reminder of God's authority over creation.

2. Fear and Repentance: The survivors' response of fear and giving glory to God suggests a potential turning point, where some may repent and acknowledge God's sovereignty in the midst of judgment (Revelation 16:9).

Verse 14: "The second woe has passed; the third woe is coming soon."

- This verse refers to the passing of the second woe and foreshadows the impending arrival of the third woe.

Interpretation and Commentary:

1. Three Woes: In Revelation, the woes are associated with intense judgments and tribulations (Revelation 8:13). The passing of the second woe signals that the final and most severe woe is imminent.

Verse 15: "The seventh angel sounded his trumpet, and there were loud voices in heaven, which said: 'The kingdom of the world has become the kingdom of our Lord and of his Messiah, and he will reign forever and ever.'"

- The seventh angel sounds his trumpet, leading to loud voices in heaven proclaiming the transfer of earthly kingdoms to the rule of the Lord and His Messiah, who will reign eternally.

Interpretation and Commentary:

1. Culmination of God's Plan: The seventh trumpet represents a pivotal moment in God's divine plan, marking the final culmination of His redemptive purposes. It signifies the establishment of God's eternal kingdom on earth, ruled by the Messiah (Revelation 19:6).
2. Fulfillment of Prophecy: This declaration fulfills numerous Old Testament prophecies, such as Daniel 7:13-14, regarding the coming of the Son of Man to establish an everlasting kingdom.

Verse 16: "And the twenty-four elders, who were seated on their thrones before God, fell on their faces and worshiped God."

- The twenty-four elders, representing heavenly beings, fall on their faces and worship God.

Interpretation and Commentary:

1. Worship and Adoration: The response of the twenty-four elders underscores the significance of the moment, as they worship God in recognition of His sovereignty and the fulfillment of His plan.

Verse 17: "'We give thanks to you, Lord God Almighty, the One who is and who was, because you have taken your great power and have begun to reign.'"

- The elders offer thanks to the Lord God Almighty, acknowledging His eternal nature and giving thanks for Him taking His great power and beginning to reign.

Interpretation and Commentary:

1. Thanksgiving: The thanksgiving of the elders highlights the praise and gratitude offered to God for His assumption of kingship over the world. It affirms His divine authority and power.

Verse 18: "'The nations were angry, and your wrath has come. The time has come for judging the dead, and for rewarding your servants the prophets and your people who revere your name, both great and small— and for destroying those who destroy the earth.'"

- The elders proclaim that the nations have expressed anger, signaling the arrival of God's wrath. They acknowledge that it is now the time for judgment, the rewarding of God's servants, and the destruction of those who harm the earth.

Interpretation and Commentary:

1. Divine Judgment and Reward: This verse signifies a turning point in God's plan, where divine judgment is meted out to those who oppose Him while rewards are given to His faithful servants. It aligns with the concept of the final judgment described elsewhere in Revelation (Revelation 20:11-15).
2. Protection of Creation: The mention of destroying those who harm the earth underscores God's concern for His creation and His commitment to justice.

Verse 19: "Then God's temple in heaven was opened, and within his temple was seen the ark of his covenant. And there came flashes of lightning, rumblings, peals of thunder, an earthquake and a severe hailstorm."

- The temple of God in heaven is opened, revealing the ark of His covenant. This vision is accompanied by dramatic displays of lightning, thunder, an earthquake, and a severe hailstorm.

Interpretation and Commentary:

1. Symbolic Meaning: The opening of God's temple and the presence of the ark of the covenant symbolize His presence, faithfulness to His covenant promises, and the imminent fulfillment of His purposes.
2. Dramatic Manifestations: The dramatic phenomena of lightning, thunder, earthquake, and hail illustrate the awesome power and majesty of God, signaling the momentous events that are unfolding in accordance with His divine plan.

Revelation Chapter 11 is a pivotal chapter that includes the ministry and martyrdom of the two witnesses, a powerful earthquake, the sounding of the seventh trumpet heralding God's kingdom, and the dramatic manifestation of God's presence and power. It sets the stage for the final judgments and the establishment of God's eternal rule over the world.

Prophetic Commentary:

In the book of Revelation, God declares, "And I will give power to my two witnesses, and they will prophesy one thousand two hundred and sixty days, clothed in sackcloth" (Revelation 11:3).

Speculation abounds regarding the identity of these two divine envoys and their 3½-year mission. Let us turn to the Bible—the singular, authentic source of information on this subject—to glean insights about these extraordinary individuals.

Connected to Zechariah and the significance of two olive trees, two lampstands, and two anointed ones The passage in Revelation further elucidates, "These are the two olive trees and the two lampstands standing before the God of the earth" (verse 4).

This statement appears to be a continuation of a prophecy bestowed by God upon the prophet Zechariah, illustrating that God accomplishes His divine purposes through the agency of His Spirit (Zechariah 4:2-10).

Olive oil symbolizes the presence of God's Holy Spirit, and God encouraged Zerubbabel—the leader of the temple reconstruction—to recognize that spiritual achievements would be realized through the empowerment of His Spirit, rather than through human efforts alone (verse 6).

After articulating this vital principle regarding the manner in which His work is achieved, God then revisited the vision of the olive trees that Zechariah had witnessed: "These are the two anointed ones, who stand beside the Lord of the whole earth" (Zechariah 4:14, emphasis added throughout).

In Revelation 11, God discloses that these two prophets, who will be abundantly filled with God's Holy Spirit to fulfill His work, will emerge prior to the return of Christ, serving as beacons of light to the world.

Just as God employed the power of His Holy Spirit during Zerubbabel's era to accomplish His purposes, He will do likewise through His two witnesses during the climactic events of the end times.

Why Two Witnesses? Throughout the Bible, we frequently encounter instances where God operates through pairs of individuals. During the period when Zechariah penned his writings, Zerubbabel held the position of governor, and a man named Joshua fulfilled the role of high priest (Zechariah 3:1). In earlier times, God had appointed Moses as the leader of the ancient Israelites and his brother Aaron as the high priest.

In the New Testament, Christ dispatched His disciples in teams of "two by two" (Mark 6:7). Although they occasionally had additional companions, Paul and Barnabas collaborated in spreading the gospel to the gentiles.

Working together as a pair often enhances productivity and effectiveness. Recognizing this principle, Ecclesiastes 4:9-10 declares, "Two are better than one because they have a good reward for their labor. For if they fall, one will lift up his companion. But woe to him who is alone when he falls, for he has no one to help him up."

Another rationale behind God's choice to appoint two witnesses is the significance of having a minimum of two individuals to bear testimony in legal matters. As stated in Deuteronomy 19:15, "One witness shall not rise against a man concerning any iniquity or any sin that he commits; by the mouth of two or three witnesses, the matter shall be established" (also see Deuteronomy 17:6).

By appointing two witnesses, God adheres to His own law. Through these two witnesses, He serves as both a warning and an opportunity for people to repent of their sins before enacting punishment should they disregard His counsel.

The Mission of the Two Witnesses The account in the book of Revelation provides insights into the mission of the two witnesses: "And if anyone wants to harm them, fire proceeds from their mouth and devours their enemies. And if anyone wants to harm them, he must be killed in this manner. These have power to shut heaven, so that no rain falls in the days of their prophecy; and they have power over waters to turn them to blood, and to strike the earth with all plagues, as often as they desire" (Revelation 11:5-6).

As these emissaries of God bear witness to the world, proclaiming the need for all individuals to repent of their sins, they will be granted access to God's Holy Spirit, enabling them to perform miraculous acts reminiscent of other prophets of God.

Similar to Elijah, they will possess the authority to halt rainfall (1 Kings 17:1) and eliminate anyone who attempts to harm them (2 Kings 1:9-12). Like Moses, they will possess the ability to transform water into blood (Exodus 7:17) and unleash plagues upon the earth (Exodus 7:14 through 12:30).

However, inflicting suffering is not their primary objective. Instead, akin to Elijah, their mission will be to inspire people to turn their hearts toward God (1 Kings 18:37).

Elijah served during an era when ancient Israel had descended into severe corruption under the rule of the wicked King Ahab and his idolatrous wife, Jezebel. Scriptural prophecies indicate that the entire world will sink into corruption prior to the return of Christ (2 Timothy 3:13), and it is within this environment that the two witnesses will carry out their ministry.

Biblical Precedents for the Two Witnesses Over the years, numerous interpretations regarding the identity and mission of the two witnesses in Revelation 11 have emerged. Many have turned to previous biblical prophets as models for understanding what these two witnesses will accomplish.

The Expositor's Bible Commentary notes, "Identifications range from two historical figures raised to life, to two groups, to two principles, such as the law and the prophets. Tertullian (d. 220) identified the two with Enoch and Elijah" (comments on Revelation 11:3).

While we've already seen that Elijah's miraculous abilities to control rain and protect himself from harm are precursors to the powers of the two witnesses, another reference to Elijah merits consideration.

Regarding the ministry of John the Baptist, Luke 1:16-17 states, "And he will turn many of the children of Israel to the Lord their God. He will also go before Him in the spirit and power of Elijah, 'to turn the hearts of the fathers to the children,' and the disobedient to the wisdom of the just, to make ready a people prepared for the Lord."

This passage illustrates that God has the capacity to send additional representatives, such as John the Baptist, with a ministry and abilities akin to the prophet Elijah's.

While John the Baptist fulfilled the prophecy in Luke 1, indicating that he would perform an Elijah-like work (Matthew 17:11-13), Malachi 4:5-6 points to another realization of an Elijah-like mission at the close of this age.

"Behold, I will send you Elijah the prophet before the coming of the great and dreadful day of the LORD. And he will turn the hearts of the fathers to the children, and the hearts of the children to their fathers, lest I come and strike the earth with a curse."

Some prophecies, as evidenced here, may have multiple fulfillments. John the Baptist unquestionably served as a type of Elijah, while Malachi 4 suggests that another "Elijah" will arise at the end of this age.

Regarding the identity of this end-time Elijah, Scripture implies that an Elijah-like message calling for repentance and obedience to God will be proclaimed by the Church of God (Matthew 24:14; 28:19-20) and by the two witnesses, who will display Elijah-like powers as they conclude their ministry (Revelation 11:5-6).

Deceptive Figures in Contrast to the Two Witnesses: The Beast and the False Prophet In the book of Revelation, God unveils a prophetic vision concerning two individuals known as "the beast" and "the false prophet," who will oppose the mission of the two witnesses. The beast will serve as the political leader whom nearly all the inhabitants of the earth, except those faithful to God, will follow (Revelation 13:8). The false prophet, on the other hand, will lead the religious system that supports the beast.

One valuable tool for comprehending prophecy is the type-antitype principle. An illustration of what lies ahead during the time of the two witnesses can be found in Exodus 7:10-12.

The account commences with the first of several encounters between Moses and Pharaoh. Acting under Moses' guidance, Aaron cast down his rod, and it transformed into a snake. The magicians (identified by the apostle Paul as Jannes and Jambres in 2 Timothy 3:8) duplicated the feat with their own rods (Exodus 7:11-12). Water was turned into blood, and the magicians replicated this miracle as well (verse 22). All these marvels took place in the presence of Pharaoh.

During the period of the Great Tribulation, the false prophet will also display miraculous abilities. In 2 Thessalonians 2:9, it is said, "The coming of the lawless one is according to the working of Satan, with all power, signs, and lying wonders."

Describing this same individual, Revelation 13:11, 13-14 reads, "Then I saw another beast coming up out of the earth, and he had two horns like a lamb and spoke like a dragon. … He performs great signs, so that he even makes fire come down from heaven on the earth in the sight of men [an Elijah-like miracle]. And he deceives those who dwell on the earth by those signs which he was granted to do in the sight of the beast."

Satan will utilize the beast and the false prophet as counterfeits to the two witnesses. Consequently, he will continue to beguile the entire world through "signs and lying wonders" (2 Thessalonians 2:9) and deceptive religious practices (see also Matthew 24:24; Revelation 12:9).

God does not desire His followers to fall prey to these impostors. Nevertheless, the sad reality is that the majority of people will be ensnared by their deception.

What Prompts the World's Celebration at the Deaths of the Two Witnesses? Following the culmination of their 3½-year ministry, during which they proclaim the gospel to the entire world, the two witnesses will lose their divine protection and be martyred.

"When they finish their testimony, the beast that ascends out of the bottomless pit will make war against them, overcome them, and kill them. And their dead bodies will lie in the street of the great city which spiritually is called Sodom and Egypt, where also our Lord was crucified.

"Then those from the peoples, tribes, tongues, and nations will see their dead bodies three-and-a-half days, and not allow their dead bodies to be put into graves. And those who dwell on the earth will rejoice over them, make merry, and send gifts to one another, because these two prophets tormented those who dwell on the earth" (Revelation 11:7-10).

Why will there be jubilation over their deaths? The majority in the world will be resistant to their message of repentance. People often recoil from being told that their actions are in error, that they are engaging in sinful behavior and need to undergo a transformation.

Their anger will stem from the plagues inflicted upon them as consequences for their refusal to turn away from their sins. Many will attribute the torment they endure to the two witnesses and, in their frustration, seek to place blame on them.

The Triumph of the Witnesses The celebration over their deaths will prove to be short-lived. After 3½ days, God will breathe life back into them, and they will stand on their feet, striking fear into the hearts of those who witness it. A resounding voice from heaven will summon them, saying, "Come up here." In a cloud, they will ascend to heaven, a sight that will astonish their enemies (Revelation 11:11-12).

This remarkable event, their ascent to heaven, is a unique occurrence reserved for the conclusion of this era, just before Jesus returns to establish His reign on Earth (for further insights, see "Where Will Jesus Return?"). It is not a phenomenon described in the Bible as happening to righteous individuals when they pass away. For more clarification on this topic, refer to our article "What Is Heaven?"

So, what's the significance? The Message of Revelation 11 The broader lesson we glean from the two witnesses is that God will send these extraordinary emissaries to caution people to repent and alter their wicked conduct, redirecting their hearts toward God.

Moreover, we should remain vigilant against the false prophets prophesied to emerge, taking care not to be deceived. It is far wiser for us to respond to God promptly, as soon as we become aware of His expectations for us.

CHAPTER TWELVE

The Woman, the Child and the Dragon

Introduction:

Chapter 12 of the Book of Revelation is a highly symbolic and visionary passage that depicts a cosmic battle between the forces of good and evil. The chapter begins with a vision of a pregnant woman clothed with the sun, with the moon under her feet and a crown of twelve stars on her head. This woman symbolizes Israel, the chosen people of God, and her child represents the Messiah, Jesus Christ, who is destined to rule all nations. As the woman is about to give birth, a great red dragon with seven heads and ten horns, identified as Satan, stands before her, ready to devour the child. However, the child is caught up to God's throne, signifying Jesus' ascension and victory over the forces of darkness.

The chapter goes on to describe a war in heaven, where Michael and his angels fight against the dragon and his angels. The dragon is defeated and cast down to the earth, no longer able to accuse the brethren before God. This heavenly battle underscores the cosmic dimensions of the spiritual conflict between God and Satan. In response to the dragon's failure in heaven, he pursues the woman (Israel) on earth, seeking to persecute and destroy her. God provides protection for the woman, nourishing her in the wilderness for a time, times, and half a time (symbolic of a period of persecution and tribulation). Chapter 12 serves as a symbolic overview of the conflict between the forces of evil and the ultimate triumph of God's redemptive plan through the Messiah. It also sets the stage for the subsequent events and judgments described in the Book of Revelation.

Verse 1: "A great sign appeared in heaven: a woman clothed with the sun, with the moon under her feet and a crown of twelve stars on her head."

- John sees a great sign in heaven: a woman clothed with the sun, the moon under her feet, and a crown of twelve stars on her head.

Interpretation and Commentary:

1. Symbolic Imagery: This woman is a symbolic figure often interpreted as representing various elements, such as the Church, the people of God, or the Virgin Mary. Her radiant appearance signifies purity and glory.

2. Crown of Twelve Stars: The twelve stars can represent the twelve tribes of Israel or the twelve apostles, emphasizing her connection to the people of God.

Verse 2: "She was pregnant and cried out in pain as she was about to give birth."

- The woman is pregnant and experiences pain as she is about to give birth.

Interpretation and Commentary:

1. Birthing of God's Plan: The pregnancy of the woman signifies the gestation of a significant event or the fulfillment of God's plan. The pain represents the travail preceding a significant birth.

Verse 3: "Then another sign appeared in heaven: an enormous red dragon with seven heads and ten horns and seven crowns on its heads."

- John sees another sign in heaven: an enormous red dragon with seven heads, ten horns, and seven crowns on its heads.

Interpretation and Commentary:

1. The Dragon: The dragon is a symbol of Satan or the forces of evil. The seven heads and ten horns signify power and authority, and the crowns indicate dominion. This imagery points to the great adversary of God's purposes.

Verse 4: "Its tail swept a third of the stars out of the sky and flung them to the earth. The dragon stood in front of the woman who was

146

about to give birth, so that it might devour her child the moment he was born."

- The dragon's tail sweeps a third of the stars from the sky to the earth, and it positions itself before the woman to devour her child upon birth.

Interpretation and Commentary:

1. War in Heaven: The dragon's action of sweeping stars from the sky symbolizes a rebellion or war in heaven, where a portion of angels joins Satan in opposing God (Revelation 12:7-9).

2. Threat to the Child: The dragon's intent to devour the woman's child signifies Satan's opposition to God's redemptive plan and his attempts to thwart the birth and ministry of Jesus.

Verse 5: "She gave birth to a son, a male child, who 'will rule all the nations with an iron scepter.' And her child was snatched up to God and to his throne."

- The woman gives birth to a male child, who is destined to rule all nations with an iron scepter. This child is caught up to God and His throne.

Interpretation and Commentary:

1. Messiah's Birth: The male child represents Jesus Christ, born to the woman (symbolic of God's people). The prophecy about ruling with an iron scepter echoes Psalm 2:9, indicating Christ's reign and authority.

2. Ascension of Christ: The child being caught up to God's throne signifies Jesus' ascension to heaven after His earthly ministry and resurrection (Acts 1:9-11). It affirms His exalted position and sovereignty.

Verse 6: "The woman fled into the wilderness to a place prepared for her by God, where she might be taken care of for 1,260 days."

- The woman flees into the wilderness to a place prepared by God, where she will be protected for 1,260 days.

Interpretation and Commentary:

1. Protection in the Wilderness: This imagery is often interpreted as a period of refuge and protection for God's people during a time of tribulation, represented by the 1,260 days (3.5 years).

It mirrors the Israelites' wilderness journey and God's provision (Exodus 16:35).

Verse 7: "Then war broke out in heaven. Michael and his angels fought against the dragon, and the dragon and his angels fought back."

- A war erupts in heaven, with Michael and his angels battling against the dragon and its angels.

Interpretation and Commentary:

1. Heavenly Conflict: This depicts a cosmic battle between the forces of good, led by Michael (often identified as an archangel), and the forces of evil, led by the dragon (Satan). The war highlights the ongoing spiritual conflict between God and Satan.

Verse 8: "But he was not strong enough, and they lost their place in heaven."

- The dragon and its angels were not strong enough, and they lost their place in heaven.

Interpretation and Commentary:

1. Defeat of Satan: This verse signifies the defeat of Satan and his rebellion in heaven, leading to his expulsion from the heavenly realms. It aligns with Jesus' statement that He saw Satan fall from heaven like lightning (Luke 10:18).

Verse 9: "The great dragon was hurled down—that ancient serpent called the devil, or Satan, who leads the whole world astray. He was hurled to the earth, and his angels with him."

- The great dragon, identified as the ancient serpent, devil, or Satan, is cast down to the earth, along with his angels.

Interpretation and Commentary:

1. Identification of the Dragon: This verse clarifies the identity of the dragon as Satan, the deceiver of the whole world. His expulsion from heaven underscores his role as the adversary of God and humanity.

Verse 10: "Then I heard a loud voice in heaven say: 'Now have come the salvation and the power and the kingdom of our God, and the authority of his Messiah. For the accuser of our brothers and sisters, who accuses them before our God day and night, has been hurled down.'"

- A loud voice in heaven proclaims the arrival of salvation, power, God's kingdom, and the authority of His Messiah, noting the expulsion of the accuser (Satan) who accuses believers before God.

Interpretation and Commentary:

1. Victory and Redemption: This verse celebrates the victory of God and His Messiah over Satan and announces the establishment of God's kingdom and the authority of Christ. It highlights the cessation of Satan's role as the accuser.

2. Accuser of Believers: Satan is described as the accuser of believers who brings accusations against them before God. This aspect of Satan's character is seen in Job 1:6-12 and Zechariah 3:1-2.

Verse 11: "They triumphed over him by the blood of the Lamb and by the word of their testimony; they did not love their lives so much as to shrink from death."

- Believers overcome Satan through the blood of the Lamb (Christ's sacrifice) and their testimony, even to the point of willingly facing death.

Interpretation and Commentary:

1. Triumph through Christ's Sacrifice: This verse underscores the central role of Christ's sacrifice (represented by the blood of the Lamb) in the victory over Satan. It is through the atoning work of Jesus on the cross that believers find forgiveness, redemption, and victory over sin and the devil (1 Peter 1:18-19).

2. Testimony: Believers' testimony of their faith in Jesus and the transformation His grace has wrought in their lives is a powerful tool against the accusations of the enemy. It also serves to inspire others to faith.

3. Willingness to Die: The phrase "did not love their lives so much as to shrink from death" emphasizes the unwavering commitment of believers to their faith, even in the face of persecution and martyrdom. This echoes Jesus' teaching in Matthew 10:39 and John 12:25.

Verse 12: "Therefore rejoice, you heavens and you who dwell in them! But woe to the earth and the sea, because the devil has gone down to you! He is filled with fury because he knows that his time is short."

- Heaven is called to rejoice, but woe is pronounced on the earth and sea because the devil, filled with fury, has been cast down and knows his time is short.

Interpretation and Commentary:

1. Heavenly Rejoicing: The call for heaven to rejoice signifies the celebration of Satan's expulsion and the impending fulfillment of God's purposes. It echoes the rejoicing in heaven over the defeat of the dragon (Satan) in verse 10.

2. Woe to the Earth: The "woe" pronounced on the earth and sea indicates impending trouble and suffering. The devil's descent to the earth is a source of danger and evil influences.

3. Satan's Short Time: Satan's fury stems from his awareness that his time is limited. This aligns with the idea that as the end times draw near, Satan intensifies his efforts to deceive and harm humanity (Revelation 20:10).

Verse 13: "When the dragon saw that he had been hurled to the earth, he pursued the woman who had given birth to the male child."

- The dragon, cast down to the earth, begins to pursue the woman who gave birth to the male child (Jesus).

Interpretation and Commentary:

1. Persecution of God's People: The pursuit of the woman (often interpreted as the Church or God's faithful people) by the dragon signifies Satan's relentless persecution of believers throughout history (Revelation 13:7). His goal is to disrupt God's plan and hinder the spread of the gospel.

Verse 14: "The woman was given the two wings of a great eagle, so that she might fly to the place prepared for her in the wilderness, where she would be taken care of for a time, times, and half a time, out of the serpent's reach."

- The woman is provided with the means to escape, likened to the wings of a great eagle, allowing her to fly to a place in the wilderness where she will be protected for a specific period.

Interpretation and Commentary:

1. Divine Protection: The imagery of the eagle's wings represents God's supernatural provision and protection for His people during times of persecution and tribulation (Exodus 19:4).

150

2. Time, Times, and Half a Time: This phrase is often interpreted as a symbolic representation of a period of tribulation, which corresponds to 3.5 years, or 1,260 days (Revelation 12:6). It mirrors the concept of a time of trouble described in Daniel 7:25.

Verse 15: "Then from his mouth the serpent spewed water like a river, to overtake the woman and sweep her away with the torrent."

- The dragon (serpent) attempts to thwart the woman's escape by spewing water like a river to engulf her in a flood.

Interpretation and Commentary:

1. Symbolic Obstacles: The serpent's attempt to drown the woman in a flood of water is symbolic and represents various obstacles, persecutions, or challenges that Satan uses to hinder the progress of God's people and the spread of the gospel (Isaiah 59:19).

Verse 16: "But the earth helped the woman by opening its mouth and swallowing the river that the dragon had spewed out of his mouth."

- The earth intervenes, helping the woman by swallowing the river spewed by the dragon.

Interpretation and Commentary:

1. Divine Intervention: This verse illustrates God's intervention on behalf of His people. The earth's action of swallowing the river is a supernatural response to the threat posed by Satan, emphasizing God's protection and care for His faithful.

Verse 17: "Then the dragon was enraged at the woman and went off to wage war against the rest of her offspring—those who keep God's commands and hold fast their testimony about Jesus."

- In his fury, the dragon turns his attention to waging war against the rest of the woman's offspring, specifically those who keep God's commands and testify about Jesus.

Interpretation and Commentary:

1. Continued Persecution: This verse indicates that despite his initial defeat, Satan continues his efforts to persecute believers, especially those who remain faithful to God's commands and bear witness to Jesus. It reflects the ongoing spiritual battle faced by the Church (Revelation 2:10).

Revelation Chapter 12 portrays a vivid cosmic conflict between the forces of good, represented by the woman and her child

(Jesus and the Church), and the forces of evil, symbolized by the dragon (Satan). It highlights the victory of Christ's sacrifice, the ongoing persecution of believers, and God's protection and intervention in the face of adversity. Ultimately, it foreshadows the triumph of God's kingdom over the forces of darkness.

Prophetic Commentary

The book of Revelation presents a vision received by Jesus Christ from God the Father. This vision unveils future events that will occur before Christ's return to establish the Kingdom of God on Earth. Often referred to as the Apocalypse, derived from the Greek word for "revelation," this prophetic book generally follows a chronological style while occasionally pausing to provide comprehensive overviews of specific subjects.

Revelation 12 is one such overview, offering a historical perspective spanning from the era predating humanity's existence to the period just prior to Christ's return as the King of Kings and Lord of Lords.

The chapter begins with the declaration, "Now a remarkable sign appeared in heaven" (verse 1). The term "sign" originates from the Greek word "semeion," signifying "a mark, token, or an extraordinary event that surpasses the ordinary course of nature" (Thayer's Greek Definitions). This first remarkable sign presents a vision featuring a woman who gives birth to a child (verse 1).

Then, in verse 3, we encounter the phrase, "And another significant sign [semeion] appeared in heaven." This signals that these three symbols—a woman, a child, and a dragon—represent concepts extending beyond the realm of ordinary natural occurrences. As we delve into the chapter, we'll come to understand that these three figures symbolize three significant spiritual forces that have been at work for millennia.

To fully grasp this chapter's meaning, we must now unravel the symbolism and decipher what the woman, the child, and the dragon represent.

Who is the woman depicted in Revelation 12? The woman described in the Apocalypse is symbolically clothed with the sun, with the moon under her feet, and wearing a garland of twelve stars on her head (verse 1). This woman symbolizes Old Testament Israel. Throughout the Old Testament, God often referred to His people as a woman whom He adorned with honor and splendor, as seen in the book of Ezekiel, among other passages. The garland adorned with twelve stars likely represents the twelve tribes of Israel, as seen in the dream of Joseph in Genesis 37:9-10.

As we continue reading Revelation 12, it becomes evident that this "woman" is repeatedly under God's protection, particularly as the time approaches for the establishment of the "kingdom of our God" on Earth (verse 10).

In the New Testament, God's Church is symbolically represented as a woman, and its members are likened to virgins (Matthew 25:1-13; Revelation 14:4; Revelation 19:7). The New Testament Church is referred to as "the Israel of God" (Galatians 6:16) and is compared to "Jerusalem above," described as "the mother of us all" (Galatians 4:26, also see Hebrews 12:22-23). Believers in the Church are characterized as "a chosen generation, a royal priesthood, a holy nation, His [God's] own special people" (1 Peter 2:9).

Upon Christ's return to Earth, He is symbolically portrayed as marrying the Church, referred to as "His wife" in Revelation 19:7. These passages clearly establish that the woman in Revelation 12 symbolizes God's people.

It is also worth noting that in Revelation 17:1, the imagery of a dishonorable woman, referred to as "the great harlot," is employed to symbolize a false church that deceives many.

Who is the Child mentioned in Revelation 12? The Child, described as destined to "rule all nations with a rod of iron" (Revelation 12:5), unequivocally represents Jesus Christ. This description aligns with the biblical narrative of Jesus' birth, as He was born into the nation of Israel. The verse further emphasizes, "And her

Child was caught up to God and His throne," clearly signifying that this "Child" is indeed Jesus Christ.

Jesus is the prophesied figure who will "strike the nations" and "rule them with a rod of iron" (Revelation 19:15). Furthermore, after His resurrection, Jesus ascended into heaven in a cloud, as documented in Acts 1:9-11. Therefore, the "Child" in Revelation 12 is undeniably a representation of Jesus Christ.

Who is the dragon in Revelation 12? The third symbol in Revelation 12, depicted as "a great, fiery red dragon" (verse 3), is explicitly identified as Satan. The dragon's actions, including drawing "a third of the stars of heaven" and seeking to devour the woman's Child at birth (verse 4), lead to this conclusion. Later in the chapter, the dragon is unmistakably named as Satan: "So the great dragon was cast out, that serpent of old, called the Devil and Satan, who deceives the whole world" (verse 9).

The reference to the dragon drawing "a third of the stars of heaven" likely signifies Satan leading a third of the angels in rebellion against God. In other passages of the Bible, stars symbolize angels (Revelation 1:20).

The Bible also reveals that Satan initiated a rebellion against God, aspiring to exalt his throne above the stars of God and be like the Most High (Isaiah 14:13-14). Subsequently, he began his work as "that serpent of old" (the one who tempted Eve in the Garden of Eden), known as the Devil and Satan, who deceives the entire world (Revelation 12:9).

Just as God has "ministers of righteousness," Satan also has his servants, both physical ministers (who may themselves be deceived and aid in deceiving others) and spirit beings who feign righteousness while encouraging humans to sin (2 Corinthians 11:15; Ephesians 6:12). Jude further describes these fallen angels or demons as those who "did not keep their proper domain" and are now "reserved in everlasting chains under darkness for the judgment of the great day" (Jude 1:6).

Revelation 12:3-17 succinctly outlines Satan's endeavors to obstruct God's plan of bringing many humans into His eternal family. Satan's actions encompass convincing a third of the angels to follow him in his bid to elevate himself to God's status, attempting to have

Christ killed in infancy (Matthew 2:13-18), deceiving the entire world, and persecuting God's people. Let's now explore in greater depth Satan's endeavors to thwart God's plan.

In Revelation 12:4, we encounter the statement that "the dragon stood before the woman who was ready to give birth, to devour her Child as soon as it was born." This passage seems to be a historical allusion to King Herod's sinister plot to eliminate the infant Jesus by ordering the massacre of all male children aged two and under in Bethlehem and its vicinity (Matthew 2:13-18). However, Joseph, forewarned by an angel, fled with his wife Mary and the infant Jesus to Egypt to safeguard the Child from harm (verse 13).

The Believer's Bible Commentary provides insights into Revelation 12:4-5, emphasizing that "the dragon is poised to consume the Child immediately upon His birth—a scenario fulfilled in the attempt of Herod the Great, a Roman vassal, to eradicate the newly born King of the Jews. The male Child unequivocally represents Jesus, destined to rule over all nations with unwavering authority."

Despite Satan's thwarted effort to annihilate Jesus in His infancy, the adversary persisted. Prior to the commencement of Jesus' ministry, He was "led up by the Spirit into the wilderness to be tempted by the devil" (Matthew 4:1). During this period of temptation, Satan endeavored to induce Jesus to transgress God's laws and worship him instead of God. The devil even proposed to grant Jesus "all the kingdoms of the world and their glory" (verse 8) in exchange for His worship. However, Jesus steadfastly refused.

As Jesus' ministry approached its culmination, and the time came for Him to offer His life as atonement for humanity's sins, Satan remained an adversary. On this occasion, it was Satan who "put it into the heart of Judas Iscariot, Simon's son, to betray Him" (John 13:2). Although Satan played a role in the crucifixion of Jesus, this was ultimately part of God's redemptive plan.

As foretold in Genesis 3:15, an enduring "enmity" was destined to persist between the serpent (Satan) and the woman (representing God's people), as well as the "Seed" (Jesus) originating from the woman. Moreover, this passage indicated that Satan would achieve limited success, symbolized by his ability to "bruise" Christ's heel through his influence on the individual who would betray Jesus.

Conversely, Jesus would "bruise" Satan's head by resisting his temptations and qualifying to supplant him as the ruler of the world.

So, why did Satan invest such relentless effort in attempting to thwart Jesus? Simply put, without a perfect Savior to pay the penalty for humanity's sins, God's divine plan would have been rendered ineffectual. In the absence of a Savior, forgiveness of human transgressions and the promise of eternal life within God's eternal family would remain unattainable.

Beyond his relentless efforts to undermine Jesus, Satan possesses a long history of persecuting God's people, particularly the members of God's Church, symbolically represented as the woman in the latter parts of Revelation 12. Despite facing fierce persecution from the early days of the New Testament Church, God ensured the woman's protection, leading her "into the wilderness, where she has a place prepared by God, that they should feed her there one thousand two hundred and sixty days" (verse 6).

This verse signifies that for 1,260 years (as supported by Numbers 14:34 and Ezekiel 4:6, where a day represents a year), the true Church enjoyed God's safeguarding hand. During this period, which may have extended into the Middle Ages, the Church found refuge from its adversaries, including the Roman Empire and false forms of Christianity.

Subsequently, the following two verses describe a momentous event—the outbreak of "war in heaven" between Satan and his angels and Michael and his angels. This celestial conflict resulted in the expulsion of Satan and his angels from heaven, as "a place was not found for them in heaven any longer," and they were "cast to the earth" (Revelation 12:7-9). It's essential to note that this battle differs from Satan's original rebellion, outlined in verse 4, which transpired long before Christ's birth.

Following this celestial clash, as detailed in verses 7-9, a resounding voice in heaven (verses 10-12) proclaims its setting and significance. This battle serves as an indicator that "the kingdom of our God, and the power of His Christ have [or will soon] come" (verse 10). Prior to this event, Satan had access to God's presence to accuse His people (Job 1:6-7; Job 2:1-2). However, he and his angels no longer possess this access and are banished to the earth.

Understanding the gravity of this development, Satan, now filled with "great wrath," recognizes that his time is short (Revelation 12:12) before Christ's return to establish the Kingdom of God on earth. Consequently, he channels his fury toward God's people, who are the continuation of the woman described in the Apocalypse and who gave birth to the male Child (verse 13).

Nevertheless, God will not permit Satan to annihilate His people. As Jesus had promised, the "gates of Hades [the grave]" would not overcome them (Matthew 16:18). To safeguard His people, the woman is granted "two wings of a great eagle," signifying her safe relocation to "her place," where she will be shielded for "a time, and times, and half a time" (likely 3½ years) from the serpent's presence (Revelation 12:14).

Even though Satan will unleash a "flood" from his mouth to assail the woman, his efforts will prove futile (verses 15-16). In this context, the concept of a "flood" likely symbolizes armies (see Isaiah 59:19; Jeremiah 46:7-8).

Subsequently, Satan sets out to "make war with the rest of her [the woman's] offspring, who keep the commandments of God and have the testimony of Jesus Christ" (Revelation 12:17). From this passage, it is evident that while certain members of God's true Church will find refuge from Satan's fury during the end times leading up to Christ's return, others will not. Those who are not in the place of protection will need to demonstrate their unwavering allegiance to God the Father and Jesus Christ in the face of Satan's relentless persecution.

The dragon vs. you

Whether you are aware of it or not, Satan harbors a deep hostility toward you and will employ every means at his disposal to hinder your love for and obedience to your Creator. His wrath is not solely directed at Jesus and the Church; it extends to all humanity. But why does he harbor such animosity toward you? It appears to stem from his recognition that humans were fashioned by God with the potential to ascend to a higher plane than he himself (Hebrews 2:6-8).

Driven by his perverse, distorted, and unsound mindset, Satan has assumed the role of an adversary to those earnestly seeking to love and follow their heavenly Father. Addressing the people of God, Peter offered a word of caution, stating, "Be sober, be vigilant, because your adversary the devil walks about like a roaring lion, seeking whom he may devour" (1 Peter 5:8).

In his correspondence with the Corinthian brethren, Paul depicted the true gospel as "veiled" or concealed due to the influence of Satan, referred to as "the god of this age," who had blinded the understanding of unbelievers (2 Corinthians 4:3-4). The encouraging news is that in Christ, this "veil is taken away" (2 Corinthians 3:14).

CHAPTER THIRTEEN

The Beast from the Sea

Introduction:

Chapter 13 of the Book of Revelation introduces two beasts that play pivotal roles in the unfolding drama of the end times. The first beast emerges from the sea and is described as having ten horns and seven heads, with blasphemous names written on its heads. This beast represents a powerful political and military empire or system that will rise to prominence during the end times. It is granted authority by the dragon (Satan) and exercises great influence over the world, leading people to worship both the dragon and the beast. The second beast, also known as the false prophet, emerges from the earth and has two horns like a lamb but speaks like a dragon. This false prophet serves as a religious leader who promotes the worship of the first beast and performs miraculous signs to deceive people. Together, these two entities—political and religious—exert control over the world, causing those who do not worship the beast to face persecution and economic hardship.

Chapter 13 underscores the themes of deception and the allure of worldly power during the end times. It warns of the rise of oppressive political and religious systems that will demand allegiance and worship, ultimately seeking to replace God. The mark of the beast, introduced in this chapter, is a symbol of allegiance to these oppressive systems, and it carries dire consequences for those who accept it. Despite the persecution and hardships faced by believers, the chapter also emphasizes the need for endurance and faithfulness in the face of worldly pressures. Ultimately, the message of Chapter 13 is a call to resist the seductive allure of worldly power and maintain unwavering faith in God, even in the midst of tribulation and persecution.

Verse 1: "The dragon stood on the shore of the sea. And I saw a beast coming out of the sea. It had ten horns and seven heads, with ten crowns on its horns, and on each head a blasphemous name."

- John observes a vision where a beast emerges from the sea, possessing ten horns, seven heads, and ten crowns on its horns, each head bearing blasphemous names.

Interpretation and Commentary:

1. The Sea and Symbolism: In biblical symbolism, the sea often represents chaos and unrest. The emergence of the beast from the sea suggests its origin in turmoil and disorder.
2. Beast's Attributes: The description of the beast with ten horns, seven heads, and blasphemous names is reminiscent of the dragon mentioned in Revelation 12, signifying a connection to Satan and his malevolent influence.

Verse 2: "The beast I saw resembled a leopard, but had feet like those of a bear and a mouth like that of a lion. The dragon gave the beast his power and his throne and great authority."

- The appearance of the beast is likened to a leopard, with bear-like feet and a lion-like mouth. It is noted that the dragon (Satan) imparts power, a throne, and great authority to the beast.

Interpretation and Commentary:

1. Composite Nature: The description of the beast as having attributes of a leopard, bear, and lion suggests its composite and formidable nature. This may symbolize the diverse and oppressive aspects of worldly power.
2. Satanic Influence: The beast derives its authority from the dragon, emphasizing its connection to Satan and his influence over worldly systems and authorities (2 Corinthians 4:4).

Verse 3: "One of the heads of the beast seemed to have had a fatal wound, but the fatal wound had been healed. The whole world was filled with wonder and followed the beast."

- One of the beast's heads appeared to have suffered a mortal wound, but the wound miraculously healed, leading the world to marvel and follow the beast.

Interpretation and Commentary:

1. Fatal Wound and Deception: The apparent healing of a fatal wound is a deceptive sign, likely designed to deceive people into believing in the beast's invincibility and divinity. This deception leads many to follow it.

Verse 4: "People worshiped the dragon because he had given authority to the beast, and they also worshiped the beast and asked, 'Who is like the beast? Who can wage war against it?'"

- People worship both the dragon (Satan) for empowering the beast and the beast itself. They marvel at the beast's apparent invincibility and challenge anyone to oppose it.

Interpretation and Commentary:

1. Idolatry and Deception: The worship of both the dragon and the beast highlights the spiritual deception orchestrated by Satan. It symbolizes the idolatry and allegiance that some will give to oppressive worldly systems or leaders.
2. Arrogance and Pride: The question, "Who is like the beast? Who can wage war against it?" reflects the arrogance and pride of those who follow the beast, believing it to be unbeatable. This mirrors the prideful defiance against God's authority.

Verse 5: "The beast was given a mouth to utter proud words and blasphemies and to exercise its authority for forty-two months."

- The beast is granted the ability to speak proud and blasphemous words and to wield authority for a period of forty-two months.

Interpretation and Commentary:

1. Blasphemous Speech: The beast's ability to speak proudly and blaspheme suggests its opposition to God and its intent to deceive and manipulate through false teachings and arrogance.
2. Forty-Two Months: This period corresponds to 3.5 years, a common symbolic timeframe for tribulation and persecution

in the book of Revelation. It represents a limited but intense season of evil influence.

Verse 6: "It opened its mouth to blaspheme God, and to slander his name and his dwelling place and those who live in heaven."

- The beast uses its mouth to blaspheme God, slander His name, His dwelling place, and those who live in heaven.

Interpretation and Commentary:

1. Blasphemy and Slander: This verse emphasizes the blasphemous nature of the beast, highlighting its intent to insult and defame God and everything associated with Him. This includes slandering God's name and His heavenly abode.

2. Persecution of Believers: The slander against "those who live in heaven" likely refers to believers who are citizens of God's kingdom. The beast not only opposes God but also targets His followers.

Verse 7: "It was given power to wage war against God's holy people and to conquer them. And it was given authority over every tribe, people, language, and nation."

- The beast is granted the power to wage war against God's holy people and to conquer them. It also receives authority over every tribe, people, language, and nation.

Interpretation and Commentary:

1. Persecution of Believers: This verse signifies a time of intense persecution against God's holy people (believers) by the beast. It is a period when the followers of Christ face significant adversity and opposition.

2. Global Influence: The authority granted to the beast over all tribes, peoples, languages, and nations suggests its widespread influence and control over various aspects of worldly authority. This aligns with the concept of a global system opposed to God's kingdom.

Verse 8: "All inhabitants of the earth will worship the beast—all whose names have not been written in the Lamb's book of life, the Lamb who was slain from the creation of the world."

- The verse predicts that all inhabitants of the earth, except those whose names are in the Lamb's book of life, will worship the beast. The Lamb is described as slain from the creation of the world.

Interpretation and Commentary:

1. Universal Worship of the Beast: This verse prophesies a time when a significant portion of the world's population will be drawn into the worship of the beast. The term "inhabitants of the earth" refers to those who align with worldly systems rather than God's kingdom.

2. The Lamb's Book of Life: The Lamb, referring to Jesus Christ, is described as slain from the creation of the world, emphasizing His eternal and foundational role in God's plan for redemption (John 1:29). The Lamb's book of life contains the names of those who are saved by faith in Him (Revelation 20:15).

Verse 9: "Whoever has ears, let them hear."

- This verse is a call for those who hear to pay attention and understand the message being conveyed.

Interpretation and Commentary:

1. Call to Discernment: This recurring phrase in the Bible, spoken by Jesus multiple times (e.g., Matthew 11:15), emphasizes the importance of spiritual discernment and understanding. It invites readers to carefully consider the message and implications of the preceding verses.

Verse 10: "If anyone is to go into captivity, into captivity they will go. If anyone is to be killed with the sword, with the sword they will be killed. This calls for patient endurance and faithfulness on the part of God's people."

- This verse acknowledges that some will face captivity and death as a consequence of their faith. It calls for patient endurance and faithfulness among God's people.

Interpretation and Commentary:

1. Inevitability of Persecution: The verse recognizes that persecution, including captivity and death, may be unavoidable for some believers during the reign of the beast. This aligns with Jesus' warnings about persecution for His followers (Matthew 24:9).

2. Endurance and Faithfulness: Believers are encouraged to endure with patience and remain faithful to God even in the

face of persecution and adversity. This reflects the broader biblical theme of persevering in faith (Hebrews 10:36).

Verse 11: "Then I saw a second beast, coming out of the earth. It had two horns like a lamb, but it spoke like a dragon."

- John sees another beast emerging from the earth, resembling a lamb but speaking with the voice of a dragon.

Interpretation and Commentary:

1. The Second Beast: The introduction of a second beast, often referred to as the False Prophet, represents a different facet of the end-times deception and opposition to God. This beast appears less overtly hostile but is equally deceptive.

2. Lamb-Like Appearance: The two horns like a lamb may symbolize an attempt to mimic Christ or godly authority. It suggests an outward appearance of religious piety or authority, which conceals the true nature of deception.

3. Dragon-Like Speech: Despite its lamb-like appearance, the beast speaks with the voice of a dragon, revealing its alignment with Satan and the deceitful messages it conveys.

Verse 12: "It exercised all the authority of the first beast on its behalf, and made the earth and its inhabitants worship the first beast, whose fatal wound had been healed."

- The second beast exercises authority on behalf of the first beast, compelling the earth and its inhabitants to worship the first beast, whose fatal wound had been healed.

Interpretation and Commentary:

1. Deceptive Influence: The second beast serves as a propagator of the first beast's authority and promotes the worship of the first beast, furthering the global deception.

2. Emphasis on the "Healed" Wound: The mention of the first beast's "fatal wound" being healed reinforces the significance of this event in deceiving people. It creates an illusion of divine or supernatural power associated with the first beast.

Verse 13: "And it performed great signs, even causing fire to come down from heaven to the earth in full view of the people."

- The second beast performs great signs, including calling fire down from heaven in full view of the people.

Interpretation and Commentary:

1. Miraculous Signs: The second beast employs miraculous signs and wonders to validate its message and further deceive people. Calling fire down from heaven mimics the power of the prophets of God and adds to the deception.

Verse 14: "Because of the signs it was given power to perform on behalf of the first beast, it deceived the inhabitants of the earth. It ordered them to set up an image in honor of the beast who was wounded by the sword and yet lived."

- The signs performed by the second beast, on behalf of the first, lead to the deception of the earth's inhabitants. They are instructed to set up an image in honor of the first beast, who survived a fatal wound.

Interpretation and Commentary:

1. Deceptive Miracles: The second beast's ability to perform miraculous signs plays a crucial role in deceiving people. Miracles have often been used in Scripture to confirm the authenticity of God's message (John 2:23; Acts 2:22), but here they serve a deceptive purpose.

2. Image in Honor of the First Beast: The directive to set up an image in honor of the first beast underscores the idolatrous nature of the worship demanded by the first beast. It may involve a physical representation symbolizing allegiance to the oppressive world system.

Verse 15: "The second beast was given power to give breath to the image of the first beast so that the image could speak and cause all who refused to worship the image to be killed."

- The second beast is granted the power to give life to the image of the first beast, enabling it to speak. Those who refuse to worship the image face the threat of death.

Interpretation and Commentary:

1. Animate Image: This verse portrays a striking deception, with the image of the first beast given apparent life and the ability to speak. This emphasizes the supernatural deception that will be at play.

2. Coercion and Persecution: The consequence for refusing to worship the image is severe—death. This reflects the coercion and persecution that will be employed against those who

remain faithful to God's commands and refuse to compromise their faith.

Verse 16: "It also forced all people, great and small, rich and poor, free and slave, to receive a mark on their right hands or on their foreheads."

- The second beast compels people of all social statuses to receive a mark on their right hands or foreheads.

Interpretation and Commentary:

1. Universal Enforcement: The mark is enforced upon all people, regardless of their social, economic, or free/slave status. This underscores the comprehensive nature of the world system's control and influence.

2. Symbolic Mark: The mark on the right hand or forehead likely carries symbolic significance, representing allegiance and submission to the oppressive system. The right hand often symbolizes actions and deeds, while the forehead symbolizes one's thoughts and beliefs.

Verse 17: "So that they could not buy or sell unless they had the mark, which is the name of the beast or the number of its name."

- The mark becomes a prerequisite for engaging in economic activities such as buying or selling. It is identified as either the name of the beast or the number of its name.

Interpretation and Commentary:

1. Economic Control: The mark's requirement for economic transactions underscores the control exerted by the oppressive system over commerce and trade. It effectively restricts participation in the economy to those who conform.

2. Name or Number: The mark is described as either the name of the beast or the number of its name. This has led to much speculation and interpretation, with various theories proposed about the specific identification of the mark.

Verse 18: "This calls for wisdom: let the one who has understanding calculate the number of the beast, for it is the number of a man, and his number is 666."

- The verse encourages those with understanding to calculate the number of the beast, which is identified as the number of a man, specifically 666.

Interpretation and Commentary:

1. The Number 666: The number 666 has been the subject of extensive speculation and interpretation throughout history. It is often associated with imperfection or incompleteness in contrast to the number seven, which symbolizes completeness and perfection in Scripture.

2. Symbolic Significance: While many interpretations have been offered, it's important to recognize that the primary significance of the number lies in its symbolic representation of imperfection and opposition to God's perfect order. The call for wisdom suggests that understanding the number requires spiritual discernment.

3. Caution against Speculation: While interest in deciphering the meaning of 666 is natural, it's important to approach such symbolism with caution and humility, as interpretations can vary widely.

Revelation Chapter 13 provides a vivid portrayal of a time of intense deception, persecution, and the emergence of oppressive world systems. The two beasts, representing political and religious powers, work together to deceive and compel people to conform to their agenda. Believers are called to exercise wisdom and discernment while remaining faithful to God's commands, even in the face of severe challenges and persecution. Ultimately, this chapter serves as a warning about the allure of worldly power and the need for unwavering faith in Christ.

Prophetic Commentary:

The Bible contains prophecies about two formidable powers, both referred to as beasts, that will emerge as dominant forces in the end times. One of these beasts rises from the sea, while the other arises from the earth (Revelation 13:1, 11).

Identifying the First and Second Beasts The first beast, ascending from the sea, is often seen as symbolizing the nations of the world and the inherent instability in their nature, as sea waters are in constant motion (Revelation 17:15; Isaiah 57:20). This beast represents a government that symbolizes the ultimate resurgence of the Roman Empire. (For more insights on this beast, you can refer to the article titled "Who Is the Beast?").

In contrast, the second beast, emerging from the earth, stands apart. While the first beast, symbolizing the Roman Empire, undergoes numerous rises and falls throughout history, the second beast maintains its power consistently from its inception until its demise, which occurs shortly before the return of Christ (Revelation 17:16).

Described in Revelation 13:11 as "another beast," this entity possesses "two horns like a lamb" but speaks with the voice of a dragon. Its resemblance to a "lamb" suggests that it appears similar to Jesus Christ, the true Lamb of God (John 1:29, 36; Revelation 12:11; 13:8; 17:14). However, instead of conveying the teachings of Christ, it communicates doctrines inspired by Satan, referred to as "the great dragon" (Revelation 12:9).

In essence, the second beast embodies a religious system that outwardly presents itself as "Christian" but, in reality, promotes doctrines aligned with Satan's agenda. Later in the book of Revelation, the leader of the second beast is identified as the "false prophet," further underscoring its religious character (Revelation 16:13; 19:20; 20:10).

This same power is depicted in the book of Daniel as a "little horn" engaging in "war against the saints," uttering "pompous words against the Most High," altering "times and laws," and persecuting "the saints" (Daniel 7:8, 21, 25). All these actions paint a picture of a religious authority that opposes God, His truth, and His followers.

Historical evidence indicates that shortly before the fall of the Roman Empire in A.D. 476, a religious power within the empire gained prominence—the Roman Catholic Church.

So, what exactly does the term "image of the beast" signify?

Some have speculated that it could manifest as a statue or a visual representation that seems to come to life and communicate. Others suggest possibilities like advanced technology such as supercomputers, holograms, human clones, cyborgs, or highly sophisticated artificial intelligence.

What's intriguing is that the concept of the "image of the beast" has been present for more than a millennium, and its influence persists in our world today.

To unravel its meaning, it's essential to recognize its connection to the "beast." The "beast" refers to a political system primarily based in Europe, with historical roots tracing back to Rome. Therefore, the "image" must be somehow associated with this empire. The Greek term used for "image" is "eikōn," signifying a likeness or resemblance.

This same word was employed in a conversation between Jesus Christ and the Pharisees when they inquired whether it was lawful to pay taxes to Caesar. In response, Jesus asked them to produce a coin and then questioned whose likeness or image was imprinted on it. Their reply was "Caesar" (Matthew 22:17-21; Mark 12:14-16; Luke 20:22-24). The coin bore a representation, or likeness, of Caesar.

Furthermore, it's crucial to understand that this "image" is intricately linked to worship (Revelation 13:15; 14:9-11; 16:2; 19:20). There will be individuals who refuse to worship the "image of the beast" and will ultimately overcome the beast (Revelation 15:2; 20:4).

Mark of the Beast

Few subjects have captured the curiosity and bewilderment of people quite like the enigmatic mark mentioned in the book of Revelation. Countless books and sermons have delved into this topic, and scholars and theologians have presented a myriad of interpretations.

Some have suggested it could be a microchip implanted in the forehead, while others propose it might be an invisible or visible mark. There are even notions that it could be linked to one's credit card or debit card.

But what does the Bible actually reveal about this perplexing mark?

The crucial passage states: "He causes all, both small and great, rich and poor, free and slave, to receive a mark on their right hand or on their foreheads, and that no one may buy or sell except one who has the mark or the name of the beast, or the number of his name" (Revelation 13:16-17).

What or who is the beast in the book of Revelation? This question has intrigued many readers, and to find an answer, we must turn to the visions recorded by John, the chosen author of the book of Revelation. In one of his visions, he witnessed the emergence of a formidable beast:

"As I stood on the sand of the sea, I saw a beast rising up out of the sea, having seven heads and ten horns, with ten crowns on his horns, and blasphemous names on his heads. Now the beast which I saw was like a leopard, his feet were like the feet of a bear, and his mouth like the mouth of a lion. The dragon gave him his power, his throne, and great authority" (Revelation 13:1-2).

To truly grasp the identity of this beast, we need to trace its origins back to the book of Daniel, specifically in Daniel 7:1-8. In these passages, Daniel employs the imagery of four animals, symbolizing the four great historical empires: a lion (representing Babylon), a bear (depicting Persia), a leopard (symbolizing Greece), and a fourth beast (representing Rome).

The key connection is made with this fourth beast, described both by Daniel and John, which is characterized by its "ten horns" and its experience of a "deadly wound" before its resurgence toward the end of this age (Daniel 7:7-8; Revelation 13:3). It is this empire that is commonly referred to as the "beast" in the book of Revelation.

Now, let's direct our focus to the identity of the figure referred to as "he" in Revelation 13:16. This verse states, "He causes all ... to receive a mark." But who is this "he"? Verse 11 provides crucial context: "Then I saw another beast coming up out of the earth, and he had two horns like a lamb and spoke like a dragon."

These characteristics point to a false religious leader, often referred to as the "false prophet" (Revelation 19:20). This religious figure plays a pivotal role in compelling "the earth and those who dwell in it to worship the first beast" (Revelation 13:12). This mark or sign signifies the resurgence of the Roman Empire at the end of days, and it is this religious leader who actively influences people to accept it.

The mark of the beast serves as a clear symbol of disobedience to God and will result in a division of humanity into two distinct groups: those who accept the mark and those who reject it.

The apostle John conveys the consequences of receiving the mark, stating, "Then a third angel followed them, saying with a loud voice, 'If anyone worships the beast and his image, and receives his mark on his forehead or on his hand, he himself shall also drink of the wine of the wrath of God, which is poured out full strength into the cup of His indignation. He shall be tormented with fire and brimstone in the presence of the holy angels and in the presence of the Lamb'" (Revelation 14:9-10).

This passage illustrates the severe suffering that will befall those who bear the mark of the beast.

Conversely, verse 12 introduces a group of individuals who refuse to accept this mark, identified as "the saints" - those who faithfully uphold God's commandments and the teachings of Jesus. Throughout the Bible, obedience to God's commands signifies those who belong to Him.

For instance, when instructing the ancient Israelites on the observance of the Days of Unleavened Bread, God explained that their obedience would serve as "a sign to you on your hand" (Exodus 13:9). The apostle Paul reinforced this concept when he urged the Christians in Corinth to "keep the feast ... with the unleavened bread of sincerity and truth" (1 Corinthians 5:8).

Therefore, the mark of the beast symbolizes rebellion against God's commandments and a rejection of the faith in Jesus.

According to the book of Revelation, those who receive the mark will face the seven last plagues, while the obedient saints will achieve "victory over the beast" (Revelation 15:2). These faithful individuals will be rewarded with eternal life and will reign alongside Christ upon His second coming (Revelation 20:4).

The mark of the beast, as previously discussed, serves as a distinct indicator that determines an individual's eligibility to engage in official business transactions. Possessing this identifying mark grants the ability to "buy and sell." The Bible clearly outlines the financial implications tied to whether one possesses this mark or not.

Furthermore, there is a specific commandment of God closely associated with one's capacity to conduct business transactions, which also distinguishes God's people. Among the Ten Commandments, the Fourth Commandment is particularly relevant in this regard, as it significantly impacts one's ability to work, earn a livelihood, and engage in business affairs.

This commandment states, "Remember the Sabbath day, to keep it holy. Six days you shall labor and do all your work, but the seventh day is the Sabbath of the LORD your God" (Exodus 20:8-10).

While many individuals may believe that the day of observance is inconsequential, it holds profound significance to God. In this present age, adhering to the Sabbath and maintaining its sanctity requires the "faith of Jesus."

In the Bible, the term "mark" carries the meaning of an identifying symbol or insignia. Specifically, the Greek word "charagma" used in Revelation 14:9 signifies "a scratch or etching, that is, stamp (as a badge of servitude)" (Strong's Hebrew and Greek Dictionaries). Therefore, a mark serves as a distinctive brand or sign of recognition.

The Bible designates the Sabbath as a "sign" representing the covenant between God and His people (Exodus 31:13, 17; Ezekiel 20:12). It serves to distinguish God's people as those sanctified and set apart by Him.

Jesus emphasized the significance of the Sabbath when He stated, "The Sabbath was made for man, and not man for the Sabbath. Therefore, the Son of Man is also Lord of the Sabbath" (Mark 2:27-28). Today, the Sabbath remains both a commandment and an emblem identifying God's people.

Another instance of marking or identifying individuals is found in the book of Ezekiel. God instructed a person with a writer's inkhorn to "Go through the midst of the city, through the midst of Jerusalem, and put a mark on the foreheads of the men who sigh and cry over all the abominations that are done within it" (Ezekiel 9:4). This mark served as a recognition of those who obeyed God and mourned over the city's sins.

In Revelation, it is mentioned that those who receive the mark of the beast will have it placed "on their right hand or on their foreheads" (Revelation 13:16). Many individuals interpret this to mean that it could be a physical mark either within or on the skin, which is a valid interpretation.

However, given the symbolic nature of the book of Revelation, it is essential to consider the possibility that these references to the "right hand" and "forehead" carry symbolic meanings. If this is the case, what might they symbolize?

In biblical symbolism, the right hand can signify our actions, deeds, and labor, while the forehead often symbolizes our inner beliefs, thoughts, and intellect. Consequently, the mark of the beast could be linked to our beliefs and thoughts in our minds, as well as our actions and deeds.

For context, consider Deuteronomy 6:8, where God instructed ancient Israel to "bind the commandments as a sign on your hand, and as frontlets between your eyes."

This association between our thoughts and our actions aligns with the concept of faith. In the Bible, the genuine "faith of Jesus" comprises two integral components: belief and the corresponding actions that demonstrate that belief.

Now that we have explored the context of Revelation 13, our attention is drawn to verse 18, which presents the following statement: "Here is wisdom. Let him who has understanding calculate the number of the beast, for it is the number of a man: His number is 666."

As previously highlighted, individuals will be required to possess either "the mark or the name of the beast, or the number of his name" to engage in buying or selling (verse 17).

By combining verses 17 and 18, we discern that the number 666 serves as an identifier for the beast, signifying a man's name who is also referred to as the beast. Additionally, this number will grant individuals authorization for economic transactions.

So, what is the significance of the number 666, and how can one "calculate" it?

Albert Barnes, in his commentary on Revelation 13:18, explains that in Greek, letters had numerical values. Several names, including "Lateinos, the Latin," "Neron Caesar," "Diocles Augustus (Diocletian)," "C.F. Julianus Caesar Atheus (the Apostate)," "Luther," "Romanus," and "Roman," collectively add up to 666.

While there may be other interpretations, Barnes also noted, "It is remarkable how many of the most obvious solutions refer to Rome and the papacy."

Furthermore, it's interesting to observe that Irenaeus, an early church writer from the second century, proposed that this number was a reference to the Latin (i.e., Roman) Empire (as mentioned in Adam Clarke's Commentary on the Bible, Revelation 13:18).

Given these insights, let's explore if the Bible provides any indications that this number relates to a revival of the Roman Empire.

God's revelation to King Nebuchadnezzar, through a dream, foretold the rise of four great world-ruling empires (Daniel 2:31-43). History has confirmed these empires as the Babylonian, Medo-Persian, Greek, and Roman Empires.

Daniel, later in the same book, received a vision of four beasts, each representing these same four empires. Concerning the fourth beast, it is noted that "it had ten horns" (Daniel 7:7). In Daniel's writings, the horn symbolizes power and is frequently used as an emblem (as explained in Albert Barnes' Notes on the Bible, Daniel 7:7-8).

Daniel further described, "I was considering the horns, and there was another horn, a little one, coming up among them, before whom three of the first horns were plucked out by the roots. And there, in this horn, were eyes like the eyes of a man, and a mouth speaking pompous words" (verse 8).

These horns represented kingdoms that would play a role in the history of the Roman Empire, while the little horn symbolized a religious power.

In his vision, Daniel saw this religious leader waging war against the saints and prevailing until the "Ancient of Days" intervened, leading to a judgment in favor of the saints, who would then inherit the kingdom (verses 21-22).

CHAPTER FOURTEEN

The Lamb and the 144,000

Introduction:

Chapter 14 of the Book of Revelation presents a vision of hope and victory in the midst of the tribulation described in earlier chapters. The chapter begins with a vision of the Lamb (Jesus Christ) standing on Mount Zion, surrounded by 144,000 redeemed ones who have the Lamb's name and the Father's name written on their foreheads. These are described as those who have been redeemed from the earth and have remained faithful to God. They are seen as offering a song of worship that no one else can learn, emphasizing their unique and intimate relationship with God. The chapter also includes messages from three angels: the first angel proclaims the eternal Gospel to the entire world, calling people to worship God and turn away from the worship of the beast; the second angel announces the fall of Babylon, signifying the impending judgment of the corrupt world system; and the third angel warns against receiving the mark of the beast and assures that those who endure in their faith will find rest in God.

Chapter 14 brings a sense of relief and reassurance to the narrative of Revelation. It reminds readers that, amidst the chaos and tribulation of the end times, there will be a faithful remnant who will remain loyal to God. The messages from the three angels highlight the importance of worshiping the true God, rejecting the allure of the world system, and avoiding the mark of the beast. The chapter reaffirms the ultimate victory of God's plan and the ultimate defeat of the forces of evil. It serves as a message of hope and a call to faithfulness for believers, encouraging them to persevere in their loyalty to God and His Gospel, even in the face of great challenges.

Verse 1: "Then I looked, and there before me was the Lamb, standing on Mount Zion, and with him 144,000 who had his name and his Father's name written on their foreheads."

- John sees a vision of the Lamb (Jesus Christ) standing on Mount Zion, accompanied by 144,000 individuals bearing His name and His Father's name on their foreheads.

Interpretation and Commentary:

1. Mount Zion: Mount Zion is often associated with Jerusalem in the Bible and symbolizes the presence of God. In this vision, it represents a place of spiritual significance and divine presence.

2. 144,000: These individuals, marked with the names of Jesus and the Father, are likely symbolic of a group of faithful and redeemed believers who have remained steadfast in their faith despite the challenges and tribulations described earlier in Revelation.

3. Forehead Markings: The markings on their foreheads signify their allegiance to God and Christ, reminiscent of the sealing mentioned in Revelation 7:3, which denotes God's protection and ownership of His people.

Verse 2: "And I heard a sound from heaven like the roar of rushing waters and like a loud peal of thunder. The sound I heard was like that of harpists playing their harps."

- John describes a heavenly sound resembling the roar of rushing waters and thunder, as well as the harmonious music of harpists playing their harps.

Interpretation and Commentary:

1. Heavenly Praise: The imagery of thunder and harp music signifies the exuberant praise and worship emanating from heaven. It highlights the joy and celebration accompanying the presence of the Lamb on Mount Zion.

2. Contrast with Earlier Chapters: This scene stands in contrast to the turmoil and chaos described in earlier chapters,

indicating a shift towards a time of victory and worship in the divine presence.

Verse 3: "And they sang a new song before the throne and before the four living creatures and the elders. No one could learn the song except the 144,000 who had been redeemed from the earth."

- The 144,000 sing a new song before the throne, the living creatures, and the elders. This song can only be learned by those who have been redeemed from the earth.

Interpretation and Commentary:

1. New Song: The "new song" signifies a song of unique praise and significance, celebrating the redemption and victory achieved through Christ. It is a song of the redeemed, emphasizing their distinct experience and testimony.

2. Redemption: Those who can sing this song are specifically those who have been redeemed from the earth. This underscores the theme of redemption and salvation through faith in Christ.

Verse 4: "These are those who did not defile themselves with women, for they remained virgins. They follow the Lamb wherever he goes. They were purchased from among mankind and offered as firstfruits to God and the Lamb."

- The 144,000 are described as those who remained pure, did not defile themselves, and followed the Lamb. They were redeemed from humanity and presented as firstfruits to God and the Lamb.

Interpretation and Commentary:

1. Purity and Faithfulness: The reference to not defiling themselves with women is likely symbolic, signifying spiritual purity and faithfulness to God. They are devoted followers of Christ, symbolically portrayed as virgins.

2. Firstfruits: The term "firstfruits" is significant. In biblical context, it represents the first and best portion offered to God as a sign of dedication and consecration. These redeemed individuals are a symbolic offering to God, signifying their special status.

Verse 5: "No lie was found in their mouths; they are blameless."

- The 144,000 are described as individuals in whom there is no falsehood, and they are considered blameless.

Interpretation and Commentary:

1. Truthfulness and Blamelessness: This verse underscores the moral and spiritual integrity of the 144,000. They are characterized by truthfulness and righteousness, and they are found blameless in the sight of God.

Verse 6: "Then I saw another angel flying in midair, and he had the eternal gospel to proclaim to those who live on the earth—to every nation, tribe, language and people."

- John sees another angel flying in midair, carrying the eternal gospel to proclaim to all inhabitants of the earth, regardless of their nationality or language.

Interpretation and Commentary:

1. Eternal Gospel: This angelic proclamation emphasizes the timeless and universal nature of the gospel message. It signifies that, even in the midst of end-times events, God's offer of salvation through faith in Christ remains available to all people.
2. Inclusivity: The message is intended for "every nation, tribe, language, and people," highlighting God's desire for the salvation of people from diverse backgrounds and cultures.

Verse 7: "He said in a loud voice, 'Fear God and give him glory, because the hour of his judgment has come. Worship him who made the heavens, the earth, the sea and the springs of water.'"

- The angel proclaims a message to fear God, give Him glory, and worship the Creator of the heavens, earth, seas, and springs of water, declaring that the hour of God's judgment has come.

Interpretation and Commentary:

1. Call to Reverence: The angel's message emphasizes reverence and worship of the one true God. It underscores the imminent arrival of God's judgment, urging people to recognize His sovereignty and turn to Him in repentance and worship.
2. Creation as Evidence: The reference to God as the Creator of all things highlights the evidence of His existence and power in the natural world. It invites people to acknowledge Him as the Creator and respond in worship.

Verse 8: "A second angel followed and said, 'Fallen! Fallen is Babylon the Great,' which made all the nations drink the maddening wine of her adulteries.'"

- A second angel follows, announcing the fall of Babylon the Great, which had led nations to partake in her adulterous actions.

Interpretation and Commentary:

1. Fall of Babylon: The announcement of Babylon's fall signifies the ultimate judgment and downfall of a symbolic entity representing worldly corruption, idolatry, and rebellion against God.

2. Spiritual Adulteries: Babylon's "maddening wine of her adulteries" symbolizes spiritual idolatry, seduction, and deception that have led people away from true worship of God. The fall of Babylon represents the defeat of worldly, anti-God systems.

Verse 9: "A third angel followed them and said in a loud voice: 'If anyone worships the beast and its image and receives its mark on their forehead or on their hand.'"

- A third angel follows, warning against worshiping the beast, its image, or receiving its mark on the forehead or hand.

Interpretation and Commentary:

1. Warning against Idolatry: This angelic proclamation serves as a stern warning against idolatry and allegiance to the oppressive world system represented by the

Certainly, let's continue with an expository commentary on Revelation Chapter 14, focusing on verses 9 to 20, with Bible references, and providing interpretation and commentary for each verse:

Verse 9: "A third angel followed them and said in a loud voice: 'If anyone worships the beast and its image and receives its mark on their forehead or on their hand.'"

- The third angel issues a warning against worshiping the beast, its image, or receiving its mark on the forehead or hand.

Interpretation and Commentary:

1. Idolatrous Worship Warning: This angelic proclamation reinforces the message of the earlier verses, emphasizing the gravity of idolatrous worship. Worshiping the beast and

receiving its mark symbolizes allegiance to worldly systems opposed to God.

Verse 10: "They, too, will drink the wine of God's fury, which has been poured full strength into the cup of his wrath. They will be tormented with burning sulfur in the presence of the holy angels and of the Lamb."

- Those who worship the beast and receive its mark will experience God's wrath in its full intensity. Their punishment involves torment with burning sulfur in the presence of the holy angels and the Lamb (Jesus Christ).

Interpretation and Commentary:

1. Divine Wrath: This verse underscores the severity of God's judgment upon those who choose to worship the beast and align with anti-God systems. The imagery of burning sulfur represents intense suffering and judgment.

2. Presence of the Holy Angels and the Lamb: The fact that this punishment occurs in the presence of the holy angels and the Lamb emphasizes the divine justice and the significance of this judgment event.

Verse 11: "And the smoke of their torment will rise for ever and ever. There will be no rest day or night for those who worship the beast and its image, or for anyone who receives the mark of its name."

- The smoke of the torment endured by those who worship the beast, its image, or receive its mark will rise forever. They will experience ceaseless suffering with no rest.

Interpretation and Commentary:

1. Eternal Consequences: This verse emphasizes the eternal nature of the consequences for choosing to align with the oppressive worldly system and rejecting God. The imagery of ceaseless smoke rising symbolizes the perpetual nature of their punishment.

2. No Rest: The absence of rest signifies the unending torment and separation from God experienced by those who refuse to repent and turn to Him.

Verse 12: "This calls for patient endurance on the part of the people of God who keep his commands and remain faithful to Jesus."

- The verse encourages God's people to exercise patient endurance while keeping His commands and remaining faithful to Jesus.

Interpretation and Commentary:

1. Endurance and Faithfulness: In the face of the intense trials and tribulations described in earlier chapters of Revelation, believers are called to persevere with patient endurance. They are urged to maintain their fidelity to God's commandments and unwavering faith in Jesus Christ.

Verse 13: "Then I heard a voice from heaven say, 'Write this: Blessed are the dead who die in the Lord from now on.' 'Yes,' says the Spirit, 'they will rest from their labor, for their deeds will follow them.'"

- A voice from heaven pronounces a blessing upon those who die in the Lord from that point onward. The Spirit confirms that they will find rest from their labors, and their deeds will accompany them.

Interpretation and Commentary:

1. Blessing for the Faithful: This pronouncement signifies a special blessing for those who remain faithful to the Lord even in the face of persecution and martyrdom. Their deaths are seen as a transition to a state of rest and reward in God's presence.

2. Eternal Impact: The assurance that "their deeds will follow them" implies that the faithful deeds and actions of believers, even in the midst of persecution, have lasting significance and will be acknowledged and rewarded by God.

Verse 14: "I looked, and there before me was a white cloud, and seated on the cloud was one like a son of man with a crown of gold on his head and a sharp sickle in his hand."

- John sees a vision of a white cloud, upon which is seated someone resembling a son of man, wearing a gold crown and holding a sharp sickle.

Interpretation and Commentary:

1. Son of Man: The figure described as "one like a son of man" is a reference to Jesus Christ. This term is frequently used in the New Testament, including by Jesus Himself, to refer to His divine and messianic identity (e.g., Daniel 7:13-14).

2. Crown and Sickle: The crown of gold symbolizes Christ's authority and kingship, while the sharp sickle suggests His role as the divine harvester of souls.

Verse 15: "Then another angel came out of the temple and called in a loud voice to him who was sitting on the cloud, 'Take your sickle and reap, because the time to reap has come, for the harvest of the earth is ripe.'"

- Another angel from the temple calls out to the one sitting on the cloud, instructing Him to use the sickle and reap the earth's harvest because the time for harvesting has arrived, and the harvest is ready.

Interpretation and Commentary:

1. Harvest of the Earth: This imagery of harvest represents the final gathering of souls, both the righteous and the unrighteous, at the culmination of God's redemptive plan. It symbolizes the time of judgment and separation.
2. Ripeness of the Harvest: The ripe harvest signifies that the appointed time for God's judgment and the gathering of souls has arrived.

Verse 16: "So, he who was seated on the cloud swung his sickle over the earth, and the earth was harvested."

- The figure seated on the cloud swings His sickle over the earth, resulting in the harvest of the earth.

Interpretation and Commentary:

1. Divine Harvest: This verse portrays the culmination of God's redemptive plan and His role as the divine harvester of souls. The act of swinging the sickle represents God's judgment and the gathering of both the righteous and the unrighteous.

Verse 17: "And another angel came out of the temple in heaven, and he too had a sharp sickle."

- Another angel emerges from the heavenly temple, holding a sharp sickle.

Interpretation and Commentary:

1. Dual Harvest: The appearance of another angel with a sharp sickle suggests a dual or successive harvest. While the first harvest represents the gathering of the righteous, this second angel may be associated with the judgment of the unrighteous.

Verse 18: "Still another angel, who had charge of the fire, came from the altar and called in a loud voice to him who had the sharp sickle, 'Take your sharp sickle and gather the clusters of grapes from the earth's vine, because its grapes are ripe.'"

- A third angel, responsible for the fire, emerges from the altar and instructs the one with the sharp sickle to gather the ripe clusters of grapes from the earth's vine.

Interpretation and Commentary:

1. Symbolic Imagery: The use of grapes and vineyard imagery is common in biblical prophecy to symbolize the people or nations (e.g., Isaiah 5:1-7). Here, the ripe grapes represent the judgment and punishment of the unrighteous.

2. Fire from the Altar: The angel associated with fire underscores the connection between the judgment and purification. Fire often symbolizes both divine judgment and purification.

Verse 19: "The angel swung his sickle on the earth, gathered its grapes and threw them into the great winepress of God's wrath."

- The angel swings his sickle on the earth, collects the grapes, and throws them into the great winepress of God's wrath.

Interpretation and Commentary:

1. Divine Wrath: This verse emphasizes the seriousness of God's judgment and the consequent outpouring of His wrath on those who have chosen to rebel against Him. The image of a winepress conveys the idea of intense pressure and suffering.

Verse 20: "They were trampled in the winepress outside the city, and blood flowed out of the press, rising as high as the horses' bridles for a distance of 1,600 stadia."

- The grapes are trampled in the winepress outside the city, resulting in a flow of blood that rises as high as horses' bridles for a distance of 1,600 stadia.

Interpretation and Commentary:

1. Symbolic Bloodshed: This graphic imagery portrays the severity of God's judgment upon the unrighteous. The flow of blood rising to the height of horses' bridles symbolizes a massive and devastating judgment.

2. 1,600 Stadia: The measurement of 1,600 stadia is symbolic and emphasizes the comprehensiveness of God's judgment. It signifies a complete and thorough judgment of the rebellious.

In Revelation Chapter 14, these verses depict the ultimate culmination of God's redemptive plan and His judgment on the unrighteous. The dual harvests symbolize the gathering of both the righteous and the unrighteous, with the latter experiencing the full weight of God's wrath. The vivid imagery of grapes being trampled in a winepress underscores the severity of the judgment and its comprehensive nature. It serves as a solemn reminder of the consequences of rejecting God's grace and choosing rebellion.

Prophetic Commentary:

The 144,000 in the Book of Revelation, as mentioned in Revelation 7 and Revelation 14, appear in three distinct references.

Revelation 7:4 tells us, "One hundred and forty-four thousand of all the tribes of the children of Israel were sealed." Within this group, there were 12,000 individuals selected from each tribe, with the exception of the tribe of Dan (as explained in verses 5-8). The reason for Dan's exclusion remains a matter of speculation.

In Revelation 14:1, we encounter the same group of "one hundred and forty-four thousand," depicted as standing alongside a Lamb on Mount Zion, bearing the name of God "written on their foreheads."

The third reference portrays this assembly singing in the presence of God, emphasizing that "no one could learn that song except the hundred and forty-four thousand who were redeemed from the earth" (verse 3).

For a more comprehensive understanding of this group, it is recommended to read Chapter 7 for additional details.

CHAPTER FIFTEEN

Prelude to the Bowl Judgments

Introduction:

Chapter 15 of the Book of Revelation serves as an introduction to the series of seven bowl judgments, also known as the "seven last plagues." John sees a vision of those who have conquered the beast and his image standing beside a sea of glass mixed with fire. These victorious individuals are seen holding harps and singing the song of Moses and the song of the Lamb, celebrating God's righteous judgments and His deliverance of His people. The sea of glass represents the purity and clarity of God's judgment, while the fire symbolizes the intensity of His wrath. This vision sets the stage for the final and most severe judgments to be poured out upon the earth.

Chapter 15 emphasizes the righteous nature of God's judgments and the ultimate vindication of His faithful followers. The songs of Moses and the Lamb echo themes of deliverance, justice, and the victory of God's people over their oppressors. This chapter also underscores the idea that God's judgments are not arbitrary or capricious but are executed with divine purpose and in accordance with His plan for the redemption of His creation. It prepares the reader for the intense and dramatic events that will follow in the subsequent chapters as the bowl judgments are unleashed, leading up to the climactic culmination of God's redemptive plan in the final chapters of Revelation.

Verse 1: "I saw in heaven another great and marvelous sign: seven angels with the seven last plagues—last, because with them God's wrath is completed."

- John sees a vision in heaven of seven angels holding the seven last plagues, signifying the completion of God's wrath.

Interpretation and Commentary;

1. Completion of God's Wrath: These seven last plagues represent the final outpouring of God's wrath upon the earth. They mark the culmination of divine judgment, indicating that God's patience has reached its limit.

2. Symbolism of Seven: The number seven is often associated with completeness and perfection in biblical symbolism, signifying that these plagues are the final and ultimate expressions of God's judgment.

Verse 2: "And I saw what looked like a sea of glass glowing with fire and, standing beside the sea, those who had been victorious over the beast and its image and over the number of its name. They held harps given them by God."

- John observes a scene in which those who had overcome the beast and its image are standing beside a sea of glass that appears to be glowing with fire. They hold harps given to them by God.

Interpretation and Commentary:

1. Triumphant Saints: The individuals standing by the sea of glass are identified as victorious over the oppressive forces represented by the beast and its image. They have remained faithful to God even in the face of persecution and idolatry.

2. Sea of Glass: The sea of glass, glowing with fire, symbolizes purity and holiness. It serves as a place of sanctification and victory for those who have overcome through their faith.

3. Harps Given by God: The harps given by God symbolize the worship and praise offered to Him. They reflect the joy and

adoration of those who have triumphed over adversity through their faith in God.

Verse 3: "And they sang the song of God's servant Moses and of the Lamb: 'Great and marvelous are your deeds, Lord God Almighty. Just and true are your ways, King of the nations.'"

- Those who have overcome sing a song that combines elements of the song of Moses and praise to the Lamb. They extol God's great deeds and declare His justice and truth.

Interpretation and Commentary:

1. Song of Praise: The song of Moses, historically found in Exodus 15, is a song of praise and deliverance. Here, it is combined with praise to the Lamb (Jesus Christ), signifying the unity of God's redemptive work throughout history.

2. Acknowledgment of God's Attributes: The lyrics of the song emphasize God's greatness, His almighty power, His just ways, and His truth. It underscores the righteousness and sovereignty of God over all nations.

Verse 4: "Who will not fear you, Lord, and bring glory to your name? For you alone are holy. All nations will come and worship before you, for your righteous acts have been revealed."

- The song continues, emphasizing that all nations will eventually fear God, give glory to His name, and worship Him because of His holiness and righteous acts.

Interpretation and Commentary:

1. Universal Worship: The lyrics of the song express a prophetic vision of universal worship. It declares that all nations will ultimately recognize God's holiness and righteousness, leading them to worship Him.

2. Revelation of Righteous Acts: The song underscores the importance of God's righteous acts being revealed to humanity. His actions and judgments are intended to bring about repentance and worship among all people.

Verse 5: "After this I looked, and I saw in heaven the temple—that is, the tabernacle of the covenant law—and it was opened."

- John sees the heavenly temple, often referred to as the tabernacle of the covenant law, and it is opened.

Interpretation and Commentary:

1. Heavenly Tabernacle: The heavenly temple or tabernacle is a symbol of God's presence and the place of divine worship. Its opening signifies a significant event or revelation.

Verse 6: "Out of the temple came the seven angels with the seven plagues. They were dressed in clean, shining linen and wore golden sashes around their chests."

*   The seven angels holding the seven plagues emerge from the temple, clothed in clean and shining linen garments with golden sashes.

Interpretation and Commentary:

1. Priestly Garments: The attire of the angels, resembling priestly garments, signifies their role in executing God's final judgments. The cleanliness and purity of their attire reflect their divine commission.
2. Temple as the Source: The fact that the angels come out of the temple reinforces the idea that their actions are in accordance with God's divine will and justice.

Verse 7: "Then one of the four living creatures gave to the seven angels seven golden bowls filled with the wrath of God, who lives for ever and ever."

*   One of the four living creatures presents the seven angels with seven golden bowls filled with God's wrath.

Interpretation and Commentary:

1. Symbolic Bowls of Wrath: These golden bowls represent the containers of God's final and complete wrath, to be poured out upon the earth. The living creature's action suggests a divine commission.
2. Eternal Nature of God: The reference to God living forever and ever underscores His eternal existence and sovereignty over all creation.

Verse 8: "And the temple was filled with smoke from the glory of God and from his power, and no one could enter the temple until the seven plagues of the seven angels were completed."

*   The temple is filled with smoke emanating from the glory and power of God, and no one can enter the temple until the seven plagues executed by the seven angels are completed.

Interpretation and Commentary:

1. Divine Presence: The smoke filling the temple symbolizes the divine presence of God and His manifest glory and power. It signifies the solemnity and seriousness of the impending judgment.

2. Restriction of Entry: The fact that no one can enter the temple until the plagues are completed suggests a period of divine judgment, during which God's presence is veiled from human access. It emphasizes the significance of the impending judgment.

Revelation Chapter 15 provides a vision of the final outpouring of God's wrath through the seven last plagues, marking the completion of His judgment. The scene also depicts the triumphant worship of those who have overcome, praising God for His righteousness and sovereignty. The heavenly temple and its opening symbolize a significant event in God's redemptive plan, leading to the execution of divine judgment by the seven angels holding the bowls of wrath.

Prophetic Commentary:

The final plagues in the Book of Revelation, also referred to as the bowls of wrath, are described in Revelation 15:7 as "golden bowls filled with the wrath of God" that will be poured out upon the earth. In some Bible translations, such as the King James Version and Young's Literal Translation, the term "vial" is used instead of "bowl" in this passage and in Revelation 16:1.

Albert Barnes, in his Notes on the Bible, explains that the word used here, "φια☐λη phialē," originally means "a bowl or goblet with more breadth than depth." He suggests that the term "vial," though derived from this word, more commonly refers to a slender, glass bottle used by apothecaries and druggists. It would be more accurate to interpret the word as "bowl" or "goblet." The reference likely alludes to drinking cups or goblets filled with a harmful substance, reminiscent of one of the methods of punishment in ancient times (comments on Revelation 15:7).

In essence, these bowls (or vials) serve as symbolic imagery that God employs to represent the seven final judgments that He will unleash upon a sinful humanity.

How do the seven final plagues align with other plagues mentioned in the Bible? There are two noteworthy historical parallels to the seven last plagues.

First, these seven last plagues draw parallels with some of the punishments God inflicted upon Egypt during the time of the Exodus, as He worked to liberate the Israelites from slavery. In the ten plagues preceding the Exodus, Egypt witnessed water turning into blood (Exodus 7:17), individuals suffering painful "sores" (Exodus 9:9), and the land being enveloped in darkness for three days (Exodus 10:21-23). These punishments bear evident similarities to the seven last plagues, as seen in the first, second, third, and fifth plagues above. Moreover, just as Pharaoh hardened his heart against God and His plan, those who experience the seven last plagues will also harden their hearts against God.

It's worth noting that in Revelation 15, which introduces the seven last plagues, the faithful sing "the song of Moses" (verse 3), a song authored by Moses after God had unleashed ten plagues upon Egypt and delivered Israel (Exodus 15:1-19).

Second, the seven last plagues in Revelation 15 and 16 exhibit similarities to the seven trumpet plagues, albeit with greater intensity. The first four trumpets result in a third of the trees being consumed by fire, a third of the sea turning to blood, a third of sea creatures perishing, a third of fresh water becoming poisonous, and a third reduction in the light of the sun, moon, and stars (Revelation 8:7-12). In contrast, the seven last plagues will transform all waters, both sea and fresh, into blood, annihilate all marine life, and cast the world into deeper darkness (Revelation 16:3, 4, 10).

The seven last plagues serve as the culmination of God's wrath, as conveyed by John: "Then I saw another sign in heaven, great and marvelous: seven angels having the seven last plagues, for in them the wrath of God is complete" (Revelation 15:1, emphasis added).

These seven final plagues in the book of Revelation are as follows:

1. First Plague: The first bowl will inflict painful sores on those who "had the mark of the beast and those who worshiped his

image" (Revelation 16:2). It appears that these painful and open sores will result from a form of skin disease or infection.

2. Second Plague: When the second bowl is poured out, the sea will turn to blood, causing all marine life within it to perish (verse 3). This will lead to the destruction of a vital food source for millions of people.

3. Third Plague: Following the pouring of the third bowl, the rivers and freshwater springs will transform into blood (verse 4). This plague will result in the demise of freshwater fish, further affecting the food supply for many.

4. Fourth Plague: The fourth bowl will intensify the heat of the sun to the point where it "scorches men with fire" (verse 8).

5. Fifth Plague: This judgment will usher in darkness, accompanied by excruciating pains and sores (verses 10-11).

6. Sixth Plague: The contents of this bowl will be emptied into the Euphrates River, causing it to dry up and facilitating land travel for the armies of "the kings of the earth and of the whole world." These armies will gather at Armageddon, an area near Megiddo, which is approximately 18 miles (30 kilometers) southeast of the modern city of Haifa. From there, they will advance toward Jerusalem for a final battle against Jesus Christ (verses 12-16).

7. Seventh Plague: This ultimate plague will manifest as "noises and thunderings and lightnings" and will unleash a "mighty and great earthquake" unlike any before. Babylon, symbolizing a powerful false religion, will fall (verse 19, compare Revelation 18:2). Additionally, there will be devastating hailstorms with hailstones weighing up to a "talent," or roughly 100 pounds (verse 21).

CHAPTER SIXTEEN

The First to the Sixth Bowl

Introduction:

Chapter 16 of the Book of Revelation unveils the pouring out of the seven bowl judgments, representing the culmination of God's wrath upon the unrepentant world. The first bowl brings painful sores upon those who bear the mark of the beast, illustrating the judgment against those who have chosen to align themselves with the oppressive system. The second bowl causes the sea to turn into blood, resulting in the death of every living creature in the sea. The third bowl turns the rivers and springs into blood, emphasizing the severity of God's judgment upon the earth's water sources. The fourth bowl brings scorching heat from the sun, causing great suffering and pain for those who are unrepentant. Despite the intense suffering, people refuse to repent of their sins and blaspheme God.

The fifth bowl leads to darkness covering the throne of the beast, symbolizing the spiritual and moral darkness that has enveloped those who have chosen to follow the beast's authority. The sixth bowl dries up the Euphrates River, making way for the kings of the east to gather for a great battle at Armageddon. The seventh and final bowl results in catastrophic earthquakes and hailstorms of unprecedented magnitude, causing cities to crumble and leading to widespread destruction. Chapter 16 highlights the unyielding nature of God's judgments and the continued refusal of many to repent and turn to Him. It serves as a stark reminder of the consequences of rejecting God's grace and choosing to follow the path of rebellion, setting the stage for the climactic events that will unfold in the final chapters of Revelation.

Verse 1: "Then I heard a loud voice from the temple saying to the seven angels, 'Go, pour out the seven bowls of God's wrath on the earth.'"

- John hears a loud voice from the temple instructing the seven angels to pour out the seven bowls containing God's wrath upon the earth.

Interpretation and Commentary:

1. Completion of God's Wrath: This chapter marks the culmination of God's judgment, as symbolized by the seven bowls of wrath. These judgments are severe and final, emphasizing God's righteous response to rebellion and sin.
2. Voice from the Temple: The voice from the temple signifies the divine origin and authority of these judgments, reinforcing that they align with God's perfect justice.

Verse 2: "The first angel went and poured out his bowl on the land, and ugly, festering sores broke out on the people who had the mark of the beast and worshiped its image."

- The first angel pours out his bowl on the land, causing painful and festering sores to afflict those who had the mark of the beast and worshiped its image.

Interpretation and Commentary:

1. Specific Judgment: This judgment specifically targets those who had aligned themselves with the oppressive forces represented by the beast and its image. The painful sores symbolize divine retribution.
2. Sign of Allegiance: The reference to the mark of the beast signifies an allegiance to worldly systems opposed to God, and these sores are a consequence of that choice.

Verse 3: "The second angel poured out his bowl on the sea, and it turned into blood like that of a dead person, and every living thing in the sea died."

- The second angel pours out his bowl on the sea, resulting in it turning into blood resembling that of a dead person, and all marine life perishes.

Interpretation and Commentary:

1. Catastrophic Impact: This judgment has a catastrophic effect on the sea, causing it to become lifeless and resembling death. It underscores the severity of God's judgment.

2. Symbolic Imagery: The transformation of the sea into blood is symbolic of divine judgment and the consequences of human rebellion. It echoes the imagery of the Exodus account (Exodus 7:20-21).

Verse 4: "The third angel poured out his bowl on the rivers and springs of water, and they became blood."

- The third angel pours out his bowl on rivers and springs of water, causing them to turn into blood.

Interpretation and Commentary:

1. Widespread Impact: This judgment extends to freshwater sources, affecting the availability of drinking water and essential resources.

2. Continuation of Symbolism: The transformation of water into blood is a recurring biblical symbol of God's judgment and the consequences of sin. It emphasizes the pervasive nature of God's wrath.

Verse 5: "Then I heard the angel in charge of the waters say: 'You are just in these judgments, O Holy One, you who are and who were;'"

- The angel overseeing the waters affirms the justice of these judgments, addressing God as the Holy One who has always existed.

Interpretation and Commentary:

1. Divine Justice Acknowledged: Even in the midst of the catastrophic judgments, there is an acknowledgment of God's justice. The judgments are seen as a righteous response to human rebellion.

2. Eternal Existence: The reference to God as "who are and who were" underscores His eternal existence and unchanging nature.

Verse 6: "for they have shed the blood of your holy people and your prophets, and you have given them blood to drink as they deserve.'"

- The angel justifies these judgments by highlighting that those on whom the bowls of wrath are poured out have shed the blood of God's holy people and prophets, and they are receiving blood to drink as a deserved consequence.

Interpretation and Commentary:

1. Retribution for Persecution: The pouring out of these judgments is seen as retribution for the persecution and violence inflicted upon God's faithful followers throughout history.

2. Deserved Consequences: The idea that they are receiving what they deserve underscores the principle of divine justice. God's judgments are proportionate and righteous.

Verse 7: "And I heard the altar respond: 'Yes, Lord God Almighty, true and just are your judgments.'"

- John hears the altar in heaven affirming the truth and justice of God's judgments.

Interpretation and Commentary:

1. Heavenly Confirmation: The response from the altar, a place of worship and sacrifice, emphasizes the heavenly affirmation of the righteousness and accuracy of God's judgments.

2. Attributes of God: The title "Lord God Almighty" is used, emphasizing God's omnipotence and sovereignty over all creation.

Verse 8: "The fourth angel poured out his bowl on the sun, and the sun was allowed to scorch people with fire."

- The fourth angel pours out his bowl on the sun, resulting in intense heat that scorches people with fire.

Interpretation and Commentary:

1. Extreme Heat: This judgment leads to unbearable heat, causing suffering and distress. It signifies a natural catastrophe with supernatural intensity.

2. Symbolic Significance: The sun, often associated with light and life, now becomes a source of suffering, symbolizing the reversal of normalcy and the catastrophic nature of God's judgment.

Verse 9: "They were seared by the intense heat and they cursed the name of God, who had control over these plagues, but they refused to repent and glorify him."

- The intense heat caused people to be seared, and they cursed the name of God, although they recognized His control over the plagues. Despite this, they refused to repent and glorify Him.

Interpretation and Commentary:

1. Stubborn Resistance: These verses highlight the stubbornness of those experiencing God's judgment. Instead of repenting and turning to God, they respond with defiance and cursing.
2. Recognition of Divine Power: Even in their rebellion, these individuals acknowledge God's control over the plagues, but their hearts remain hardened.

Verse 10: "The fifth angel poured out his bowl on the throne of the beast, and its kingdom was plunged into darkness. People gnawed their tongues in agony"

- The fifth angel pours out his bowl on the throne of the beast, resulting in the kingdom of the beast being engulfed in darkness. People experience intense agony, symbolized by gnawing their tongues.

Interpretation and Commentary:

1. Symbolism of Darkness: Darkness often symbolizes spiritual blindness and the absence of God's presence and guidance. This judgment signifies the spiritual darkness that engulfs those aligned with the oppressive forces of the beast.
2. Agonizing Consequences: The description of people gnawing their tongues underscores the excruciating nature of God's judgment. Their suffering is both physical and spiritual.

Verse 11: "and cursed the God of heaven because of their pains and their sores, but they refused to repent of what they had done."

- Despite their suffering, those under the judgment of the fifth bowl continue to curse God and refuse to repent for their actions.

Interpretation and Commentary:

1. Hardened Hearts: These individuals demonstrate a tragic pattern of hardening their hearts even in the face of severe

judgment and suffering. Instead of turning to God in repentance, they persist in their rebellion.

2. Cursing God: Their cursing of the God of heaven reveals their deep-seated hostility toward the divine and underscores their refusal to acknowledge His authority.

Verse 12: "The sixth angel poured out his bowl on the great river Euphrates, and its water was dried up to prepare the way for the kings from the East."

- The sixth angel pours out his bowl on the Euphrates River, causing its waters to dry up, facilitating the arrival of kings from the East.

Interpretation and Commentary:

1. Drying of the Euphrates: The drying up of the Euphrates River is a significant event, as the Euphrates has historical and symbolic importance in biblical prophecy (e.g., Revelation 9:14). It signifies a preparation for a significant event.

2. Kings from the East: The arrival of these kings from the East is a part of the unfolding of God's divine plan. Their specific role and identity are not provided in this verse but are important to the broader context of Revelation.

Verse 13: "Then I saw three impure spirits that looked like frogs; they came out of the mouth of the dragon, out of the mouth of the beast and out of the mouth of the false prophet."

- John sees three impure spirits resembling frogs coming out of the mouths of the dragon, the beast, and the false prophet.

Interpretation and Commentary:

1. Symbolic Imagery: The use of impure spirits resembling frogs is symbolic and signifies deceitful and demonic influences. These spirits are associated with the dragon (Satan), the beast (representing oppressive worldly systems), and the false prophet (a deceitful religious figure).

2. Deceptive Influence: The emergence of these spirits highlights the prevalence of deception and spiritual warfare in the events leading up to the final judgment.

Verse 14: "They are demonic spirits that perform signs, and they go out to the kings of the whole world, to gather them for the battle on the great day of God Almighty."

- These impure spirits are described as demonic, performing signs and going to the kings of the entire world to gather them for the great battle on the day of God Almighty.

Interpretation and Commentary:

1. Deceptive Signs: These spirits deceive through miraculous signs, drawing the allegiance of the world's leaders to participate in a final confrontation. This gathering foreshadows the climactic battle that will take place at the end of the age.

2. Day of God Almighty: The reference to the "great day of God Almighty" signifies a decisive and eschatological event, likely referring to the final battle between the forces of evil and the sovereignty of God.

Verse 15: "Look, I come like a thief! Blessed is the one who stays awake and remains clothed, so as not to go naked and be shamefully exposed."

- A warning is given: Jesus declares that He will come like a thief, and those who stay awake, spiritually prepared, and remain clothed with righteousness will be blessed.

Interpretation and Commentary:

1. Imminent Return of Christ: The declaration of Jesus coming like a thief emphasizes the unexpected nature of His return. Believers are urged to remain spiritually alert and prepared for His coming.

2. Clothed in Righteousness: Being clothed symbolizes spiritual readiness and righteousness. Those who maintain their faith and righteousness will not be exposed to shame when Christ returns.

Verse 16: "Then they gathered the kings together to the place that in Hebrew is called Armageddon."

- The kings, influenced by the impure spirits, gather together at a place known in Hebrew as Armageddon.

Interpretation and Commentary:

1. Armageddon: Armageddon has become a well-known term symbolizing the final apocalyptic battle between the forces of good and evil. It is a place of eschatological significance, representing the ultimate conflict.

2. Worldwide Gathering: The influence of the impure spirits leads to the gathering of world leaders at this pivotal location, setting the stage for the climax of end-time events.

Verse 17: "The seventh angel poured out his bowl into the air, and out of the temple came a loud voice from the throne, saying, 'It is done!'"

- The seventh angel pours out his bowl into the air, and a loud voice from the throne in the temple declares, "It is done!"

Interpretation and Commentary:

1. Culmination of Judgment: The pouring out of the seventh bowl represents the culmination of God's judgment. The declaration "It is done!" signifies the completion of His divine plan.

2. Finality: This statement underscores the finality and irreversibility of the events leading to the ultimate resolution of God's redemptive plan.

Verse 18: "Then there came flashes of lightning, rumblings, peals of thunder and a severe earthquake. No earthquake like it has ever occurred since mankind has been on earth, so tremendous was the quake."

- As a result of the seventh bowl, there are intense displays of lightning, thunder, and a severe earthquake of unprecedented magnitude.

Interpretation and Commentary:

1. Cosmic Upheaval: The dramatic natural phenomena, such as lightning, thunder, and a severe earthquake, signify cosmic upheaval and the profound impact of God's judgment.

2. Unprecedented Earthquake: The description emphasizes that this earthquake surpasses any previous in human history, highlighting the exceptional and unparalleled nature of the events.

Verse 19: "The great city split into three parts, and the cities of the nations collapsed. God remembered Babylon the Great and gave her the cup filled with the wine of the fury of his wrath."

- In this verse, we see significant events unfolding as a result of the pouring out of the seventh bowl of God's wrath.

Interpretation and Commentary:

1. Division of the Great City: The "great city" often symbolizes worldly systems opposed to God. Its division into three parts

signifies its disintegration and downfall. This could symbolize the collapse of political, economic, and religious structures opposed to God.

2. Collapse of the Cities of the Nations: The collapse of these cities suggests widespread destruction and upheaval on a global scale. It reflects the consequences of human rebellion against God.

3. God's Remembrance of Babylon: Babylon the Great represents a spiritual and moral system that stands in opposition to God's kingdom. God's "remembering" implies that judgment has come upon this system, and it receives the full measure of His wrath.

4. Cup of God's Wrath: The image of a cup filled with the wine of God's fury is a recurring motif in Revelation (Revelation 14:10; 18:6). It symbolizes the pouring out of God's righteous judgment on those who persist in rebellion.

Verse 20: "Every island fled away, and the mountains could not be found."

- This verse describes the dramatic and catastrophic physical changes that occur as part of God's judgment.

Interpretation and Commentary:

1. Geological Catastrophe: The imagery of islands fleeing and mountains disappearing represents an extreme geological upheaval, possibly indicating widespread earthquakes and natural disasters. These events underscore the profound impact of God's judgment.

2. Symbolism of Stability Shaken: Islands and mountains are often seen as symbols of stability and permanence. Their disappearance signifies the complete disruption of the natural order and the frailty of human structures when confronted by divine judgment.

Verse 21: "From the sky huge hailstones, each weighing about a hundred pounds, fell on people. And they cursed God on account of the plague of hail because the plague was so terrible."

- The final verse of Chapter 16 portrays a devastating hailstorm with immense hailstones, causing intense suffering and leading to people cursing God.

Interpretation and Commentary:
1. Hailstorm of Unprecedented Scale: The hailstones, each weighing about a hundred pounds, are exceptionally large and destructive. This imagery reinforces the severity of God's judgment during this final phase of His wrath.
2. Response of Humanity: Despite the catastrophic events and suffering, many people persist in cursing God. Their response reveals the hardness of their hearts and their refusal to acknowledge God's sovereignty even in the face of undeniable divine intervention.

These verses in Revelation Chapter 16 depict a series of climactic and catastrophic events, symbolizing the culmination of God's judgment on a world marked by rebellion and opposition to His divine authority. They emphasize the consequences of human choices, the persistence of rebellion, and the righteousness of God's judgment as part of the unfolding of His redemptive plan.

Prophetic Commentary:

The term "Armageddon" is found only once in the Bible, denoting a pivotal moment at the culmination of this age. Armageddon serves as the gathering point for what is described as "the battle of that great day of God Almighty" (Revelation 16:14, 16).

Interest in Armageddon is fervent, and rightfully so. Given the state of global affairs, it appears that the realization of this end-time prophecy is drawing nearer (refer to "Where Are We Now in Bible Prophecy?").

The word "Armageddon" has its origins in Hebrew, signifying the "hill" or "mountain" of Megiddo. Megiddo, located approximately 80 miles (about 130 kilometers) north of Jerusalem by road, has been the backdrop for numerous historic battles.

Who will assemble at Armageddon? Armies from across the globe will convene. In Revelation 16:13-14, the involvement of malevolent spirits in the gathering of these armies is described:

"I saw three unclean spirits like frogs coming out of the mouth of the dragon, out of the mouth of the beast, and out of the mouth of the false prophet. For they are spirits of demons, performing signs, which go out to the kings of the earth and of the whole world, to gather them to the battle of that great day of God Almighty."

The armies amassed at Armageddon will comprise:

1. The army of the beast (Revelation 16:13-14; 19:19). The primary forces of the beast will originate from Europe.
2. Kings from the east, leading vast armies (Revelation 16:12). This likely represents a coalition of Asian powers.
3. All nations, including formidable warriors (Joel 3:9-11).

To comprehend why all these armies congregate at Armageddon, we must delve into the sequence of events leading up to these end-time conflicts, as prophesied in the years preceding the Armageddon gathering.

God paves the path to Armageddon In spite of the devastation, humanity will persist in rebellion against God. People will persist in their sinful ways and continue to venerate false deities, including demons (Revelation 16:20).

Following the sounding of the seventh trumpet, a declaration will be made that the kingdoms of this world have become the kingdoms of our Lord and His Christ (Revelation 11:15). Strangely, instead of rejoicing, the deluded inhabitants of the earth will mourn.

God's wrath will persist, as seen through the outpouring of the seven last plagues. These plagues will inflict painful sores on the followers of the beast, transform the seas and freshwater into blood, unleash scorching heat, and shroud the world in complete darkness. Yet, despite these catastrophic events, humanity will remain unrepentant and continue to blaspheme against God (Revelation 16:11).

The sixth plague will dry up the Euphrates River, making way for the kings of the east to journey to Armageddon.

It's worth noting that Armageddon is approximately a nine-hour drive (835 kilometers or 518 miles) from the Euphrates at Ramadi, Iraq. However, the Bible does not specify the exact location of the Euphrates crossing.

Where will the so-called Armageddon conflict occur? Despite the armies gathering at Armageddon, the decisive battle will unfold in Jerusalem.

The sounding of the trumpet will serve as a divine summons to warfare, rallying nations to assemble (Joel 2:1; 3:9-12). A vast multitude will journey approximately 1½ hours south, covering a distance of 132 kilometers or 82 miles, from Armageddon to reach Jerusalem. These assembled forces will enter the Valley of Decision (verse 14).

The Valley of Decision is situated between the Temple Mount and the Mount of Olives, alternatively recognized as the Valley of Jehoshaphat or Kidron Valley (verse 12). It is located on the east side of the Old City of Jerusalem.

Who will participate in the battle on that momentous day ordained by God Almighty in Jerusalem? The assembled armies from Armageddon, comprising kings, captains, mighty individuals, and people both small and great, will be among the combatants (Revelation 19:17-19).

Who else will be engaged in the battle at Jerusalem?

1. Jesus Christ: The King of Kings and Lord of Lords, who will take part in the conflict (Zechariah 14:3; Revelation 19:11-19).
2. Michael: The eminent angelic prince appointed to watch over God's people will also be present (Daniel 12:1).
3. The heavenly armies: A formidable host of supernatural beings will join the fray (Revelation 19:14).
4. The resurrected saints: As foretold in Psalm 149:5-9, the saints who have been raised from the dead will participate in the battle.
5. The people of Judah: The inhabitants of Judah will also play a role in the Jerusalem conflict (Zechariah 14:14).

What transpires in the midst of this colossal battle?

As the momentous conflict unfolds, all eyes will turn skyward to witness the arrival of the Son of Man, who will return in resplendent power and glory (Matthew 24:30). The Lord will descend to engage the nations in battle (Zechariah 14:3). Christ, accompanied by the resurrected saints, will descend from the heavens (1 Thessalonians 4:16) and alight upon the Mount of Olives (Zechariah 14:4; Acts 1:9-

11) (Matthew 24:31; Zechariah 14:5; 1 Thessalonians 4:16-17; Jude 1:14).

In a startling turn of events, the bodies of the human armies gathered at Armageddon will abruptly begin to disintegrate while they are still standing, leaving behind a valley filled with lifeless bodies (Zechariah 14:12; Revelation 19:21).

Furthermore, the beast and false prophet will be apprehended and cast "into the lake of fire burning with brimstone," where they will be consumed by the flames (Revelation 19:20).

What insights can we glean from the events of Armageddon?

Those who converge upon Armageddon will be ensnared by a powerful delusion, embracing Satan's falsehood. They will shun the truth (2 Thessalonians 2:9-11) and ultimately find themselves in opposition to God.

Those who stand in defiance of God will become His adversaries, and they will face divine destruction as this age draws to a close.

Armageddon, while a source of fascination for many, offers us critical lessons. Within the context of Armageddon, a warning is sounded:

"Behold, I am coming as a thief. Blessed is he who watches, and keeps his garments, lest he walk naked and they see his shame" (Revelation 16:15).

In the absence of God's revelation and guidance, individuals may succumb to the lure of battling against God. Therefore, let us draw near to God and remain vigilant against the deceptions that may entice us astray.

CHAPTER SEVENTEEN

The Scarlet Woman and the Scarlet Beast

Introduction:

Chapter 17 of the Book of Revelation unveils a vision of a great prostitute sitting on a scarlet beast with seven heads and ten horns. The prostitute is described as arrayed in luxurious attire and holding a golden cup filled with abominations. She is identified as the "great city" that reigns over the kings of the earth, symbolizing a corrupt and idolatrous system that seduces and manipulates the nations. The seven heads of the beast represent both the seven hills of Rome and seven kings, while the ten horns signify ten future rulers who will receive authority for a short time, aligned with the beast's agenda. This vision provides insight into the spiritual and political corruption that will characterize the end times, with a focus on a powerful and deceptive world system that opposes God's kingdom.

Chapter 17 also reveals the eventual judgment of the great prostitute. The angel explains to John that the waters on which the prostitute sits represent peoples, multitudes, nations, and languages, highlighting her global influence. However, the ten kings who have aligned themselves with the beast will turn against the prostitute, leading to her destruction. This chapter emphasizes the ultimate fate of those who participate in this corrupt system, serving as a warning against pursuing worldly power, wealth, and influence at the expense of faithfulness to God. It underscores the contrast between the fallen world's values and God's ultimate judgment and sovereignty, setting the stage for the unfolding events in the latter part of Revelation.

Verse 1: "One of the seven angels who had the seven bowls came and said to me, 'Come, I will show you the punishment of the great prostitute, who sits by many waters.'"

- John is approached by one of the angels who had the seven bowls, inviting him to witness the judgment of the great prostitute sitting by many waters.

Interpretation and Commentary:

1. The Great Prostitute: In this context, the great prostitute symbolizes a spiritual entity or system that leads people away from true worship of God. She is depicted as a seducer of nations.

2. Sitting by Many Waters: The image of sitting by many waters can be understood as her influence spreading far and wide, potentially representing her sway over various nations and peoples.

Verse 2: "With her the kings of the earth committed adultery, and the inhabitants of the earth were intoxicated with the wine of her adulteries."

- The great prostitute has led the kings of the earth into spiritual adultery, and the inhabitants of the earth have been spiritually intoxicated by her seductive allure.

Interpretation and Commentary:

1. Spiritual Adultery: The reference to kings committing adultery emphasizes their alliance with this seductive spiritual entity, forsaking their allegiance to God. This is symbolic of idolatry and rebellion against God's commandments.

2. Intoxication: The metaphor of intoxication signifies spiritual delusion and deception. People are ensnared by false beliefs and practices that lead them away from God.

Verse 3: "Then the angel carried me away in the Spirit into a wilderness. There I saw a woman sitting on a scarlet beast that was covered with blasphemous names and had seven heads and ten horns."

- John is transported in the Spirit to a wilderness, where he sees a woman seated on a scarlet beast with blasphemous names, seven heads, and ten horns.

Interpretation and Commentary:

1. Wilderness Symbolism: The wilderness can symbolize a place of spiritual desolation or a state of moral decay. John's vision indicates that this spiritual entity is connected to spiritual corruption.

2. Woman and Beast: The woman represents the same great prostitute mentioned earlier, while the scarlet beast is a symbol of worldly power and oppressive systems. The presence of blasphemous names, seven heads, and ten horns signifies the evil nature and authority of this system.

Verse 4: "The woman was dressed in purple and scarlet, and was glittering with gold, precious stones, and pearls. She held a golden cup in her hand, filled with abominable things and the filth of her adulteries."

- The woman is adorned with luxurious attire and holds a golden cup filled with abominations and the filth of her adulteries.

Interpretation and Commentary:

1. Luxurious Attire: The woman's attire, described as purple, scarlet, gold, precious stones, and pearls, reflects opulence and wealth. This imagery contrasts her external appearance with the spiritual corruption within.

2. Golden Cup: The golden cup she holds symbolizes the allure and deception of her false teachings and practices, which lead people away from God's truth.

Verse 5: "The name written on her forehead was a mystery: Babylon the Great, the mother of prostitutes, and of the abominations of the earth."

- The woman's forehead bears a mysterious name: "Babylon the Great, the mother of prostitutes, and of the abominations of the earth."

Interpretation and Commentary:

1. Babylon the Great: The name "Babylon" is used symbolically here. It draws a connection to the ancient city of Babylon, known for its rebellion against God. In this context, it

represents a spiritually corrupt and rebellious system that seduces people away from God.

2. Mother of Prostitutes: This title underscores her influence in leading many astray into spiritual prostitution, symbolizing idolatry and false worship.

3. Abominations of the Earth: This further emphasizes her role in promoting detestable practices and false beliefs on a global scale.

Verse 6: "I saw that the woman was drunk with the blood of God's holy people, the blood of those who bore testimony to Jesus. When I saw her, I was greatly astonished."

- John observes that the woman is intoxicated with the blood of God's faithful martyrs, those who testified about Jesus. This sight astonishes him.

Interpretation and Commentary:

1. Persecution of the Faithful: The woman's drunkenness with the blood of God's holy people signifies her role in persecuting and martyring believers who remained faithful to Jesus.

2. Astonishment: John's reaction reflects the shocking and abhorrent nature of her actions. The suffering of God's faithful followers at the hands of this seductive system is deeply troubling.

Verse 7: "Then the angel said to me: 'Why are you astonished? I will explain to you the mystery of the woman and of the beast she rides, which has the seven heads and ten horns.'"

- The angel reassures John and promises to explain the mystery of the woman and the beast with seven heads and ten horns.

Interpretation and Commentary:

1. Divine Revelation: John's astonishment prompts the angel to provide him with deeper insight into the symbolism and significance of the woman and the beast. This indicates that these symbols hold crucial meaning within the context of God's divine plan.

Verse 8: "The beast, which you saw, once was, now is not, and yet will come up out of the Abyss and go to its destruction. The inhabitants of the earth whose names have not been written in the book of life from the creation of the world will be astonished when they see the beast, because it once was, now is not, and yet will come."

- The angel begins to explain the nature of the scarlet beast. It had a past existence, disappeared, and will return from the Abyss, leading to astonishment among those whose names are not in the book of life.

Interpretation and Commentary:

1. Temporal Phases: The beast undergoes temporal phases: past existence, absence, and future reappearance. This suggests a cycle of oppressive systems throughout history.
2. Return from the Abyss: The beast's return from the Abyss signifies a resurgence of oppressive worldly power with the potential for increased persecution.
3. Book of Life: The mention of the book of life highlights the importance of one's spiritual destiny. Those whose names are not in the book of life will be astonished when they witness the beast's reappearance, emphasizing the significance of God's sovereignty over salvation.

Verse 9: "This calls for a mind with wisdom. The seven heads are seven hills on which the woman sits."

- The angel emphasizes the need for wisdom in understanding the symbolism, explaining that the seven heads of the beast represent seven hills on which the woman sits.

Interpretation and Commentary:

1. Symbolic Interpretation: The angel underscores the importance of spiritual discernment and wisdom when interpreting these symbols. In this case, the seven hills refer to a geographical location associated with the woman's influence.
2. Seven Hills: Historically, Rome has been referred to as the "City of Seven Hills." The connection between the woman and these hills could indicate a link between the spiritual entity represented by the woman and the city of Rome.

Verse 10: "They are also seven kings. Five have fallen, one is, the other has not yet come; but when he does come, he must remain for only a little while."

- The seven heads of the beast are also explained as representing seven kings, with specific historical phases: five have fallen, one is, and another will come briefly.

214

Interpretation and Commentary:
1. Symbolic Kings: The seven kings represent rulers or leaders of kingdoms or empires. These rulers are connected to the oppressive system symbolized by the beast.
2. Historical Phases: The explanation points to a historical sequence of rulers. Five have already come and gone, one is in power at the time of John's writing, and another is yet to come but will have a brief reign.
3. Transitory Nature: The brief reign of the seventh king suggests that these worldly powers are ultimately temporary and subject to divine sovereignty.

Verse 11: "The beast who once was, and now is not, is an eighth king. He belongs to the seven and is going to his destruction."

- The explanation continues, identifying the scarlet beast as an eighth king who has a connection to the seven kings and is destined for destruction.

Interpretation and Commentary:
1. Eighth King: The scarlet beast, which John saw earlier, represents an additional ruler (eighth king) who is connected to the previous seven. This ruler is characterized by his association with the oppressive system represented by the seven heads.
2. Destruction Foretold: Despite his prominence, this eighth king is ultimately doomed to destruction. This reaffirms the theme of divine judgment on worldly powers that oppose God's authority.

Verse 12: "The ten horns you saw are ten kings who have not yet received a kingdom, but who for one hour will receive authority as kings along with the beast."

- The ten horns on the beast represent ten future kings who will receive authority for a short time in conjunction with the beast.

Interpretation and Commentary:
1. Ten Kings: The ten kings symbolize political leaders who align themselves with the oppressive system represented by the beast. Their reign is relatively short-lived, suggesting a temporary consolidation of power.

2. Collaboration with the Beast: These kings receive authority in association with the beast, indicating their allegiance to its agenda and the role they play in furthering its objectives.

Verse 13: "They have one purpose and will give their power and authority to the beast."

- These ten kings share a common purpose and willingly delegate their power and authority to the beast.

Interpretation and Commentary:

1. Unified Agenda: The unity of purpose among these kings signifies a coordinated effort to support and empower the oppressive system represented by the beast. Their actions are in alignment with the agenda of the beast.

Verse 14: "They will wage war against the Lamb, but the Lamb will triumph over them because he is Lord of lords and King of kings—and with him will be his called, chosen and faithful followers."

- The ten kings, in alliance with the beast, will engage in a conflict against the Lamb (Jesus), but ultimately, the Lamb will emerge victorious due to His divine authority. He is Lord of lords and King of kings, accompanied by His faithful followers.

Interpretation and Commentary:

1. Conflict and Victory: This verse anticipates a great spiritual battle between the forces of evil (represented by the ten kings and the beast) and the Lamb (Jesus Christ). Despite the opposition, Jesus is declared as the ultimate victor, emphasizing His supreme authority.
2. Called, Chosen, and Faithful Followers: Those who align themselves with Christ, identified as His called, chosen, and faithful followers, will participate in His victory. This highlights the importance of faithfulness to Christ in the face of opposition.

Verse 15: "Then the angel said to me, 'The waters you saw, where the prostitute sits, are peoples, multitudes, nations and languages.'"

- The angel explains that the waters on which the woman sits represent a diverse array of peoples, multitudes, nations, and languages.

Interpretation and Commentary:

1. Symbolic Waters: The waters symbolize the widespread influence and control exerted by the seductive spiritual entity represented by the woman. It underscores her sway over diverse populations from different parts of the world.

Verse 16: "The beast and the ten horns you saw will hate the prostitute. They will bring her to ruin and leave her naked; they will eat her flesh and burn her with fire."

- The beast and the ten horns, despite their previous alliance, will turn against the woman, causing her destruction in a gruesome manner.

Interpretation and Commentary:

1. Betrayal of the Woman: The beast and the ten kings, at some point, will betray the woman who previously symbolized their shared agenda. This could signify political or ideological shifts in alliances.

2. Violent Destruction: The language used to describe the woman's fate is graphic, suggesting a sudden and violent end to her influence. This serves as a stark reminder of the unpredictable and treacherous nature of worldly powers.

Verse 17: "For God has put it into their hearts to accomplish his purpose by agreeing to hand over to the beast their royal authority, until God's words are fulfilled."

- The actions of the beast and the ten kings, including their betrayal of the woman, are attributed to God's sovereignty and His purpose being accomplished through their actions.

Interpretation and Commentary:

1. Divine Sovereignty: This verse underscores God's ultimate control over world events, even using the actions of those who oppose Him to fulfill His divine purpose.

2. Temporary Authority: The beast and the ten kings are allowed to wield authority for a specific period, but this authority is subject to God's timing and His plan for history.

Verse 18: "The woman you saw is the great city that rules over the kings of the earth."

- In this verse, the angel provides a clear interpretation, stating that the woman John saw represents the great city that exercises authority over the kings of the earth.

Interpretation and Commentary:
1. Identification of the Woman: The woman, previously described as a great prostitute, is now identified as a symbolic representation of a great city. This city holds significant influence and power over the rulers of the world.
2. The Great City: The identity of the great city is a subject of interpretation and debate among scholars. Historically, many have associated it with the city of Rome, given its status as a dominant world power during the time of the Apostle John. Others have suggested symbolic interpretations related to worldly systems and centers of power throughout history.
3. Ruling over Kings: The woman's authority extends to the kings of the earth, signifying her political, economic, and possibly religious influence. She plays a central role in guiding and manipulating the actions of world leaders.
4. Symbolic Significance: Beyond any specific historical or geographical identification, the verse underscores the theme of worldly systems and powers that oppose God's authority. These systems, represented by the great city, often lead humanity away from God and toward idolatry, rebellion, and moral corruption.
5. Prophetic Warning: The overall message of Revelation is to provide a prophetic warning about the consequences of aligning with worldly powers and systems that oppose God. Ultimately, these powers will face divine judgment, and God's sovereignty will prevail.

As with many verses in Revelation, interpretation may vary among theologians and scholars. However, the central message remains clear: God's ultimate authority and justice will prevail, even in the face of powerful worldly systems and those who oppose His truth.

Prophetic Commentary:

Revelation 17 commences with verse 1, identifying the woman featured in this chapter as a "whore" (as per the King James Version) or a "harlot" (as in the New King James Version), who engaged in illicit relations with "the kings of the earth" (verse 2).

This portrayal appears to allude to political entanglements where the leaders of these nations collaborated in spiritual misconduct with this immoral woman, each party pursuing its own interests. Similarly, God previously characterized Israel's disobedience to Him as adultery and harlotry (Jeremiah 3:8-9; Jeremiah 5:7; Jeremiah 13:27; Ezekiel 16:32).

The fallen woman wields significant influence both historically and in contemporary times. Beyond her sway over the rulers of the earth, she exerts control over a substantial portion of the global population.

The reference to her as one "who sits on many waters" (Revelation 17:1) is later clarified: "The waters which you saw, where the harlot sits, are peoples, multitudes, nations, and tongues" (verse 15).

Verse 2 further characterizes her actions as intoxicating "the inhabitants of the earth with the wine of her fornication."

How is the harlot of Babylon depicted?

The woman in this chapter is described as being adorned in "purple and scarlet, and adorned with gold and precious stones and pearls, having in her hand a golden cup full of abominations and the filthiness of her fornication" (verse 4). Due to the color of her attire, she is also commonly referred to as the scarlet woman in the context of Revelation.

During the period when the book of Revelation was written, in the first century, clothing of a reddish-purple hue was highly esteemed and typically worn by individuals of rank and affluence. This color, often called "purple," contained a greater proportion of blue than crimson, though the precise boundaries were not precisely defined, and the terms were sometimes used interchangeably. For instance, the mock robe placed on Jesus is referred to as both "purple" in Mark 15:17 and "crimson" in Matthew 27:28 (Albert Barnes' Notes on the Bible, Revelation 17:4).

The significance of her attire in purple and scarlet lies in the impression of wealth and authority it conveys. This choice of clothing complements her possession of gold, precious gemstones, and pearls, as well as her holding a golden cup.

However, beneath this visually striking exterior, her cup is filled with "abominations and the filthiness of her fornication" (verse 4). In other words, her appearance is deceptive. Although she presents herself as beautiful and possesses the symbols of opulence and power, her actions are abhorrent to God.

Babylon the Great

In verse 5, we encounter the woman's name: "MYSTERY, BABYLON THE GREAT, THE MOTHER OF HARLOTS AND OF THE ABOMINATIONS OF THE EARTH."

Although the original Greek manuscripts did not use capital letters for this passage, numerous translators have employed them here (similarly to Matthew 27:37; Mark 15:26; Luke 23:38; John 19:19) to emphasize that this was a title or inscription.

The reference to Babylon signifies that, just as Babylon, the first of four world-ruling empires predicted by God in the book of Daniel, had propagated and enforced its false and idolatrous form of worship, so would this woman. As the mother of harlots, she would also give rise to daughters who would teach similar abominable doctrines—teachings contrary to those of Jesus and His disciples.

Furthermore, we are informed that this woman is accountable for the deaths of the faithful "martyrs of Jesus" (Revelation 17:6) and that she is "that great city which reigns over the kings of the earth" (verse 18).

When we examine history since the time of Christ, we find that the Roman Catholic Church, located in Rome (in the autonomous Vatican territory), did indeed exert authority over rulers of the earth in the past. Although it bore the name Christian, this institution also persecuted God's faithful followers throughout the ages and introduced substantial alterations to the fundamental doctrines taught by Christ and the apostles of the first century.

What or who is the beast in Revelation 17?

In this portion of Scripture, the term "the beast" refers to the Roman Empire, while in Revelation 19:20, it also designates the human leader of this empire. Here, in Revelation 17:3, the focus is on the empire itself.

A particularly intriguing description of the woman in Revelation 17 is found in verse 3: "And I saw a woman sitting on a scarlet beast which was full of names of blasphemy, having seven heads and ten horns."

As clarified in our article titled "Mark of the Beast," the beast in the book of Revelation is a continuation of the fourth great historical empire—the Roman Empire—foretold in Daniel 7:1-8. This kingdom was prophesied to suffer a "deadly wound" before experiencing a revival prior to the end of this age (Revelation 13:1, 3).

The woman seated on the beast appears to exert control or authority over the beast, much like a rider guides a horse.

In Adam Clarke's commentary, we find further insight: "This is a representation of the Latin [Roman] Church in her highest state of antichristian prosperity, for she sits upon the scarlet coloured beast, a striking emblem of her complete domination over the secular Latin [Roman] empire" (Adam Clarke's Commentary on the Bible, Revelation 17:3).

Thus, the term "The Holy Roman Empire" denoted the empire centered in Europe and under the authority of the Roman Catholic Church.

Regarding the seven heads of the beast, these represent "seven mountains on which the woman sits. There are also seven kings. Five have fallen, one is, and the other has not yet come. And when he comes, he must continue a short time" (Revelation 17:9-10).

Regarding the ten horns, Revelation 17 explains: "The ten horns which you saw are ten kings who have received no kingdom as yet, but they receive authority for one hour as kings with the beast. These are of one mind, and they will give their power and authority to the beast" (verses 12-13).

When we piece together this information, we find that the scarlet woman—the Roman Catholic Church—was prophesied to wield influence over successive iterations of the Roman Empire. The last of these will emerge at the end of this age.

John, during his vision, was transported to a time near the end of days. When he wrote that five kings had fallen, one existed, and another had not yet come, he referred to the Roman Empire. A final resurgence of the Roman Empire—the one John mentioned as "not yet come" (verse 10)—will comprise ten kings who will unite to create a brief, final revival of this historical fourth empire from Daniel 7.

This end-times empire, briefly controlled by the harlot, will derive its power from Satan the devil. Revelation 13:4 states, "So they worshiped the dragon who gave authority to the beast."

Previously, the dragon—representing Satan—was described as "having seven heads and ten horns, and seven diadems on his heads" (Revelation 12:3). This passage underscores that as the god of this current evil age, Satan exercises control and authority over the kingdoms of the world (2 Corinthians 4:4; Galatians 1:4; Matthew 4:8-9).

The demise of the scarlet-clad woman (the whore of Babylon)

Due to the influence of Satan and the woman adorned in scarlet, the ten horns or kings will "cede their power and authority to the beast" (Revelation 17:13) and "be granted authority as kings with the beast for one hour" (verse 12). However, their brief reign will culminate in a conflict with the Lamb, but the Lamb will prevail, for He is the Lord of lords and the King of kings (verse 14).

Evidently recognizing that they were misled or disillusioned by the scarlet woman, these nations will then turn against her and bring about her destruction. "And the ten horns that you saw on the beast, they will hate the harlot, make her desolate and bare, consume her in flesh, and reduce her to ashes by fire. For it is God's purpose that they unite, share a common resolve, and bestow their kingdom upon the beast, until the words of God are fulfilled" (verses 16-17).

CHAPTER EIGHTEEN

The Fall of Babylon the Great

Introduction:

Chapter 18 of the Book of Revelation continues the theme of judgment against the great city, which symbolizes a corrupt and idolatrous world system. This chapter portrays the fall of this powerful city in dramatic terms, as an angel descends from heaven, announcing its destruction with great authority and causing the earth to be illuminated with his glory. The chapter describes the city's decadence and opulence, as well as its participation in the exploitation and persecution of God's people. It is a city characterized by luxury, wealth, and commerce, and it has become a dwelling place for demons and a haunt for every unclean spirit. In response to the angel's proclamation, a voice from heaven calls God's people to come out of the city to avoid sharing in its sins and receiving its plagues. The destruction of the city is described as sudden, complete, and catastrophic, with merchants and kings mourning over its fall, symbolizing the economic and political ramifications of its demise.

Chapter 18 serves as a vivid depiction of the world's systems of power, wealth, and influence coming to a tragic end. It warns against the seductive allure of materialism and the pursuit of worldly gain at the expense of faithfulness to God. The call for God's people to come out of the city highlights the importance of maintaining a distinct identity as followers of Christ, even in a corrupt world. Ultimately, this chapter points to the inescapable judgment that awaits those who reject God's ways and choose to participate in systems that oppose His kingdom, while also highlighting the ultimate triumph of God's righteousness and justice.

Verse 1: "After this I saw another angel coming down from heaven. He had great authority, and the earth was illuminated by his splendor."

- John sees another angel descending from heaven, radiating great authority and illuminating the earth with his splendor.

Interpretation and Commentary:

1. Angel's Authority: This angel possesses significant authority, indicating the divine nature of his mission. His purpose is to convey a message of great importance.
2. Illumination: The angel's splendor illuminates the earth, symbolizing the revelation of divine truth and judgment that is about to be proclaimed.

Verse 2: "With a mighty voice he shouted: 'Fallen! Fallen is Babylon the Great! She has become a dwelling for demons and a haunt for every impure spirit, a haunt for every unclean bird, a haunt for every unclean and detestable animal.'"

- The angel proclaims with a powerful voice that Babylon the Great has fallen and has become a dwelling place for demons and unclean spirits.

Interpretation and Commentary:

1. Babylon's Fall: Babylon the Great symbolizes a corrupt and oppressive system or city, often associated with worldly powers opposed to God. Its fall signifies divine judgment and the end of its influence.
2. Dwelling for Demons: The imagery of Babylon becoming a dwelling for demons and impure spirits emphasizes the spiritual corruption and depravity associated with this system.
3. Unclean and Detestable: Babylon's transformation into a haunt for unclean birds and animals underscores its moral decay and defilement. It has become a place of spiritual filth.

Verse 3: "For all the nations have drunk the maddening wine of her adulteries. The kings of the earth committed adultery with her, and the merchants of the earth grew rich from her excessive luxuries."

- This verse explains the reasons for Babylon's judgment. The nations, kings, and merchants have all participated in her sinful ways.

Interpretation and Commentary:

1. Maddening Wine: Babylon's allure is described as "maddening wine," symbolizing the intoxicating and deceptive nature of its influence, which leads nations astray.
2. Adulteries: Metaphorically, the nations and their rulers have committed "adultery" by aligning themselves with this corrupt system, forsaking their allegiance to God.
3. Merchants' Wealth: Babylon's excessive luxuries and economic power have led merchants to grow rich through their association with her. This highlights the temptation of material wealth and the moral compromise that can result from pursuing it.

Verse 4: "Then I heard another voice from heaven say: 'Come out of her, my people, so that you will not share in her sins, so that you will not receive any of her plagues.'"

- A voice from heaven calls for God's people to come out of Babylon to avoid sharing in her sins and facing the resulting plagues.

Interpretation and Commentary:

1. Call to Separation: This is a call to spiritual separation from the corrupt and sinful systems of the world, represented by Babylon. God's people are urged to disassociate themselves from worldly values and practices.
2. Avoidance of Plagues: The call to come out of Babylon is not just about physical separation but also about escaping the spiritual consequences of aligning with ungodly systems. Those who remain entangled in Babylon's sins will face divine judgment.

Verse 5: "For her sins are piled up to heaven, and God has remembered her crimes."

- Babylon's sins have reached a point where they have accumulated to the heavens, and God is now mindful of her wrongdoing.

Interpretation and Commentary:

1. Accumulated Sins: Babylon's sins have become so numerous and grievous that they have reached a point of no return. This imagery conveys the idea of divine patience and forbearance eventually coming to an end.

2. Divine Remembrance: God's remembrance of her crimes signifies that divine judgment is imminent. God, who is just and righteous, cannot overlook persistent wickedness indefinitely.

Verse 6: "Give back to her as she has given; pay her back double for what she has done. Pour her a double portion from her own cup."

- This verse announces that Babylon will receive retribution in proportion to her sins, even a double portion of the judgment she has meted out.

Interpretation and Commentary:

1. Retribution: Babylon's judgment is in accordance with the principle of divine justice, known as "lex talionis" or "eye for an eye." She will face the consequences of her actions.

2. Double Portion: The double portion signifies the severity of her judgment. Babylon will experience a punishment commensurate with her sins.

Verse 7: "Give her as much torment and grief as the glory and luxury she gave herself. In her heart she boasts, 'I sit enthroned as queen. I am not a widow; I will never mourn.'"

- Babylon, which reveled in glory and luxury, will now experience torment and grief in proportion to her self-indulgence. She boasted of her power and permanence.

Interpretation and Commentary:

1. Torment and Grief: The contrast between Babylon's past extravagance and her impending torment underscores the justice of her judgment. She will suffer in proportion to her arrogance and wickedness.

2. Boasting and Pride: Babylon's pride and arrogance are highlighted in her self-proclamation as a queen who will never experience mourning or widowhood. This reflects her deluded sense of invincibility.

Verse 8: "Therefore in one day her plagues will overtake her: death, mourning, and famine. She will be consumed by fire, for mighty is the Lord God who judges her."

- In a sudden turn of events, Babylon will face swift and comprehensive judgment, including death, mourning, famine, and fiery destruction. The Lord God is the mighty judge who executes this judgment.

Interpretation and Commentary:

1. Sudden Destruction: The phrase "in one day" suggests the sudden and overwhelming nature of Babylon's downfall. Her judgment will be swift and inescapable.
2. Plagues and Destruction: The description of her plagues—death, mourning, famine, and fire—underscores the completeness of her judgment. These are symbolic of physical, spiritual, and moral devastation.
3. Mighty Judge: The judgment of Babylon is attributed to the omnipotent authority of the Lord God, emphasizing His sovereignty over the affairs of the world and His commitment to justice.

Verse 9: "When the kings of the earth who committed adultery with her and shared her luxury see the smoke of her burning, they will weep and mourn over her."

- The earthly rulers and leaders who had aligned with Babylon, benefiting from her wealth and luxury, witness her destruction and mourn her fall.

Interpretation and Commentary:

1. Kings' Grief: The response of these earthly kings and leaders underscores the significant impact of Babylon's fall. They had willingly embraced her corrupt system for their own gain and now face the consequences.
2. Loss of Allies: Babylon's sudden downfall not only results in her own demise but also disrupts the alliances and power structures that relied on her. This highlights the interconnectedness of worldly powers and systems.

Verse 10: "Terrified at her torment, they will stand far off and cry: 'Woe! Woe to you, great city, you mighty city of Babylon! In one hour your doom has come!'"

- The kings and leaders, terrified by Babylon's torment, stand at a distance and lament her destruction, recognizing the swiftness of her judgment.

Interpretation and Commentary:

1. Fear and Awe: The fear and awe of these rulers at the suddenness and severity of Babylon's judgment reflect the shockwaves sent throughout the world by her fall.
2. Swift Doom: The mention of "one hour" emphasizes the astonishing speed with which Babylon's doom arrives. It reinforces the theme of unexpected judgment.

Verse 11: "The merchants of the earth will weep and mourn over her because no one buys their cargoes anymore—"

- The merchants of the earth, who had profited from trade with Babylon, now lament her demise because their businesses suffer from the loss of her patronage.

Interpretation and Commentary:

1. Economic Collapse: Babylon's fall results in a severe economic downturn as the flow of commerce ceases. This highlights the economic entanglement of the world with her and the consequences of moral compromise for financial gain.

Verse 12: "cargoes of gold, silver, precious stones and pearls; fine linen, purple, silk and scarlet cloth; every sort of citron wood, and articles of every kind made of ivory, costly wood, bronze, iron and marble—"

- The verse lists the various commodities and luxury goods that Babylon traded in, revealing the extent of her material wealth.

Interpretation and Commentary:

1. Wealth and Luxury: Babylon was characterized by immense material wealth and opulence. This list of commodities reflects the extravagance and affluence associated with her.

Verse 13: "cargoes of cinnamon and spice, of incense, myrrh and frankincense, of wine and olive oil, of fine flour and wheat; cattle and sheep; horses and carriages; and human beings sold as slaves."

- The verse continues to enumerate the items traded by Babylon, including spices, perfumes, foodstuffs, livestock, and even human beings as slaves.

Interpretation and Commentary:
1. Comprehensive Trade: Babylon's trade network was extensive, involving a wide range of goods, from luxury items like spices and perfumes to essential commodities like food, livestock, and slaves.
2. Moral Corruption: The mention of human beings being sold as slaves highlights the moral depravity associated with Babylon, where human lives were commodified.

Verse 14: "They will say, 'The fruit you longed for is gone from you. All your luxury and splendor have vanished, never to be recovered.'"

- Those who profited from Babylon's trade lament the loss of the desirable goods they had once enjoyed. Babylon's luxury and splendor are now irretrievably lost.

Interpretation and Commentary:
1. Loss of Desires: Babylon's fall not only affects her but also those who were enticed by her prosperity. The verse underscores the transient nature of worldly wealth and pleasures.
2. Irreversible Decline: The mention of never being recovered emphasizes the finality of Babylon's downfall. It serves as a reminder of the temporal nature of earthly riches.

Verse 15: "The merchants who sold these things and gained their wealth from her will stand far off, terrified at her torment. They will weep and mourn"

- The merchants who had grown wealthy through trade with Babylon are now filled with fear and sorrow as they witness her torment.

Interpretation and Commentary:
1. Sudden Loss of Wealth: The fear and mourning of the merchants highlight the abrupt loss of their wealth and prosperity. This reflects the fragility of material success tied to corrupt systems.

Verse 16: "and cry out: 'Woe! Woe to you, great city, dressed in fine linen, purple and scarlet, and glittering with gold, precious stones and pearls!'"

- The merchants join in lamentation, exclaiming "woe" upon Babylon the great city, known for its opulence and adorned in luxurious attire.

Interpretation and Commentary:

1. Emphasis on Luxury: The merchants' cries emphasize Babylon's extravagance, characterized by fine clothing and dazzling displays of wealth, including gold, precious stones, and pearls.

Verse 17: "In one hour such great wealth has been brought to ruin!' Every sea captain, and all who travel by ship, the sailors, and all who earn their living from the sea, will stand far off."

- The suddenness of Babylon's fall is emphasized, leading to the ruination of great wealth. Even those associated with maritime trade are filled with fear and stand at a distance.

Interpretation and Commentary:

1. Sudden Wealth Ruin: The verse underscores the astonishing speed with which Babylon's immense wealth is obliterated. This serves as a cautionary tale about the transient nature of worldly riches.

2. Impact on Maritime Trade: The fear of sea captains, sailors, and those dependent on maritime commerce highlights the widespread consequences of Babylon's fall, affecting various sectors of the economy.

Verse 18: "When they see the smoke of her burning, they will exclaim, 'Was there ever a city like this great city?'"

- Those observing Babylon's destruction marvel at the sight, acknowledging the greatness of the city.

Interpretation and Commentary:

1. Astonishment at Ruin: The observers express astonishment at the extent of Babylon's destruction, recognizing the city's former grandeur and influence.

Verse 19: "They will throw dust on their heads, and with weeping and mourning cry out: 'Woe! Woe to you, great city, where all who had ships on the sea became rich through her wealth! In one hour she has been brought to ruin!'"

- Those who profited from Babylon's wealth lament her downfall, using symbols of mourning, such as throwing dust on their heads.

Interpretation and Commentary:

1. Repentant Lamentation: The weeping, mourning, and cries of "woe" express sorrow and, in a sense, repentance for having benefited from Babylon's corrupt system.
2. Economic Collapse: The verse highlights the economic impact of Babylon's fall, particularly on those involved in maritime trade. It underscores the interconnectedness of the world's economic systems.

Verse 20: "Rejoice over her, you heavens! Rejoice, you people of God! Rejoice, apostles and prophets! For God has judged her with the judgment she imposed on you.'"

-   In contrast to the mourning on earth, there is a call for rejoicing in heaven and among God's people because God has executed judgment on Babylon.

Interpretation and Commentary:

1. Heavenly Rejoicing: Heaven and God's faithful rejoice because God's justice has been served, and Babylon, which persecuted and oppressed God's people, has been judged.
2. Retributive Justice: The principle of retributive justice is evident here, as Babylon is judged according to the judgment she imposed on God's people, including the apostles and prophets who suffered for their faith.

Verse 21: "Then a mighty angel picked up a boulder the size of a large millstone and threw it into the sea, and said: 'With such violence the great city of Babylon will be thrown down, never to be found again.'"

-   A powerful angel symbolically demonstrates the force and finality of Babylon's destruction by casting a massive stone into the sea, declaring that Babylon will be utterly obliterated.

Interpretation and Commentary:

1. Symbolic Act: The angel's action with the millstone represents the irrevocable and catastrophic nature of Babylon's fall. It emphasizes that there will be no recovery or restoration.
2. Finality of Judgment: The declaration that Babylon will never be found again reinforces the permanence of her judgment. Babylon's corrupt system and influence are eradicated.

Verse 22: ""The music of harpists and musicians, pipers and trumpeters, will never be heard in you again. No worker of any trade will ever be found in you again. The sound of a millstone will never be heard in you again.'"

- Babylon's once-thriving cultural, economic, and industrial activities will cease entirely.

Interpretation and Commentary:

1. Cultural Silence: The cessation of music and artistic expression signifies the cultural desolation of Babylon. Its once-vibrant cultural scene will vanish.

2. Economic Collapse: The absence of workers and the sound of millstones allude to the complete economic collapse of Babylon. It will no longer be a center of trade or industry.

Verse 23: "'The light of a lamp will never shine in you again. The voice of bridegroom and bride will never be heard in you again. Your merchants were the world's important people. By your magic spell all the nations were led astray.'"

- The verse underscores the utter darkness and spiritual corruption of Babylon. It highlights her role in leading nations astray.

Interpretation and Commentary:

1. Spiritual Darkness: The absence of lamp light symbolizes the spiritual darkness that now shrouds Babylon. It is no longer a place of spiritual enlightenment or revelation.

2. End of Celebrations: The silence of bridegrooms and brides reflects the cessation of joyous celebrations and life's milestones. Babylon's fall brings an end to such festivities.

3. Deceptive Influence: Babylon's ability to lead nations astray is described as a "magic spell." This points to the seductive and deceptive nature of her influence, which lured people away from God.

Verse 24: "'In her was found the blood of prophets and of God's holy people, of all who have been slaughtered on the earth.'"

- The verse affirms Babylon's guilt in shedding the blood of God's prophets and faithful followers throughout history.

Interpretation and Commentary:

1. Blood of the Martyrs: Babylon is held responsible for the persecution and martyrdom of God's prophets and holy people. This indictment emphasizes her long history of opposition to God's purposes.

2. Divine Retribution: Babylon's judgment is not arbitrary but a divine response to her wicked deeds. God's justice is meted out in accordance with her actions.

In these concluding verses of Revelation Chapter 18, we witness the finality of Babylon's judgment. The chapter serves as a stark reminder of the consequences of aligning with corrupt and oppressive systems, as well as the ultimate triumph of God's justice over all earthly powers.

Prophetic Commentary:

The downfall of Babylon the great

Jesus Christ instructs John through His angel, saying, "I will reveal to you the judgment of the great harlot" (Revelation 17:1). The ultimate judgment unfolds in the subsequent chapter, declaring, "Babylon the great has fallen, has fallen, and has become a dwelling place for demons, a prison for every unclean spirit" (Revelation 18:2).

Interestingly, God inspired the prophet Isaiah to use similar language to depict the fall of the Babylonian Empire (Isaiah 21:9; 47:9). This secular authority, which also coerced people into practicing false religious worship (Daniel 3:1-6), served as a precursor or archetype of the false religious authority referred to as Babylon in Revelation 17-18.

When God's judgment befalls Babylon the great—the formidable, counterfeit church—it will be swift. As the Scriptures emphasize, it will occur "in one day" (Revelation 18:8) and "in one hour" (verses 10, 17, 19) of that day. "In this manner, the great city Babylon shall be violently overthrown, and shall never be found again" (verse 21).

This judgment will serve as God's retribution for all His saints who were martyred by her throughout the centuries (verses 20, 24).

Judgment accompanied by a warning

In His judgment against this woman and the ungodly society that will exist at the end times, Jesus Christ issues a solemn warning to all of us. John records, "And I heard another voice from heaven saying, 'Come out of her, my people, lest you share in her sins, and lest you receive of her plagues'" (verse 4). This warning imparts two vital lessons for us.

First, we are called to wholly disengage from any doctrines and practices that deviate from God's Word—the Bible. Christians are tasked with "contending earnestly for the faith which was once for all delivered to the saints" (Jude 3). This entails a commitment to follow the teachings and doctrines of the faithful woman described in Revelation 12.

Second, Christians must refrain from reverting to the false doctrines and teachings of this deceptive woman once they have separated from her. History has shown that Christians have erred by compromising and returning to false doctrines, and the Bible suggests that this error may recur in the future (Revelation 2-3). Worshiping God "in spirit and truth" (John 4:24) necessitates an unwavering commitment to avoid mixing or returning to erroneous teachings.

Jesus Christ has unveiled the identity of "BABYLON THE GREAT" to the reader, dispelling the mystery. She is no longer an enigma. The question remains: will you heed your Savior's counsel to "come out of her" in order to evade the impending consequences destined for her and all who embrace her misleading teachings?

CHAPTER NINETEEN

Heaven Exults over Babylon

Introduction:

Chapter 19 of the Book of Revelation is a triumphant and celebratory passage that portrays the culmination of God's redemptive plan and the ultimate victory of Christ over the forces of evil. It begins with a resounding chorus of praise in heaven, as a great multitude of voices declares "Hallelujah!" (which means "Praise the Lord!") in response to the judgment and destruction of the great prostitute (the corrupt world system) described in the previous chapters. The chapter emphasizes the righteousness and justice of God's judgments, and the heavenly multitude rejoices over God's avenging of the blood of His servants. The scene then transitions to a vision of the marriage supper of the Lamb, symbolizing the union of Christ (the Lamb) with His bride, the Church. This joyous occasion marks the consummation of the covenant between Christ and His people, and believers are invited to partake in this glorious celebration.

Chapter 19 also depicts the return of Christ as a conquering warrior riding a white horse. He is called "Faithful and True," and His robe is dipped in blood, symbolizing His victorious triumph over the forces of evil. He leads the armies of heaven, and with the sharp sword of His mouth, He defeats the beast and the false prophet and casts them into the lake of fire. The chapter culminates with the capture of the beast and the false prophet, and the rest of the enemies are killed by the sword that comes from Christ's mouth. Chapter 19 is a powerful proclamation of the ultimate victory of Christ and the establishment of His reign over the earth. It is a vivid portrayal of the fulfillment of God's promises and the vindication of His people, serving as a source of hope and encouragement for believers facing trials and tribulations.

Verse 1: "After this I heard what sounded like the roar of a great multitude in heaven shouting: 'Hallelujah! Salvation and glory and power belong to our God,'"

- John hears a multitude in heaven rejoicing and praising God for His salvation, glory, and power.

Interpretation and Commentary:

1. Heavenly Celebration: This scene marks a dramatic shift from the previous chapter's mourning over Babylon's fall. The heavenly multitude's joyful declaration underscores the triumph of God's justice and the redemption of His people.

2. Hallelujah: "Hallelujah" is an expression of praise and adoration, signifying the exuberant worship of God in heaven.

Verse 2: "for true and just are His judgments. He has condemned the great prostitute who corrupted the earth by her adulteries. He has avenged on her the blood of His servants.'"

- The multitude praises God for His righteous judgments, specifically mentioning the judgment of the great prostitute (Babylon) and the avenging of the blood of His servants.

Interpretation and Commentary:

1. Righteous Judgments: The praise highlights the justice of God's judgments. He judges with truth and equity, ensuring that the wickedness of Babylon is addressed.

2. Vengeance for the Martyrs: God's judgment on Babylon includes avenging the blood of His servants, particularly the martyrs who suffered for their faith. This theme of divine justice and retribution is significant.

Verse 3: "And again they shouted: 'Hallelujah! The smoke from her goes up forever and ever.'"

- The heavenly multitude continues to praise God, declaring that the smoke from Babylon's destruction ascends eternally.

Interpretation and Commentary:

1. Eternal Consequence: The rising smoke symbolizes the everlasting consequences of Babylon's judgment. It serves as a stark reminder of the irrevocable nature of her fall.

Verse 4: "The twenty-four elders and the four living creatures fell down and worshiped God, who was seated on the throne. And they cried: 'Amen, Hallelujah!'"

- The heavenly elders and living creatures join in worshiping God on His throne, affirming the praise of the multitude with an "Amen" and "Hallelujah."

Interpretation and Commentary:

1. Unified Worship: This scene portrays a unified worship of God in heaven, emphasizing the harmony and agreement among the heavenly beings in praising God for His righteous acts.

Verse 5: "Then a voice came from the throne, saying: 'Praise our God, all you His servants, you who fear Him, both great and small!'"

- A voice from the throne calls upon all God's servants, regardless of their station or status, to praise Him.

Interpretation and Commentary:

1. Inclusive Worship: The call to praise God extends to all His servants, emphasizing inclusivity in worship. It doesn't matter whether one is great or small in the eyes of the world; all are invited to fear and worship God.

Verse 6: "Then I heard what sounded like a great multitude, like the roar of rushing waters and like loud peals of thunder, shouting: 'Hallelujah! For our Lord God Almighty reigns.'"

- The description of the multitude's praise is likened to the sound of rushing waters and thunder. They exclaim "Hallelujah" because God, the Almighty, reigns.

Interpretation and Commentary:

1. Majestic Praise: The imagery of rushing waters and thunder emphasizes the grandeur and power of the multitude's praise. It signifies the awe and reverence with which they acknowledge God's reign.

2. Divine Sovereignty: The declaration that "our Lord God Almighty reigns" underscores God's absolute sovereignty and authority over all creation.

Verse 7: "Let us rejoice and be glad and give Him glory! For the wedding of the Lamb has come, and His bride has made herself ready."

- The multitude calls for rejoicing and giving glory to God because the long-anticipated wedding of the Lamb (Christ) has arrived, and His bride (the Church) has prepared herself.

Interpretation and Commentary:

1. Joyful Anticipation: The call to rejoice reflects the joy and celebration surrounding the union of Christ and His Church, which is a central theme in the book of Revelation.

2. Preparation of the Bride: The mention of the bride making herself ready symbolizes the sanctification and purification of the Church in preparation for the glorious union with Christ.

Verse 8: "Fine linen, bright and clean, was given her to wear.' (Fine linen stands for the righteous acts of God's holy people.)"

- The bride is given fine linen garments, which represent the righteous deeds of God's holy people.

Interpretation and Commentary:

1. Symbolic Attire: The fine linen garments symbolize the purity and righteousness of God's people. These righteous acts are not achieved through human effort alone but are graciously provided by God.

Verse 9: "Then the angel said to me, 'Write this: Blessed are those who are invited to the wedding supper of the Lamb!' And he added, 'These are the true words of God.'"

- The angel instructs John to write down a blessing for those who are invited to the wedding feast of the Lamb, affirming the truth of these words.

Interpretation and Commentary:

1. Blessed Invitation: This verse underscores the profound blessing of being invited to participate in the wedding feast of Christ and His Church. It represents the ultimate fellowship and communion with God.

2. Divine Affirmation: The angel emphasizes that these words are from God Himself, underscoring their importance and authenticity.

Verse 10: "At this I fell at his feet to worship him. But he said to me, 'Don't do that! I am a fellow servant with you and with your brothers and sisters who hold to the testimony of Jesus. Worship God! For it is the Spirit of prophecy who bears testimony to Jesus.'"

- John is so overwhelmed that he falls at the angel's feet to worship him, but the angel corrects him, stating that they are fellow servants and that worship should be directed to God alone.

Interpretation and Commentary:

1. Prohibition of Worship: The angel's response reinforces the absolute prohibition of worshiping anyone other than God. Even heavenly beings are fellow servants in the presence of God.

2. Testimony to Jesus: The verse highlights the central role of the Spirit of prophecy in bearing testimony to Jesus. All worship and adoration should ultimately lead to God through Christ.

Verse 11: "I saw heaven standing open and there before me was a white horse, whose rider is called Faithful and True. With justice, He judges and wages war."

- John witnesses a vision of heaven opening, and he sees a white horse. The rider of this horse is named "Faithful and True," and He comes to judge and engage in a just war.

Interpretation and Commentary:

1. Faithful and True Rider: The rider on the white horse is none other than Jesus Christ, symbolized by His title "Faithful and True." This imagery reflects His divine character and faithfulness to God's purposes.

2. Justice in Judgment: The description of the rider waging war with justice emphasizes that His judgment is perfectly fair and righteous. He comes to bring justice to a world marred by sin and oppression.

Verse 12: "His eyes are like blazing fire, and on His head are many crowns. He has a name written on Him that no one knows but He Himself."

- The rider's eyes are described as blazing fire, signifying His penetrating and all-seeing gaze. He wears many crowns and possesses a mysterious name known only to Himself.

Interpretation and Commentary:

1. Fiery Eyes: The fiery eyes symbolize Christ's divine knowledge and discernment. He sees all and judges with perfect insight.

2. Many Crowns: The multiple crowns on His head symbolize His authority over all dominions and kingdoms. He is the King of kings and Lord of lords.

3. Mysterious Name: The undisclosed name emphasizes the transcendence and uniqueness of Christ. It signifies His divine nature and attributes beyond human comprehension.

Verse 13: "He is dressed in a robe dipped in blood, and His name is the Word of God."

- The rider is clothed in a robe dipped in blood, and He is identified as the "Word of God."

Interpretation and Commentary:

1. Robe Dipped in Blood: The robe dipped in blood is a symbol of Christ's sacrificial death on the cross, where His blood was shed for the redemption of humanity. It also symbolizes His role as a righteous warrior in executing judgment.

2. The Word of God: This title, "the Word of God," harkens back to John 1:1, where Jesus is described as the Word who was with God and was God. It emphasizes His divine identity and the role of communication and revelation.

Verse 14: "The armies of heaven were following Him, riding on white horses and dressed in fine linen, white and clean."

- Christ is accompanied by the heavenly armies, riding on white horses and clothed in clean, white linen.

Interpretation and Commentary:

1. Heavenly Armies: These armies represent the redeemed saints and angels who follow Christ in His triumphant return. They participate in His righteous judgment.

2. White Horses and Garments: The white horses symbolize purity, and the white linen represents the righteousness of those who are with Christ. This underscores the holiness of the heavenly host.

Verse 15: "Coming out of His mouth is a sharp sword with which to strike down the nations. 'He will rule them with an iron scepter.' He treads the winepress of the fury of the wrath of God Almighty."

- From the rider's mouth comes a sharp sword, signifying His authority to defeat the nations. He will rule with an iron scepter and execute the wrath of God.

Interpretation and Commentary:

1. Sword of Authority: The sharp sword symbolizes Christ's authority and power to bring judgment upon the rebellious nations. His word is sufficient to defeat His enemies.
2. Rule with an Iron Scepter: This phrase indicates Christ's absolute sovereignty and His role as the divine ruler who enforces God's righteous reign.
3. Winepress of Wrath: The imagery of treading the winepress of God's wrath signifies the severity of the judgment that will be executed. It emphasizes the finality and completeness of God's judgment.

Verse 16: "On His robe and on His thigh He has this name written: KING OF KINGS AND LORD OF LORDS."

- The rider's robe and thigh bear the title "KING OF KINGS AND LORD OF LORDS."

Interpretation and Commentary:

1. Supreme Authority: This title unequivocally declares Christ's supreme authority and rulership over all kings and lords. He is the ultimate sovereign.

Verse 17: "And I saw an angel standing in the sun, who cried in a loud voice to all the birds flying in midair, 'Come, gather together for the great supper of God,'"

- John sees an angel in the sun, calling the birds to gather for the great supper of God.

Interpretation and Commentary:

1. Symbolic Gathering: The gathering of birds for the "supper of God" symbolizes the aftermath of the battle and the judgment that will take place. It is a vivid image of God's judgment upon the wicked.

Verse 18: "'so that you may eat the flesh of kings, generals, and the mighty, of horses and their riders, and the flesh of all people, free and slave, great and small.'"

- The angel invites the birds to feast on the flesh of those who have been defeated in the battle, including kings, generals, soldiers, and people of all statuses.

Interpretation and Commentary:

1. Symbolic Destruction: This imagery represents the catastrophic and final defeat of the enemies of God. The

invitation to birds underscores the completeness of God's judgment.

Verse 19: "Then I saw the beast and the kings of the earth and their armies gathered together to wage war against the rider on the horse and His army."

- John sees a gathering of the beast (representing the forces of evil), the kings of the earth, and their armies, preparing to wage war against the rider on the white horse and His heavenly army.

Interpretation and Commentary:

1. Final Battle: This verse describes the culmination of human rebellion against God, as the forces of evil and earthly powers make a futile attempt to resist the return of Christ and His victorious army.

Verse 20: "But the beast was captured, and with it the false prophet who had performed the signs on its behalf. With these signs he had deluded those who had received the mark of the beast and worshiped its image. The two of them were thrown alive into the fiery lake of burning sulfur."

- The beast and the false prophet, who had deceived people with miraculous signs, are captured and thrown alive into the lake of burning sulfur.

Interpretation and Commentary:

1. Defeat of Evil: This marks the ultimate defeat of the forces of evil represented by the beast and the false prophet. Their capture and judgment illustrate the finality of God's justice.
2. Lake of Fire: The lake of burning sulfur symbolizes the place of eternal punishment and separation from God, reserved for the wicked.

Verse 21: "The rest were killed with the sword coming out of the mouth of the rider on the horse, and all the birds gorged themselves on their flesh."

- The remaining enemies who gathered to wage war against the rider on the white horse are killed by the sword that comes from the rider's mouth, and the birds feed on their flesh.

Interpretation and Commentary:

1. Divine Word of Judgment: The sword coming from the rider's mouth symbolizes the powerful, decisive, and effective nature of God's Word in executing judgment. It's a reminder that God's spoken word has the authority to bring about both salvation and judgment.
2. Complete Victory: This verse emphasizes the completeness of the victory of Christ and His heavenly army. All opposition is defeated, and the enemies of God are vanquished.
3. Symbolic Imagery: The imagery of birds feeding on the flesh of the slain represents the aftermath of God's judgment. It's a vivid and symbolic way to depict the finality and totality of God's justice.

Bible References:
- The imagery of the sword coming from the rider's mouth reflects earlier biblical passages, such as:
    - Isaiah 11:4: "But with righteousness, he will judge the needy, with justice, he will give decisions for the poor of the earth. He will strike the earth with the rod of his mouth; with the breath of his lips, he will slay the wicked."
    - Hebrews 4:12: "For the word of God is alive and active. Sharper than any double-edged sword, it penetrates even to dividing soul and spirit, joints and marrow; it judges the thoughts and attitudes of the heart."

Interpretation and Commentary Summary:

Revelation 19:21 serves as the concluding scene of Christ's victorious return. The powerful imagery of the sword from His mouth and the birds feeding on the slain emphasizes the authority, finality, and completeness of God's judgment. It underscores the certainty of God's justice prevailing over all opposition and the ultimate triumph of Christ over the forces of evil. This chapter paints a vivid picture of the culmination of God's redemptive plan and the establishment of His righteous kingdom.

Prophetic Commentary:

The return of Jesus and the Battle of Armageddon are significant events described in the Bible.

Following the marriage supper of the Lamb and the pouring of the Vials, Jesus descends to Earth and destroys the armies of the nations at Armageddon, ultimately casting the Antichrist and the False Prophet into the lake of fire (Revelation 19:11-21). This battle, as described in Revelation 19:11-21, is more of a decisive action than a traditional "battle," with Jesus' mere word bringing about the destruction of the enemy.

Notably, Jesus is hailed as the "KING OF KINGS, AND LORD OF LORDS!" (Revelation 19:16).

Verse 15 emphasizes that Jesus will rule with a "rod of iron" during the Millennial Reign of Christ that follows these events, marking the end of the period of grace. It is a time when individuals are encouraged to accept Jesus and repent of their sins.

The "bride" mentioned in verses 7-9, and again in verse 14, represents the saints who follow Jesus into battle. In Chapter 21, verses 2 and 9, the symbolism suggests that the New Jerusalem will be the dwelling place of the saints, possibly signifying it as a home where they will reside with God for eternity.

The Antichrist and the False Prophet are cast alive into the Lake of Fire, as described in Revelation 19:20.

These events coincide with passages in Ezekiel 39:17-20 and Revelation 19:17-21, in which both describe the fowl of the air and the beasts of the earth feasting on the flesh of kings and mighty men. This indicates that these two events are indeed the same.

Comparing various scripture passages where God returns, such as Revelation 11:14-19 (7th trumpet), Revelation 6:12-17 (6th seal), and Revelation 16:17-21 (7th vial), the return of the Lord is depicted as a significant and catastrophic event marked by God's wrath, great shaking, and a global impact.

Additional references in Daniel 2, 7, 8, 11, and 12 further clarify the connection between these events and the return of Jesus.

These passages speak of the last world-dominating power, the role of the four kings, the Antichrist's actions and eventual downfall, and the time of trouble followed by the deliverance of God's people.

In Matthew 24:30, Mark 13, and Luke 17:24, the Bible indicates that immediately after the tribulation, the return of Jesus will be accompanied by celestial phenomena, God's wrath, and a worldwide revelation of His glory. The angels will be sent to gather His elect.

2 Thessalonians 2:1-8 emphasizes that the coming of the Lord and the gathering of His followers will occur only after the revelation of the Antichrist through the Abomination of Desolation. The Lord will consume the Antichrist with a word, and His coming will be bright.

1 Thessalonians 4:16-17 describes the Lord's return with a shout, gathering the elect to meet Him in the clouds.

Revelation 1:7 indicates that Jesus will return with clouds, and every eye shall see Him.

Revelation 19:11-16 portrays the marriage supper of the Lamb followed by the Battle of Armageddon. In this battle, Jesus treads the winepress of the wrath of God. The Antichrist and the False Prophet meet their end by being cast into the lake of fire.

1 Thessalonians 5:1-4 and Luke 17:24-30 highlight that the Lord's return will be unexpected, like a thief in the night, for those living in darkness. Their false sense of "peace and safety" will be disrupted by sudden destruction.

Zechariah 14 prophesies the splitting of the Mount of Olives, the Lord's return with all saints, the gathering of all nations against Jerusalem, and the subsequent divine intervention and victory (Battle of Armageddon).

Joel foretells the Lord roaring out of Zion, a ripe harvest, the day of the Lord, and the gathering of nations in the valley of Jehoshaphat (Battle of Armageddon).

Ezekiel 38-39 describes the Lord bringing nations against Israel (Battle of Armageddon) and the ensuing wrath, great shaking, and divine intervention.

All these passages collectively point to a sequence of events that include Jesus' return with His saints, His triumphant victory over evil forces, the inauguration of His kingdom, and cataclysmic events on Earth and in the heavens.

CHAPTER TWENTY

Satan Bound 1,000 Years

Introduction:

Chapter 20 of the Book of Revelation is a pivotal and highly debated passage that introduces the concept of the thousand-year reign of Christ, often referred to as the "Millennium." The chapter begins with the binding of Satan and his imprisonment in the abyss for a thousand years, during which time he is prevented from deceiving the nations. This period of time is characterized by the reign of Christ and His faithful followers, often understood as a symbolic representation of the Church Age. Those who have been martyred for their faith are seen as coming to life and reigning with Christ for this duration. This is commonly referred to as the "first resurrection," signifying the spiritual resurrection of believers who share in Christ's victory.

The chapter goes on to describe a final rebellion led by Satan after the thousand years have ended, in which he deceives the nations and gathers them for battle against the saints and the beloved city. However, this rebellion is swiftly crushed by God's intervention, as fire from heaven consumes the armies of the enemy. Satan is then cast into the lake of fire, where the beast and the false prophet are already, marking the ultimate defeat and eternal judgment of these malevolent figures. Chapter 20 concludes with a description of the "second resurrection," in which the rest of the dead are raised and judged according to their deeds, and those whose names are not found in the Book of Life are cast into the lake of fire. This chapter raises important theological questions about the nature and timing of the Millennium and the final judgment, and interpretations vary among different Christian traditions.

Verse 1: "And I saw an angel coming down out of heaven, having the key to the Abyss and holding in his hand a great chain."

- John sees an angel descending from heaven with the key to the Abyss and a great chain.

Interpretation and Commentary:

1. Angel and the Abyss: This angel is granted authority over the Abyss, which is often associated with a place of imprisonment for evil spirits or demonic forces. The presence of the key and chain signifies control and restriction over the forces of darkness.

Bible References:

- The concept of angels having authority over spiritual realms is found in various biblical passages, such as Matthew 16:19 and Revelation 9:1.

Verse 2: "He seized the dragon, that ancient serpent, who is the devil, or Satan, and bound him for a thousand years."

- The angel seizes the dragon, identified as the ancient serpent, who is the devil or Satan, and binds him for a thousand years.

Interpretation and Commentary:

1. Binding of Satan: This verse portrays the binding of Satan, rendering him powerless for a specified period, often referred to as the "millennium." This binding restricts his ability to deceive the nations during this time.

2. Ancient Serpent: The reference to the "ancient serpent" harks back to Genesis, identifying Satan as the deceiver who led humanity astray in the Garden of Eden.

3. A Thousand Years: The duration of a thousand years is symbolic and represents a significant, but not necessarily literal, period of time. It signifies a long era of Christ's reign and the relative peace and righteousness on earth during this time.

Bible References:
- The idea of Satan as the ancient serpent and deceiver is rooted in Genesis 3:1-15.
- The concept of a thousand-year reign is unique to Revelation and is referred to as the "millennium."

Verse 3: "He threw him into the Abyss, and locked and sealed it over him, to keep him from deceiving the nations anymore until the thousand years were ended. After that, he must be set free for a short time."

- Satan is cast into the Abyss, which is locked and sealed, preventing him from deceiving the nations for the duration of the thousand years. However, he will be released for a short time afterward.

Interpretation and Commentary:
1. Temporary Restraint: Satan's imprisonment in the Abyss signifies a period of restraint during which his influence and ability to deceive are curtailed. This corresponds to the peaceful reign of Christ during the millennium.
2. Future Release: The verse also foreshadows that Satan will be released for a short time at the end of the thousand years, which will lead to a final conflict before God's ultimate judgment.

Bible References:
- The concept of Satan's temporary restraint aligns with Revelation 20:7-10, which describes his release and subsequent rebellion.

Verse 4: "I saw thrones on which were seated those who had been given authority to judge. And I saw the souls of those who had been beheaded because of their testimony about Jesus and because of the word of God. They had not worshiped the beast or its image and had not received its mark on their foreheads or their hands. They came to life and reigned with Christ a thousand years."

- John observes thrones with individuals seated on them, granted authority to judge. He also sees the souls of martyrs who were beheaded for their testimony about Jesus. These resurrected martyrs did not worship the beast, its image, or receive its mark; they come to life and reign with Christ for a thousand years.

Interpretation and Commentary:

1. Reigning with Christ: This verse introduces the idea of believers who, after enduring persecution and martyrdom, are resurrected and given authority to reign with Christ during the millennium. This reflects the fulfillment of Christ's promise of rewards to His faithful followers.

2. Martyrs for Their Faith: The mention of those beheaded for their testimony underscores the cost of faith in Christ during the tribulation period. These faithful believers are granted a special role in Christ's reign.

3. Resistance to Idolatry: The martyrs' refusal to worship the beast and its image and to receive its mark exemplifies their unwavering faith and allegiance to God.

Bible References:

- The concept of believers reigning with Christ aligns with passages like Revelation 2:26-27 and 2 Timothy 2:12.
- The resistance to idolatry and refusal to worship false gods is consistent with biblical teachings on worshiping the one true God (Exodus 20:3-4).

Verse 5: "The rest of the dead did not come to life until the thousand years were ended. This is the first resurrection."

- The rest of the dead, aside from those who were resurrected to reign with Christ, do not come to life until the thousand years have concluded. This is referred to as the first resurrection.

Interpretation and Commentary:

1. First Resurrection: The "first resurrection" mentioned here is understood by some as the resurrection of believers to participate in Christ's millennial reign. It is a spiritual resurrection that involves being raised to a new spiritual life and sharing in Christ's reign during the thousand years.

2. Second Resurrection: The implication is that there will be a subsequent resurrection, often associated with the final judgment (Revelation 20:12-13), which includes both the righteous and the unrighteous.

Bible References:

- The concept of resurrection is central to Christian eschatology and is found throughout the New Testament, including John 5:28-29.

Verse 6: "Blessed and holy are those who share in the first resurrection. The second death has no power over them, but they will be priests of God and of Christ and will reign with him for a thousand years."

- Those who partake in the first resurrection are considered blessed and holy. The second death holds no power over them, and they are appointed as priests of God and Christ, reigning with Him for a thousand years.

Interpretation and Commentary:

1. Blessed and Holy: Those who are part of the first resurrection are described as "blessed and holy." They have been redeemed by Christ and are set apart for a special purpose.
2. Freedom from the Second Death: The reference to the second death indicates that these believers will not face eternal separation from God but will enjoy eternal life with Him. The second death is the final judgment of the wicked.
3. Priests and Reigning: Believers are appointed as priests of God and Christ, emphasizing their role as mediators and worshipers. They also participate in the reign of Christ during the millennium.

Bible References:

- The concept of believers as a royal priesthood is found in 1 Peter 2:9.
- The idea of reigning with Christ is mentioned in passages like Revelation 2:26-27 and 2 Timothy 2:12.

Verse 7: "When the thousand years are over, Satan will be released from his prison."

- After the conclusion of the thousand-year reign of Christ and His saints, Satan will be released from his imprisonment.

Interpretation and Commentary:

1. Release of Satan: This verse introduces the notion that Satan's restraint during the millennium is not permanent. His release signifies the fulfillment of God's plan and a test for humanity.

Bible References:

- The release of Satan is further elaborated in Revelation 20:8-9. Verse 8: "And he will go out to deceive the nations in the four corners of the earth—Gog and Magog—and to gather them for battle. In number, they are like the sand on the seashore."
  - Satan is released with the purpose of deceiving the nations, specifically "Gog and Magog," and gathering them for battle. These deceived nations are described as numerous as the sand on the seashore.

Interpretation and Commentary:

1. Deception of the Nations: Satan's release leads to a period of deception, where nations are enticed into rebellion against God. "Gog and Magog" are symbolic terms representing the enemies of God.
2. Numerous Opposition: The imagery of their number being "like the sand on the seashore" conveys the magnitude of this final rebellion. It underscores the extent to which Satan can lead people astray.

Bible References:

- The reference to "Gog and Magog" is reminiscent of Ezekiel 38-39, where these names are used to describe hostile nations.

Verse 9: "They marched across the breadth of the earth and surrounded the camp of God's people, the city he loves. But fire came down from heaven and devoured them."

- The deceived nations gather and encircle God's people and the beloved city, but divine fire descends from heaven, consuming them.

Interpretation and Commentary:

1. Final Conflict: This verse describes the climactic battle between the forces of rebellion and God's people. The enemy surrounds the "beloved city," often understood as Jerusalem, and God's faithful.
2. Divine Intervention: God intervenes with judgment by sending fire from heaven, annihilating the rebellious forces. This is reminiscent of God's historical judgments in the Old Testament, such as Sodom and Gomorrah.

Bible References:

- The concept of divine judgment by fire is found in numerous biblical accounts, including Genesis 19:24 and 2 Kings 1:10-12.

Verse 10: "And the devil, who deceived them, was thrown into the lake of burning sulfur, where the beast and the false prophet had been thrown. They will be tormented day and night for ever and ever."

- The devil, the deceiver of the nations, is cast into the lake of burning sulfur, the same place where the beast and the false prophet were cast. They will experience eternal torment.

Interpretation and Commentary:

1. Final Defeat of Evil: This verse signifies the ultimate defeat of Satan, the beast, and the false prophet. Their eternal torment in the lake of burning sulfur reflects the righteous judgment of God.
2. Eternal Punishment: The phrase "day and night forever and ever" emphasizes the unending nature of their punishment. It is a sobering reminder of the consequences of rebellion against God.

Bible References:

- The lake of burning sulfur is a symbol of eternal punishment, comparable to the concept of hell.

Verse 11: "Then I saw a great white throne and him who was seated on it. The earth and the heavens fled from his presence, and there was no place for them."

- John sees a magnificent white throne with the One seated on it. The earth and heavens flee from His presence, leaving no place for them.

Interpretation and Commentary:

1. The Great White Throne: This vision represents the final judgment of all humanity. The white throne symbolizes purity, righteousness, and the absolute authority of the Judge.
2. The Earth and Heavens Flee: The imagery of the earth and heavens fleeing underscores the magnitude and awe-inspiring nature of this judgment. Nothing can withstand the presence of the Judge.

Bible References:
- The concept of a great white throne judgment is unique to Revelation but aligns with the broader biblical teaching of a final judgment, as seen in passages like Matthew 25:31-46.

Verse 12: "And I saw the dead, great and small, standing before the throne, and books were opened. Another book was opened, which is the book of life. The dead were judged according to what they had done as recorded in the books."
- John witnesses the resurrection of the dead, both great and small, who stand before the throne. Books are opened, including the book of life, and the dead are judged based on their deeds recorded in the books.

Interpretation and Commentary:
1. The Resurrection of All: This verse describes a universal resurrection, including both significant and ordinary individuals. All will stand before God's judgment seat.
2. Books and the Book of Life: The "books" represent records of people's deeds, while the "book of life" contains the names of the redeemed. The judgment is based on one's actions and whether their name is in the book of life.
3. Judgment by Deeds: The judgment is not solely based on faith but also takes into account individuals' actions. This aligns with biblical teachings emphasizing both faith and works as aspects of salvation.

Bible References:
- The concept of a final judgment is found in passages like Matthew 25:31-46.
- The idea of a book of life is mentioned in Revelation 3:5 and Philippians 4:3.

Verse 13: "The sea gave up the dead that were in it, and death and Hades gave up the dead that were in them, and each person was judged according to what they had done."
- All realms, including the sea, death, and Hades, give up their dead, and each individual is judged based on their deeds.

Interpretation and Commentary:
1. Universal Resurrection: This verse emphasizes the comprehensive nature of the resurrection. No one can escape

this final reckoning, as even those lost at sea or buried in Hades will be raised.

2. Judgment by Works: The repetition of the judgment being based on one's deeds underscores the importance of personal accountability and actions in the final judgment.

Bible References:

- The concept of the dead being raised is found in passages like Daniel 12:2 and John 5:28-29.

Verse 14: "Then death and Hades were thrown into the lake of fire. The lake of fire is the second death."

- Death and Hades are cast into the lake of fire, symbolizing their ultimate defeat. The lake of fire is referred to as the second death.

Interpretation and Commentary:

1. Defeat of Death and Hades: This verse signifies the triumph of God's judgment over death and Hades. Death and the realm of the dead will no longer have power over humanity.
2. The Second Death: The lake of fire is identified as the "second death," distinct from physical death. It represents eternal separation from God and is a consequence of rejecting Him.

Bible References:

- The concept of the lake of fire as the final punishment is consistent with Revelation 19:20 and Revelation 21:8.

Verse 15: "Anyone whose name was not found written in the book of life was thrown into the lake of fire."

- Those whose names were not recorded in the book of life are cast into the lake of fire.

Interpretation and Commentary:

1. The Final Verdict: This verse encapsulates the finality of God's judgment. Those whose names are absent from the book of life face eternal separation from God.
2. The Importance of Faith: It underscores the importance of faith in Christ, as those who believe and are redeemed have their names written in the book of life, securing eternal life.

Bible References:

- The concept of eternal separation from God is mentioned in passages like Matthew 25:46 and Revelation 21:8.

Summary and Conclusion:
Revelation Chapter 20, verses 12 to 15, describe the grand culmination of human history and the final judgment. The resurrection of all individuals, the opening of the books, and the distinction between the book of life and deeds underscore the comprehensive nature of God's judgment. This judgment results in the ultimate defeat of death, Hades, and the eternal separation of those whose names are not in the book of life in the lake of fire. It serves as a sobering reminder of the consequences of one's faith and deeds, highlighting the need for a personal relationship with God through Christ for eternal salvation.

Prophetic Commentary:

1,000 years of tranquility

In a world fraught with instability, marked by the specter of wars, terrorism, climatic upheavals, and natural disasters, the notion of a 1,000-year era of peace, often referred to as the Millennium, captivates our imagination.

It is only natural for people to harbor a deep curiosity about the future. What is truly surprising, however, is the scarcity of reliable information available regarding the Bible's portrayal of the Millennium, and how little most individuals grasp about this subject.

In actuality, the Bible stands as the sole dependable source for comprehending this topic. Remarkably, it has a wealth of insight to offer concerning an imminent 1,000-year period. Despite the absence of the term "millennium" in most common English translations of Scripture, and the relatively few direct references to a "thousand years" in the Bible, it is replete with valuable information concerning the approaching Millennium. Above all, it unequivocally affirms its forthcoming arrival.

1,000 years in biblical perspective

Let's delve into the passages that address the concept of "a thousand years."

In Psalm 90:4, we find the profound statement that "a thousand years in Your sight are like yesterday when it is past, and like a watch in the night." This verse underscores the disparity between God's perception of time and our own. As the eternal and self-sustaining Creator, God's relationship with time differs significantly from our human experience.

Apostle Peter further contributes to this understanding with his words: "But, beloved, do not forget this one thing, that with the Lord one day is as a thousand years, and a thousand years as one day" (2 Peter 3:8). This verse emphasizes the divine timelessness and infinite perspective of the Creator.

1,000 years in the book of Revelation

The first direct reference to a 1,000-year reign of the Kingdom of God on earth can be found in the concluding book of the Bible, Revelation.

Revelation 19 vividly depicts the glorious return of Jesus Christ, as He comes in majestic power to establish His dominion over the kingdoms of the world and usher in a new era of righteousness and justice on our planet (verses 11-16). During this momentous event, Christ will quell all opposition, dismantle the last vestiges of human rule, and inaugurate the divine government's rule for a literal 1,000-year period known as the Millennium.

We adhere to the interpretation that these passages indeed signify a factual thousand-year reign following the return of Jesus Christ. This perspective is commonly referred to as premillennialism, in which Christ returns before the commencement of the thousand years—a viewpoint we find to be consistent with the biblical narrative, distinguishing it from postmillennialism and amillennialism.

Satan's Binding Preceding the Millennium

Following the triumphant return of Jesus Christ, a significant event unfolds. The apostle John provides a vivid description: "Then I witnessed an angel descending from heaven, holding the key to the abyss and a mighty chain in his hand. He seized the dragon, that ancient serpent known as the Devil and Satan, and bound him for a period of one thousand years. The angel cast him into the abyss, sealed it shut, and ensured that he would not deceive the nations any longer until the thousand years had elapsed. After this, a brief release is ordained for him" (Revelation 20:1-3).

In this passage, we encounter the first mention of the duration of this initial stage within God's reign on earth—a remarkable 1,000 years! Moreover, we gain a profound understanding of the reason behind this extraordinary period: Satan, the adversary of God and His divine purpose, will be restrained for the entirety of these 1,000 years. Welcome to the Millennium!

The Thousand-Year Reign of Jesus

Continuing our exploration, John goes on to write, "I saw thrones, and they were seated on them, and judgment was committed to them [the faithful followers of God]. Then I saw the souls of those who had been martyred for their testimony of Jesus and for the Word of God. They had not worshiped the beast or its image, nor had they accepted its mark on their foreheads or their hands. They came to life and reigned with Christ for a thousand years" (Revelation 20:4).

In this passage, we witness that God's devoted saints, those who steadfastly refused to yield to the oppressive influence of the beastly power in the last days, will enjoy the extraordinary privilege of reigning alongside Jesus Christ for a full millennium.

The 1,000-year reign of Jesus Christ is the central theme of numerous enchanting messianic prophecies. Some cherished descriptions of this era of peace include:

- "They shall not harm or destroy on all My holy mountain, for the earth will be full of the knowledge of the LORD as the waters cover the sea" (Isaiah 11:9).

- "Then the eyes of the blind will be opened, and the ears of the deaf unstopped. Then the lame will leap like a deer, and the tongue of the mute will sing. For waters will burst forth in the wilderness, and streams in the desert" (Isaiah 35:5-6).

- "In the latter days, the mountain of the LORD's house will be established as the highest of the mountains; it will be lifted up above the hills, and peoples will stream to it. Many nations will come and say, 'Come, let us go up to the mountain of the LORD, to the house of the God of Jacob. He will teach us His ways so that we may walk in His paths.' The law will go forth from Zion, and the word of the LORD from Jerusalem. He will judge between many peoples and will settle disputes for strong nations far and wide. They will beat their swords into plowshares and their spears into pruning hooks. Nation will not take up sword against nation, nor will they train for war anymore. Everyone will sit under their own vine and under their own fig tree, and no one will make them afraid, for the LORD Almighty has spoken" (Micah 4:1-4).

- The apostle Peter summarized these prophecies with these words: "Repent, then, and turn to God, so that your sins may be wiped out, that times of refreshing may come from the Lord, and that He may send the Messiah, who has been appointed for you—even Jesus. Heaven must receive Him until the time comes for God to restore everything, as He promised long ago through His holy prophets" (Acts 3:19-21).

What Occurs After the Millennium?

"But the rest of the dead did not live again until the thousand years were finished. This is the first resurrection" (Revelation 20:5).

Who precisely are "the rest of the dead"? This group encompasses the vast majority of humanity, excluding the saints, who will remain in their graves for a period of 1,000 years until they experience a resurrection that is distinct and separate from that of the saints. The "first resurrection" will transpire at the return of Jesus Christ (1 Thessalonians 4:14-17), while a second resurrection will occur a millennium later.

Which resurrection is superior? The book of Revelation offers a clear answer: "Blessed and holy is he who has part in the first resurrection. Over such, the second death has no power, but they shall be priests of God and of Christ and shall reign with Him for a thousand years" (Revelation 20:6).

Those who participate in the first resurrection, which takes place at the onset of the Millennium, will no longer be subject to death. For a more comprehensive understanding of this topic, we encourage you to read our article titled "Resurrections: What Are They?"

Satan's Release After the Millennium

Verse 7 introduces the release of Satan the devil after the completion of the 1,000-year period. During this time, he will have one final opportunity to venture out and deceive the nations of the world before ultimately being cast into the lake of fire and brimstone (verses 10-11).

Revelation 20 emphasizes the phrase "thousand years" six times. This chapter unequivocally affirms the existence of a millennial reign of Jesus Christ on earth, underscoring that it will be a vastly superior era compared to the present age of humanity that precedes it.

More Prophecies of the Millennium

However, the mention of the phrase "thousand years" is just a part of the broader narrative. Beyond this specific phrase, we find a wealth of information about the coming Millennium throughout various passages of the Bible.

In particular, the writings of the Old Testament prophets shed light on the profound impact of the ruling Kingdom of God during this period. These prophecies encompass a wide range of subjects, including global peace, economic stability, the restoration of genuine education and moral values, the significant role of the resurrected saints, the roles of different nations, and even transformations in the behavior of animals.

The Millennium promises to be a remarkable and exhilarating era, something to eagerly anticipate.

CHAPTER TWENTY ONE

All Things Made New

Introduction:

Chapter 21 of the Book of Revelation presents a breathtaking vision of the new heaven and the new earth that God creates after the final judgment. The chapter begins with John seeing a "new heaven and a new earth," signifying a complete renewal and restoration of the created order. He also witnesses a new Jerusalem coming down from heaven, symbolizing the dwelling place of God among His people. This holy city is described as adorned like a bride, prepared for her husband, and its brilliance and beauty radiate with the glory of God. In this new creation, God's presence will be with His people, and there will be no more suffering, death, or tears. He promises, "Behold, I am making all things new."

Chapter 21 provides a glimpse of the ultimate fulfillment of God's redemptive plan. It emphasizes the hope of a future where God's dwelling place is among humanity, and He will be their God, wiping away every sorrow and pain. The vision of the new Jerusalem reflects the intimate relationship between God and His people, portraying the culmination of God's covenant promises. This chapter serves as a source of great comfort and encouragement to believers, assuring them of the glorious future that awaits those who remain faithful to God's calling, ultimately leading to the eternal fellowship with Him in a world free from sin and suffering.

Verse 1: "Then I saw 'a new heaven and a new earth,' for the first heaven and the first earth had passed away, and there was no longer any sea."

- John sees a vision of a new heaven and a new earth, replacing the old ones, which had passed away, and there is no longer a sea.

Interpretation and Commentary:

1. A New Creation: This vision represents the culmination of God's plan for the restoration of creation. The new heaven and earth signify a renewed, perfect order, free from the effects of sin and decay.
2. No More Sea: The absence of the sea can be symbolic of the removal of chaos and separation. In the ancient world, the sea was often associated with unpredictability and danger.

Bible References:

- The idea of a new heaven and earth is also found in Isaiah 65:17 and 2 Peter 3:13.

Verse 2: "I saw the Holy City, the new Jerusalem, coming down out of heaven from God, prepared as a bride beautifully dressed for her husband."

- John beholds the Holy City, the new Jerusalem, descending from heaven, appearing radiant and prepared, like a bride adorned for her husband.

Interpretation and Commentary:

1. The New Jerusalem: The new Jerusalem is a central symbol in Revelation, representing the dwelling place of God and His redeemed people. Its descent signifies the union of heaven and earth.
2. Bride of Christ: The imagery of the city as a bride beautifully dressed reflects the intimate relationship between Christ and His Church. It highlights the joyous union between Christ and His redeemed followers.

Bible References:

- The concept of the new Jerusalem is also found in Revelation 3:12 and Revelation 21:10.

Verse 3: "And I heard a loud voice from the throne saying, 'Look! God's dwelling place is now among the people, and he will dwell with them. They will be his people, and God himself will be with them and be their God.'"

- A voice from the throne announces that God's dwelling place is now with humanity, and He will reside among them. The people will be His, and He will be their God.

Interpretation and Commentary:

1. God's Presence: This verse emphasizes the ultimate fulfillment of God's desire for intimacy with His creation. His dwelling among people signifies a profound closeness and communion with His redeemed.

2. Covenant Language: The language of "His people" and "their God" echoes the covenant promises in the Old Testament, underlining the unbreakable relationship between God and His chosen ones.

Bible References:

- Similar themes of God dwelling with His people are found in Ezekiel 37:27 and Revelation 7:15.

Verse 4: "He will wipe every tear from their eyes. There will be no more death' or mourning or crying or pain, for the old order of things has passed away."

- God will personally comfort His people by wiping away their tears. In the new creation, there will be no more death, mourning, crying, or pain because the former things have passed away.

Interpretation and Commentary:

1. Divine Comfort: This verse portrays the tender care of God for His people, personally wiping away their tears. It symbolizes the removal of all suffering and sorrow.

2. The End of Suffering: The absence of death, mourning, crying, and pain signifies the complete restoration of creation. These were consequences of sin, which will no longer have a place in the new order.

Bible References:

- Similar promises of a tearless existence are found in Isaiah 25:8 and Revelation 7:17.

Verse 5: "He who was seated on the throne said, 'I am making everything new!' Then he said, 'Write this down, for these words are trustworthy and true.'"

- The One on the throne declares that He is making everything new and instructs John to record these words because they are trustworthy and true.

Interpretation and Commentary:

1. The Divine Creator: The statement "I am making everything new" underscores God's role as the Creator and the One who brings about the renewal of all things.
2. Trustworthy and True: God's words are emphasized as reliable and truthful, assuring John and readers of the certainty of His promises.

Bible References:

- God's creative power is evident in passages like Genesis 1:1, and the trustworthiness of His words is affirmed throughout the Bible.

Verse 6: "He said to me: 'It is done. I am the Alpha and the Omega, the Beginning and the End. To the thirsty I will give water without cost from the spring of the water of life.'"

- God declares, "It is done," and identifies Himself as the Alpha and Omega, the Beginning and the End. He promises to provide the water of life freely to the thirsty.

Interpretation and Commentary:

1. Divine Sovereignty: God's declaration, "It is done," signifies the fulfillment of His divine plan. He is the ultimate source and culmination of all things.
2. Water of Life: The offer of "water without cost" symbolizes the gift of eternal life through Christ. It represents spiritual refreshment and nourishment for those who seek Him.

Bible References:

- The titles Alpha and Omega are also found in Revelation 1:8 and Revelation 22:13. The water of life is mentioned in Revelation 22:17.

Verse 7: "Those who are victorious will inherit all this, and I will be their God, and they will be my children."

- The victorious ones will inherit all the blessings of the new creation. God will be their God, and they will be His children.

Interpretation and Commentary:

1. Victorious Inheritance: Those who have overcome through faith in Christ are promised an inheritance in the new heaven and earth. This reflects the biblical concept of believers as heirs of God's promises.

2. Adopted as Children: The language of "children" signifies an intimate relationship with God, where believers become part of His family through faith in Christ.

Bible References:

- The idea of believers as children of God is found in John 1:12 and Romans 8:16-17.

Verse 8: "But the cowardly, the unbelieving, the vile, the murderers, the sexually immoral, those who practice magic arts, the idolaters and all liars—they will be consigned to the fiery lake of burning sulfur. This is the second death."

- In this verse, a list of sinful behaviors and those who practice them is provided, and it is stated that they will face the fiery lake of burning sulfur, which is the second death.

Interpretation and Commentary:

1. Consequences of Sin: This verse emphasizes various sinful behaviors and their consequences. Those who persist in unbelief and unrepentant sin will face eternal judgment.

2. The Second Death: The fiery lake of burning sulfur symbolizes eternal punishment, often referred to as the second death. This is a stark contrast to the eternal life promised to the faithful.

Bible References:

- The concept of eternal punishment is also found in Matthew 25:41 and Revelation 20:14.

Verse 9: "One of the seven angels who had the seven bowls full of the seven last plagues came and said to me, 'Come, I will show you the bride, the wife of the Lamb.'"

- One of the angels with authority over the plagues invites John to witness the bride, the wife of the Lamb.

Interpretation and Commentary:

1. The Bride of the Lamb: The bride represents the Church, the redeemed people of God, and the Lamb is Jesus Christ. This

imagery signifies the intimate relationship between Christ and His followers.

2. Angelic Guidance: John receives guidance from one of the angels entrusted with the final plagues, underscoring the significance of the vision he is about to witness.

Bible References:

- The Church as the bride of Christ is a recurring theme in the New Testament, seen in passages like Ephesians 5:25-27 and 2 Corinthians 11:2.

Verse 10: "And he carried me away in the Spirit to a mountain great and high, and showed me the Holy City, Jerusalem, coming down out of heaven from God."

- John is transported in the Spirit to a high mountain where he sees the Holy City, Jerusalem, descending from heaven, a continuation of the vision.

Interpretation and Commentary:

1. Supernatural Revelation: John's experience of being carried away in the Spirit emphasizes the supernatural nature of this vision. It transcends ordinary human perception.

2. The Holy City: The Holy City represents the dwelling place of God and His redeemed people. Its descent from heaven symbolizes the union of heaven and earth.

Bible References:

- Similar themes of heavenly visions are found in Ezekiel 40:2 and Ezekiel 48:35.

Verse 11: "It shone with the glory of God, and its brilliance was like that of a very precious jewel, like a jasper, clear as crystal."

- The Holy City radiates with the glory of God, shining brilliantly like a valuable jewel, particularly a jasper, and is clear as crystal.

Interpretation and Commentary:

1. Divine Radiance: The radiance and clarity of the Holy City signify the presence of God's glory. It is described with imagery of purity and splendor.

2. Precious Jewel: The comparison to a jasper, known for its brilliance and variety of colors, highlights the beauty and preciousness of the Holy City.

Bible References:

- The imagery of God's glory shining is found in passages like Ezekiel 43:2 and Revelation 22:5.

Verse 12: "It had a great, high wall with twelve gates, and with twelve angels at the gates. On the gates were written the names of the twelve tribes of Israel."

- The Holy City is surrounded by a high wall with twelve gates, each guarded by an angel. The gates are inscribed with the names of the twelve tribes of Israel.

Interpretation and Commentary:

1. Symbolic Significance: The twelve gates and the names of the tribes of Israel symbolize the inclusion of God's covenant people in the new Jerusalem. It signifies the continuity of God's promises.
2. Angel Guardians: The presence of angels at the gates underscores the security and sanctity of the Holy City. They ensure that only those who belong can enter.

Bible References:

- The twelve tribes of Israel are foundational in Old Testament history and are mentioned throughout the Bible.

Verse 13: "There were three gates on the east, three on the north, three on the south, and three on the west."

- The twelve gates of the Holy City are evenly distributed, with three gates on each side: east, north, south, and west.

Interpretation and Commentary:

1. Symmetry and Completeness: The arrangement of the gates in four sets of three adds to the sense of completeness and symmetry in the vision, emphasizing its divine design.
2. Access from All Directions: The placement of gates on all sides signifies that people from all corners of the earth have access to the Holy City, highlighting God's universal invitation.

Bible References:

- The use of numbers to convey symbolism is seen throughout the Bible, such as twelve representing completeness and four representing universality.

Verse 14: "The wall of the city had twelve foundations, and on them were the names of the twelve apostles of the Lamb."

- The city's wall has twelve foundations, and each foundation bears the names of the twelve apostles of the Lamb.

Interpretation and Commentary:

1. Apostolic Foundation: The twelve foundations, with the names of the apostles, signify the foundational role of the apostles in the Church. They played a central role in spreading the Gospel.
2. Continuity and Unity: The inclusion of both the twelve tribes of Israel and the twelve apostles demonstrates the continuity between the Old and New Testaments and the unity of God's people.

Bible References:

- The role of the apostles as foundational is mentioned in Ephesians 2:20 and Ephesians 4:11-14.

Verse 15: "The angel who talked with me had a measuring rod of gold to measure the city, its gates and its walls."

- The angel guiding John carries a golden measuring rod to measure the dimensions of the city, including its gates and walls.

Interpretation and Commentary:

1. Symbol of Precision: The use of a measuring rod symbolizes precision and accuracy in God's design. It signifies the exactness and order of God's plans.
2. Divine Planning: The act of measuring implies that God has a specific plan and purpose for the Holy City, ensuring that everything aligns perfectly with His design.

Bible References:

- The use of measuring instruments in biblical visions is also found in Ezekiel 40:3 and Zechariah 2:1.

Verse 16: "The city was laid out like a square, as long as it was wide. He measured the city with the rod and found it to be 12,000 stadia in length, and as wide and high as it is long."

- The Holy City is described as a perfect square, with each side measuring 12,000 stadia, and its height matches its length and width.

Interpretation and Commentary:

1. Divine Perfection: The perfect square shape of the Holy City symbolizes divine perfection, order, and completeness. It reinforces the idea of God's meticulous planning and design.
2. Equal Dimensions: The equal dimensions in length, width, and height emphasize the balance and symmetry of the city. It is a place of perfect harmony.

Bible References:

*   The use of measurements in visions is also found in Ezekiel 40:5 and Ezekiel 48:20.

Verse 17: "The angel measured the wall using human measurement, and it was 144 cubits thick."

*   The angel measured the thickness of the city wall, and it was 144 cubits.

Interpretation and Commentary:

1. Human Measurement: The mention of "human measurement" suggests that the thickness of the wall is expressed in familiar terms, making it understandable to the reader. It reinforces the realness of the vision.
2. Symbolic Number: The number 144 is significant in the Bible, as it is the square of 12 (12 x 12). It signifies completeness and perfection.

Bible References:

*   The use of numbers to convey symbolism is seen throughout the Bible, and 12 represents completeness and governance.

Verse 18: "The wall was made of jasper, and the city of pure gold, as pure as glass."

*   The composition of the wall is described as jasper, while the city itself is made of pure gold as clear as glass.

Interpretation and Commentary:

1. Precious Materials: The choice of jasper and pure gold symbolizes the extraordinary beauty and value of the Holy City. It emphasizes its heavenly and divine nature.
2. Purity and Transparency: The clarity of gold as glass underscores the purity and transparency of the city, suggesting that nothing impure or corrupt can exist in its presence.

Bible References:

*   The use of precious materials in describing heavenly places is also found in Ezekiel 28:13 and Revelation 4:6.

Verse 19: "The foundations of the city walls were decorated with every kind of precious stone. The first foundation was jasper, the second sapphire, the third agate, the fourth emerald."

- The foundations of the city walls are adorned with various precious stones, with each foundation featuring a different stone, starting with jasper.

Interpretation and Commentary:

1. Symbolic Beauty: The use of precious stones to decorate the foundations symbolizes the splendor and beauty of the city. It reflects the richness of God's blessings.

2. Foundation of Faith: The mention of twelve foundations with different stones may symbolize the diverse nature of the apostolic ministry and the foundational role of faith in Christ.

Bible References:

- The use of precious stones in describing heavenly places is also found in Ezekiel 28:13 and Revelation 4:3.

Verse 20: "The fifth onyx, the sixth ruby, the seventh chrysolite, the eighth beryl, the ninth topaz, the tenth turquoise, the eleventh jacinth, and the twelfth amethyst."

- The list continues, describing the remaining precious stones adorning the foundations of the city walls.

Interpretation and Commentary:

1. Diverse Beauty: The diversity of precious stones highlights the multifaceted beauty and richness of the Holy City. It conveys the idea of heavenly abundance.

2. Spiritual Symbolism: While these stones are undoubtedly beautiful, they may also hold symbolic significance, representing various aspects of God's character and His relationship with His people.

Bible References:

- The symbolic use of precious stones in the Bible is also seen in Exodus 28:17-21 and Ezekiel 28:13.

Verse 21: "The twelve gates were twelve pearls, each gate made of a single pearl. The great street of the city was of gold, as pure as transparent glass."

- The twelve gates of the city are described as pearls, each gate being a single pearl. The main street of the city is made of pure gold as clear as glass.

Interpretation and Commentary:

1. Pearl Gates: The gates made of pearls symbolize their extreme value and preciousness. They also convey the idea of purity and exclusivity, as pearls are formed through a process of transformation.

2. Golden Street: The golden street represents the purity, holiness, and magnificence of the city. It signifies the splendor of the pathway leading to God's presence.

Bible References:

- The use of pearls and gold to depict heavenly elements is also seen in Matthew 13:45-46 and Revelation 21:21.

Verse 22: "I did not see a temple in the city, because the Lord God Almighty and the Lamb are its temple."

- In the Holy City, John observes that there is no temple, as the Lord God Almighty and the Lamb serve as its temple.

Interpretation and Commentary:

1. Divine Presence: The absence of a temple signifies direct and unmediated access to God's presence. In the new heaven and earth, God's presence is fully revealed, and there is no need for an earthly sanctuary.

2. Unity of God: The reference to both "the Lord God Almighty" and "the Lamb" as the temple emphasizes the unity of the Godhead—Father, Son, and Holy Spirit—as the central focus of worship.

Bible References:

- Similar themes of direct access to God's presence are found in Hebrews 10:19-22 and Revelation 7:15.

Verse 23: "The city does not need the sun or the moon to shine on it, for the glory of God gives it light, and the Lamb is its lamp."

- In the Holy City, there is no need for natural light sources like the sun or the moon because the glory of God provides illumination, and the Lamb serves as its lamp.

Interpretation and Commentary:

1. Divine Illumination: The absence of natural light sources underscores the supernatural nature of the Holy City. It

emphasizes that God's presence and glory are sufficient to provide light and revelation.

2. The Lamb as Lamp: The Lamb, representing Jesus Christ, is not only the light but also the source of spiritual revelation and guidance for the inhabitants of the city.

Bible References:

- The concept of God as the source of light and illumination is found in Psalm 27:1 and Isaiah 60:19-20.

Verse 24: "The nations will walk by its light, and the kings of the earth will bring their splendor into it."

- The nations will walk in the light of the Holy City, and the kings of the earth will bring their glory and honor into it.

Interpretation and Commentary:

1. Universal Access: This verse emphasizes that the blessings of the Holy City are not limited to a specific group but are accessible to people from all nations. It underscores the inclusive nature of God's salvation.

2. Honor and Tribute: The image of kings bringing their splendor signifies the acknowledgment of God's sovereignty and the recognition of His majesty by earthly rulers. It portrays a scene of worship and homage.

Bible References:

- Similar themes of the nations coming to worship God are found in Isaiah 60:3 and Revelation 15:4.

Verse 25: "On no day will its gates ever be shut, for there will be no night there."

- The gates of the Holy City will never be closed, and there will be no night.

Interpretation and Commentary:

1. Continuous Access: The perpetual openness of the gates signifies continuous access to God's presence. There are no restrictions or barriers in the new creation.

2. No Darkness: The absence of night underscores the eternal nature of God's light and the absence of evil. It is a place of eternal day, symbolizing purity and holiness.

Bible References:

- The concept of God's eternal presence and light is found in Revelation 22:5 and Psalm 84:11.

Verse 26: "The glory and honor of the nations will be brought into it."

- The glory and honor of the nations will be brought into the Holy City.

Interpretation and Commentary:

1. Recognition of God's Majesty: This verse reinforces the idea that all the splendor, achievements, and cultural richness of the nations will ultimately find their highest purpose in acknowledging and honoring God.

2. Transformation of Glory: The glory and honor of the nations will be purified and sanctified in the presence of God. What is brought into the city will be transformed and made holy.

Bible References:

- The idea of the nations bringing their glory to God is also found in Isaiah 60:5 and Revelation 21:24.

Verse 27: "Nothing impure will ever enter it, nor will anyone who does what is shameful or deceitful, but only those whose names are written in the Lamb's book of life."

- The verse emphasizes that nothing impure, shameful, or deceitful will enter the Holy City. Only those whose names are written in the Lamb's book of life will gain access.

Interpretation and Commentary:

1. Purity and Holiness: This verse underscores the absolute purity and holiness of the Holy City. It is a place free from sin, deception, and anything that defiles.

2. The Lamb's Book of Life: Salvation and entrance into the city are exclusively for those whose names are written in the Lamb's book of life. This book contains the names of the redeemed, those who have accepted Jesus Christ as their Lord and Savior.

Bible References:

- The concept of the Lamb's book of life is also mentioned in Revelation 13:8 and Revelation 20:15. The idea of purity and holiness is found in passages like Psalm 24:3-4 and Hebrews 12:14.

In conclusion, Revelation 21:24-27 paints a vivid picture of the Holy City, emphasizing its accessibility to people from all nations, the perpetual openness of its gates, and the transformation of worldly glory into divine honor. It also highlights the city's absolute purity and holiness, allowing entry only to those whose names are written in the Lamb's book of life. These verses provide a powerful glimpse into the eternal dwelling place of God and His redeemed people, where His light shines continuously, and His presence is fully realized.

Prophetic Commentary:

Revelation 21 unfolds an extraordinary prophecy regarding the future of our world. In this vision, John describes what he witnessed:

"I saw a new heaven and a new earth, for the first heaven and the first earth had passed away. Also, there was no more sea" (Revelation 21:1).

What does the concept of "a new heaven and a new earth" signify? What will characterize this fresh heaven and earth? And what is destined to become of our existing heaven and earth?

To grasp the meaning of this prophecy, it's crucial to discern the context and the specific time it alludes to. The book of Revelation contains prophecies that pertain to events leading up to the return of Christ to Earth and the subsequent establishment of God's Kingdom on Earth.

Upon His return, Christ will rule alongside His glorified saints for a period of 1,000 years. These saints will experience resurrection into immortal, spiritual life during the first resurrection, which will occur at the return of Christ (1 Corinthians 15:50-52; Revelation 20:4, 6).

For a deeper understanding of the return of Jesus Christ, please refer to our article titled "Second Coming of Christ."

Following this initial 1,000-year reign, known as the Millennium, Revelation 20:5 reveals that all other humans who have lived and died throughout human history will be resurrected. It states, "But the rest of the dead did not live again until the thousand years [the Millennium] were finished."

The term "rest of the dead" denotes the vast majority of individuals who have lived and died. Verses 12-13 indicate that these individuals will experience a resurrection followed by a period of judgment. (It's important to note that the present era is the time of judgment for those God calls out of this present world, as outlined in 1 Peter 4:17. Nevertheless, the standards for judgment—the teachings of the Bible, God's revealed guidance—are uniform for all individuals, regardless of which resurrection they are part of.)

By the conclusion of this judgment period, those who embrace God's way will be granted eternal life, with their names inscribed in the Book of Life. Conversely, those who reject God's path will be "cast into the lake of fire" (Revelation 20:15).

Verse 14 clarifies that this consignment to the lake of fire represents "the second death" (emphasis added throughout). The first death corresponds to the termination of earthly life (also discussed in Revelation 21:8). This "second death" is definitive—a demise from which there is no possibility of resurrection.

In various Scriptures, this "lake of fire" is also referred to as "hell fire." In many instances, the Greek word for "hell" is "Gehenna," which designates the valley of Hinnom located in the southern part of Jerusalem.

It seems that the "lake of fire" will be situated within the valley of Hinnom in Jerusalem. However, the book of Revelation suggests that it will encompass a much broader scope than just this valley. Ultimately, it will play a pivotal role in the establishment of the new heaven and earth.

The lake of fire's expansion is depicted in 2 Peter 3, where it's stated that the heavens and the earth are preserved until the day of judgment and the destruction of ungodly individuals: "But the heavens and the earth which are now preserved by the same word, are reserved for fire until the day of judgment and perdition of ungodly men" (verse 7). Consequently, after all "ungodly" individuals are consumed in the lake of fire, the heavens and the earth will undergo destruction by fire.

Consider verse 10: "But the day of the Lord will come as a thief in the night, in which the heavens will pass away with a great noise, and the elements will melt with fervent heat; both the earth and the works that are in it will be burned up."

In this verse, the Greek term for "heavens" encompasses the sky and the atmosphere above the earth, which will also be set ablaze. Therefore, both the earth and its surrounding atmosphere will be "burned up."

Peter proceeds, "Looking for and hastening the coming of the day of God, because of which the heavens will be dissolved, being on fire, and the elements will melt [liquefy] with fervent heat?" (verse 12). The physical constituents of our planet and the sky will dissolve and liquefy due to intense heat.

New heaven(s) and earth are anticipated in accordance with God's promise: "Nevertheless we, according to His promise, look for new heavens and a new earth in which righteousness dwells" (verse 13).

The Greek term Peter employs for "new" is "kainos," which implies a state of freshness rather than "neos," which denotes newness in terms of age. Regardless of whether the earth is entirely consumed by the fire or its surface is melted and thus purified, the outcome remains a "new" planet, reconstituted or reshaped by God. It will still be referred to as the "earth," and the heavens will likewise be made "new."

Psalm 102:25-26 likens this future transformation to putting on a fresh garment: "Of old You laid the foundation of the earth, and the heavens are the work of Your hands. They will perish, but You will endure; yes, they will all grow old like a garment; like a cloak You will change them, and they will be changed."

Whether God replaces existing stars and planets with new ones or transforms the current ones into a different state or arrangement that endures eternally is a question we will only find the answer to when the time comes.

In Revelation 21:1, John writes, "Now I saw a new heaven and a new earth, for the first heaven and the first earth had passed away. Also there was no more sea."

John employs the same Greek term for "new" that Peter used, signifying a state of freshness. He also uses the singular term "heaven," instead of the plural used by Peter. It's possible that John is referring to everything visible from Earth, encompassing the atmosphere and everything visible in the night sky.

The Greek word John uses for "passed away" in Revelation 21:1 conveys the notion that these things have perished and no longer exist.

Why will there be a new heaven and earth? If heaven, which is God's current abode, were the eternal reward of the righteous, as traditional Christianity teaches, then there would be no purpose for a new earth. However, the Bible clearly reveals that heaven is not the reward of the righteous. Instead, Jesus explicitly taught: "Blessed are the meek, for they shall inherit the earth" (Matthew 5:5).

So, what is so special about inheriting the earth rather than heaven? First and foremost, we know that God will transform this earth into a pure, fresh, and beautiful new earth.

Consider what will transpire: "Then I, John, saw the holy city, New Jerusalem, coming down out of heaven from God, prepared as a bride adorned for her husband" (Revelation 21:2).

Upon this newly refashioned earth will descend a dazzling and immense city that stretches a remarkable 1,500 miles in each direction!

Verses 9-27 provide more detailed descriptions of this incredible city. Even Abraham, known as the "father of all those who believe" (Romans 4:11), eagerly anticipated this future city: "For he waited for the city which has foundations, whose builder and maker is God" (Hebrews 11:10).

Verse 16 makes it clear that God has prepared this city for His faithful elect: "Therefore God is not ashamed to be called their God, for He has prepared a city for them." Furthermore, Hebrews 13:14 affirms: "For here we have no continuing city, but we seek the one to come."

But why such a vast city? In the near future, when Christ returns, He will establish His reign in Jerusalem, making it the capital of the earth. Yet, when New Jerusalem descends to earth, it will become the capital of the entire universe!

This city will even serve as the new residence of God the Father Himself! Observe Revelation 21:3: "And I heard a loud voice from heaven saying, 'Behold, the tabernacle of God is with men, and He will dwell with them, and they shall be His people. God Himself will be with them and be their God.'" Verse 22 further emphasizes:

"But I saw no temple in it, for the Lord God Almighty and the Lamb are its temple."

Indeed, God the Father and Jesus Christ will ultimately reside on earth! There is no mention of us going to heaven to dwell with God.

Now, why will the heavens, including all the planets, stars, and galaxies, also be made new or fresh? God has offered some hints in Scripture. Romans 8:19, 21-22 states: "For the earnest expectation of the creation eagerly waits for the revealing of the sons of God. ... Because the creation itself also will be delivered from the bondage of corruption [decay] into the glorious liberty of the children of God. For we know that the whole creation groans and labors with birth pangs together until now."

Here, the apostle Paul offers a glimpse of our future and connects it to the "whole creation." He implies that the entire universe will eventually come under the care of glorified saints!

Currently, the physical creation is subject to entropy, the continual decline of all physical things. Left unchecked, the earth would eventually deteriorate and become uninhabitable. Similarly, all stars, including our sun, would ultimately deplete their fuel and extinguish. This is precisely why God intends to "make all things new" (Revelation 21:5).

God's glorified and immortal saints will not inhabit a world in a perpetual state of decay. Instead, they will reside on an earth and under a heaven that are eternal and free from decay.

CHAPTER TWENTY TWO
The River of Life

Introduction:

Chapter 22 of the Book of Revelation serves as a profound conclusion to the entire biblical narrative, offering a glimpse of the eternal state of God's kingdom. John describes a river of the water of life flowing from the throne of God and the Lamb in the center of the city, providing nourishment and healing to the inhabitants. The tree of life is also found there, bearing twelve kinds of fruit, and its leaves are for the healing of the nations. This imagery harks back to the Garden of Eden, symbolizing the restoration of humanity's close relationship with God and the eternal life offered through Christ. The curse of sin is no more, and God's people will see His face and bear His name on their foreheads, signifying an intimate and eternal communion with Him.

Chapter 22 concludes with a series of final assurances and warnings. Jesus, the Alpha and the Omega, declares His imminent return, and He promises to reward the faithful according to their deeds. The invitation to come and partake of the water of life is extended to all who thirst, emphasizing the universal offer of salvation through faith in Christ. However, a solemn warning is given against altering the words of the book of Revelation, reminding readers of the seriousness of God's revealed truth. The chapter closes with the repeated promise of Jesus' return and the earnest plea, "Come, Lord Jesus." Chapter 22 encapsulates the themes of redemption, restoration, and the hope of eternal life, offering a glimpse of the glorious future that awaits those who trust in Christ and remain faithful to His teachings. It serves as a fitting conclusion to the entire Bible, echoing the words of Christ's invitation to all to come and find salvation and eternal life in Him.

Verse 1: "Then the angel showed me the river of the water of life, as clear as crystal, flowing from the throne of God and of the Lamb."
Interpretation and Commentary:
1. River of Life: This verse depicts a beautiful image of the river of the water of life. It symbolizes the eternal source of life, purity, and refreshment that flows from the very throne of God and Jesus (the Lamb).
2. Clear as Crystal: The clarity of the water emphasizes its purity and the absence of any impurity or contamination. It symbolizes the spiritual purity and perfection found in God's presence.

Bible References:
- Similar imagery of a river of life is found in Ezekiel 47:1 and Psalm 36:8-9.

Verse 2: "Down the middle of the great street of the city. On each side of the river stood the tree of life, bearing twelve crops of fruit, yielding its fruit every month. And the leaves of the tree are for the healing of the nations."
Interpretation and Commentary:
1. Tree of Life: In this verse, the tree of life is reintroduced, echoing the Garden of Eden. It symbolizes eternal life and nourishment for God's people.
2. Twelve Crops of Fruit: The abundance of fruit and its monthly yield symbolizes continuous and abundant provision for the redeemed. It signifies the perpetual blessings of eternal life.
3. Healing of the Nations: The leaves of the tree being for the healing of the nations suggest the restoration and reconciliation of all people in God's presence. It signifies the end of suffering and division.

Bible References:
- The concept of the tree of life originates in Genesis 2:9 and is also mentioned in Revelation 2:7.

Verse 3: "No longer will there be any curse. The throne of God and of the Lamb will be in the city, and his servants will serve him."
Interpretation and Commentary:
1. Cursed Removed: This verse declares the removal of the curse that has plagued creation since the fall of humanity. In the new creation, there will be no more suffering, sin, or death.
2. The Throne of God: The presence of God's throne in the city symbolizes His eternal sovereignty and rule over the redeemed creation.
3. Eternal Service: The promise that His servants will serve Him indicates a purposeful, joyous service in God's presence. It reflects the fulfillment of the believer's calling.

Bible References:
- The removal of the curse is foretold in passages like Isaiah 65:25 and Revelation 21:4.

Verse 4: "They will see his face, and his name will be on their foreheads."
Interpretation and Commentary:
1. Intimate Fellowship: Seeing God's face represents intimate, unhindered fellowship with Him. It signifies the full revelation and presence of God to His people.
2. His Name on Their Foreheads: Having His name on their foreheads indicates ownership, identity, and belonging to God. It symbolizes the close relationship between God and His redeemed.

Bible References:
- The concept of seeing God's face is also found in Psalm 17:15 and 1 Corinthians 13:12.

Verse 5: "There will be no more night. They will not need the light of a lamp or the light of the sun, for the Lord God will give them light. And they will reign forever and ever."
Interpretation and Commentary:
1. End of Darkness: The absence of night and the need for artificial or natural light symbolize the eternal presence of God's light. In His presence, there is no darkness or need for external illumination.

2. Reign Forever: The promise that believers will reign forever and ever underscores their coheirs with Christ. They will share in His eternal kingdom and authority.

Bible References:

- The idea of God being the source of light is found in Psalm 27:1 and Revelation 21:23.

Verse 6: "The angel said to me, 'These words are trustworthy and true. The Lord, the God who inspires the prophets, sent his angel to show his servants the things that must soon take place.'"

Interpretation and Commentary:

1. Trustworthy Revelation: The angel confirms the reliability and truthfulness of the words and visions John has received. It underscores the divine source of this revelation.

2. Prophetic Inspiration: The reference to God inspiring the prophets emphasizes that this revelation is in line with the prophetic tradition of conveying God's will to His people.

Bible References:

- The trustworthiness of God's words is affirmed in passages like Psalm 19:7 and Psalm 111:7.

Verse 7: "Look, I am coming soon! Blessed is the one who keeps the words of the prophecy written in this scroll."

Interpretation and Commentary:

1. Imminent Return: Jesus reaffirms His promise of coming soon. This is a reminder of the urgency and anticipation of His second coming.

2. Blessed Obedience: Blessing is pronounced upon those who faithfully heed and obey the prophecies contained in this book. It emphasizes the importance of living in accordance with God's revealed will.

Bible References:

- The promise of Jesus' return is central in passages like Matthew 24:44 and Revelation 22:12.

Verse 8: "I, John, am the one who heard and saw these things. And when I had heard and seen them, I fell down to worship at the feet of the angel who had been showing them to me."

Interpretation and Commentary:

1. John's Experience: John reiterates that he is the one who personally witnessed and heard these visions. His response of

falling down to worship at the feet of the angel reveals his deep reverence and awe.

Bible References:

- Instances of people falling down to worship angels can be found in Revelation 19:10 and Revelation 22:9.

Verse 9: "But he said to me, 'Don't do that! I am a fellow servant with you and with your fellow prophets and with all who keep the words of this scroll. Worship God!'"

Interpretation and Commentary:

1. Angel's Correction: The angel immediately corrects John's act of worship, emphasizing his shared status as a servant of God, rather than an object of worship. He directs all worship toward God alone.

Bible References:

- The command to worship God alone is central to the biblical message (Exodus 34:14; Matthew 4:10).

Verse 10: "Then he told me, 'Do not seal up the words of the prophecy of this scroll, because the time is near.'"

Interpretation and Commentary:

1. Unsealed Prophecy: Unlike some Old Testament prophecies that were sealed until a later time (e.g., Daniel 12:4), this prophecy is not to be sealed. It is meant to be understood and shared because its fulfillment is imminent.
2. Imminent Fulfillment: The mention of "the time is near" emphasizes the urgency of the events described in this prophecy. It serves as a reminder that the fulfillment of these prophecies is not in the distant future.

Bible References:

- Similar themes of unsealed prophecies can be found in Daniel 8:26 and Daniel 12:9.

Verse 11: "Let the one who does wrong continue to do wrong; let the vile person continue to be vile; let the one who does right continue to do right; and let the holy person continue to be holy."

Interpretation and Commentary:

1. End of Probation: This verse seems to convey a sense of finality, suggesting that when Christ returns, people's character and choices will be fixed. Those who persist in evil will

continue in that path, and those who are righteous will remain so.

2. Free Will Acknowledged: While it may seem that choices are fixed, this verse also acknowledges that people continue in the paths they have chosen. It doesn't negate the importance of personal responsibility and free will.

Bible References:

*   A similar concept of finality can be seen in Daniel 12:10, which speaks of the righteous becoming more righteous and the wicked becoming more wicked.

Verse 12: "Look, I am coming soon! My reward is with me, and I will give to each person according to what they have done."

Interpretation and Commentary:

1. Imminent Return: Jesus reiterates His promise of coming soon. He emphasizes the certainty and proximity of His return.

2. Just Reward: This verse underscores the principle of divine justice. When Christ returns, He will bring rewards in accordance with each person's actions, whether good or bad. It speaks to the accountability of every individual.

Bible References:

*   The concept of Jesus coming with rewards is also mentioned in Matthew 16:27 and 1 Corinthians 3:8.

Verse 13: "I am the Alpha and the Omega, the First and the Last, the Beginning and the End."

Interpretation and Commentary:

1. Divine Identity: Jesus declares His divinity by using these titles. "Alpha and Omega" represent the first and last letters of the Greek alphabet, signifying completeness and all-encompassing existence. "First and Last" and "Beginning and End" emphasize His eternal and preeminent nature.

2. Ultimate Authority: These titles affirm that Jesus is the ultimate source, sustainer, and goal of all things. He is the beginning and end of creation and redemption.

Bible References:

*   Similar titles are used in Revelation 1:8 and Isaiah 44:6.

Verse 14: "Blessed are those who wash their robes, that they may have the right to the tree of life and may go through the gates into the city."

Interpretation and Commentary:

1. Blessedness of the Redeemed: This verse pronounces a blessing on those who have purified themselves through faith in Christ's atonement. They have the privilege of eternal life symbolized by access to the tree of life and entrance into the Holy City (New Jerusalem).
2. Cleansing Symbolism: "Washing their robes" symbolizes the cleansing from sin through faith in Jesus. It underscores the importance of repentance and faith in Christ's sacrifice.

Bible References:

*   Similar themes of cleansing and access to the tree of life are found in Revelation 7:14 and Revelation 21:27.

Verse 15: "Outside are the dogs, those who practice magic arts, the sexually immoral, the murderers, the idolaters and everyone who loves and practices falsehood."

Interpretation and Commentary:

1. Exclusion from God's Presence: This verse describes those who are excluded from the blessings of the New Jerusalem. It lists various sinful practices that separate people from God's presence.
2. Moral Accountability: The inclusion of specific sins emphasizes the moral accountability of individuals. Those who persist in unrepentant sin will remain outside God's eternal kingdom.

Bible References:

*   Similar lists of sins and their consequences can be found in 1 Corinthians 6:9-10 and Galatians 5:19-21.

Verse 16: "I, Jesus, have sent my angel to give you this testimony for the churches. I am the Root and the Offspring of David, and the bright Morning Star."

Interpretation and Commentary:

1. Jesus' Identity: Jesus reaffirms His identity as the sender of the angel and as the fulfillment of Old Testament prophecies. He is the Root and Offspring of David, connecting His divine nature (Root) with His human lineage (Offspring).
2. Bright Morning Star: Jesus also identifies Himself as the bright Morning Star, symbolizing His role as the source of spiritual light and guidance. He brings hope and the dawn of salvation.

Bible References:

- The titles "Root of David" and "Morning Star" are used in connection with the Messiah in Isaiah 11:1 and Numbers 24:17, respectively.

Verse 17: "The Spirit and the bride say, 'Come!' And let the one who hears say, 'Come!' Let the one who is thirsty come; and let the one who wishes take the free gift of the water of life."

Interpretation and Commentary:

1. Universal Invitation: This verse presents a universal invitation to salvation. The Holy Spirit and the bride (the Church) join in inviting all to come to Jesus for salvation.

2. Thirst for God: The invitation is extended to those who are spiritually thirsty, emphasizing the soul's longing for God. It underscores that salvation is freely available to all who desire it.

3. Free Gift: The offer of "the water of life" symbolizes the life-giving, spiritually satisfying nature of salvation through Jesus Christ. It is a free gift available to all who believe.

Bible References:

- Similar invitations to come to God are found in Isaiah 55:1 and Matthew 11:28.

Verse 18: "I warn everyone who hears the words of the prophecy of this scroll: If anyone adds anything to them, God will add to that person the plagues described in this scroll."

Interpretation and Commentary:

1. Serious Warning: This verse issues a solemn warning against adding to the words of the prophecy in the book of Revelation. It underscores the importance of preserving the integrity of God's Word.

2. Consequences of Tampering: The warning states that those who add to these prophecies will face the plagues described in the book. This serves as a deterrent against distorting or misrepresenting God's revealed truth.

Bible References:

- Similar warnings about not adding to God's words can be found in Deuteronomy 4:2 and Proverbs 30:6.

Verse 19: "And if anyone takes words away from this scroll of prophecy, God will take away from that person any share in the tree of life and in the Holy City, which are described in this scroll."
Interpretation and Commentary:
1. Serious Consequence: This verse delivers another solemn warning, this time against subtracting or removing words from the prophecy in Revelation. It emphasizes the gravity of altering God's Word.
2. Loss of Blessings: The consequence for tampering with the prophecy is the forfeiture of one's share in the tree of life and exclusion from the Holy City. This underscores the eternal significance of obedience to God's Word.
Bible References:
- The concept of losing access to the tree of life is reminiscent of Genesis 3:24, where Adam and Eve were barred from it.

Verse 20: "He who testifies to these things says, 'Yes, I am coming soon.' Amen. Come, Lord Jesus."
Interpretation and Commentary:
1. Confirmation of Jesus: The verse confirms that the speaker is Jesus Himself, who testifies to the contents of this book. He reiterates His promise of coming soon, affirming the certainty of His return.
2. Amen: The word "Amen" is an expression of agreement and affirmation, emphasizing the truth and certainty of Christ's return.
3. Prayer for Christ's Return: The phrase "Come, Lord Jesus" is a prayer and expression of longing for Jesus' return. It reflects the eager anticipation of believers for the fulfillment of His promise.
Bible References:
- The affirmation "Amen" is used throughout the Bible as a confirmation of truth and agreement (e.g., Numbers 5:22, Revelation 3:14).

Verse 21: "The grace of the Lord Jesus be with God's people. Amen."
Interpretation and Commentary:
1. Final Blessing: This verse closes the Book of Revelation with a final blessing invoking the grace of the Lord Jesus upon

God's people. It is a prayer for God's favor, mercy, and empowerment to rest upon believers.

2. Unity: The phrase "God's people" reflects the unity of all believers in Christ, irrespective of time, place, or background. It signifies the shared grace that is available to all who follow Jesus.

Bible References:

- Similar blessings invoking God's grace can be found in 2 Corinthians 13:14 and Romans 16:20.

In conclusion, Revelation Chapter 22 contains profound warnings about the integrity of God's Word, affirmations of Christ's imminent return, and blessings of grace upon God's people. It encourages believers to eagerly anticipate the fulfillment of God's promises and to faithfully adhere to His revealed truth. The Book of Revelation as a whole serves as a reminder of the ultimate victory of Christ over evil and the hope of eternal life for those who remain faithful to Him.

Prophetic Commentary:

In Revelation 22:1, we find a profound reflection of the Trinity of God.

"River of water of life":

This symbolic depiction represents the Holy Spirit, through whom we are reborn, indwelled, and granted eternal life. It highlights the promise of dwelling eternally in the "holy city" through our faith in Christ.

"Throne of God and of the Lamb":

This signifies the co-rule of the Father and the Son in the Eternal Kingdom. Christ's kingdom currently exists through the Church and will culminate in the future Eternal Kingdom, as described in Revelation 21 and 22. However, according to 1 Corinthians 15:24-28, Jesus will eventually yield the kingdom to God the Father, signifying the completion of the current order and God's renewal of all things.

Nevertheless, Revelation 22:1 underscores that both the Father and the Son are co-rulers in the eternal city. In our present world, the emphasis is on Christ as the central figure, ruling over His spiritual kingdom. In the New Covenant, the focus is on Jesus as Lord, Savior, and Redeemer. However, in the eternal state, the focus shifts to the physical kingdom described in Revelation 21 and 22, where the Father and the Son reign together, and the redeemed dwell in glorified, physical bodies.

"The Lamb":

This title reminds us of Christ's sacrificial death on the cross. The Old Testament animal sacrifices foreshadowed Jesus as the "Lamb of God, who takes away the sin of the world" (John 1:29), emphasizing His role as the ultimate sacrifice for mankind.

Revelation 22:2 describes the presence of the "tree of life" on both sides of the symbolic river. This tree signifies our salvation in Christ, akin to a "tree of salvation." It represents the ongoing production of the "fruit" of eternal life, emphasizing our eternal security in Christ.

While it's possible that this tree is symbolic, it could also be a literal reference, perhaps reminiscent of the tree in the Garden of Eden (Genesis 2:9; 3:22-24). The absence of a curse in the next verse (Revelation 22:3) aligns with the idea that the eternal "new earth" (Revelation 21:1) mirrors the sinless state of Eden. The Eternal Kingdom may resemble the Garden of Eden before sin entered the world, and humanity will dwell in sinless bodies similar to Adam and Eve's original state.

"Healing of the nations":

This phrase does not imply the presence of distinct nations in the eternal city, as discussed in Revelation 21:24. Instead, it refers to the redeemed individuals from various nations in our current world, as indicated in Revelation 5:9 and 7:9. "Healing" encompasses both spiritual and physical aspects, reflecting our eternal security and wholeness in Christ. We will no longer experience physical pain or suffering in our glorified, immortal bodies, symbolizing the permanence of our healing, both spiritual and physical.

Revelation 22:3-10 contains crucial insights into the final chapters of the Book of Revelation.

"No curse": This verse references the curse placed on the ground in Genesis 3:17-19 due to sin's entry into the world. The eternal city described in Revelation will resemble the original perfection of the Garden of Eden, free from the toil and struggles caused by the curse. It represents a self-sustaining, beautiful, and perfect creation.

"Throne of God and of the Lamb": As mentioned earlier in Revelation 22:1, this verse reaffirms the co-rule of God the Father and Jesus Christ in the Eternal Kingdom, combining both the spiritual kingdom (the Church) and the future physical kingdom (the Eternal Kingdom described in Revelation 21 and 22). This transition from spiritual to physical signifies the culmination of God's plan and the renewal of all things.

"His servants shall serve him": In the eternal city, believers will continue to serve God in various capacities, finding joy and fulfillment in their roles. While the exact nature of this service is not specified, it emphasizes that Christians should faithfully serve God throughout their lives, continuously growing in their relationship with Him, ultimately finding fulfillment in their glorified, immortal bodies in the new creation.

"They shall see his face": This phrase reflects the longing of believers to see Jesus face-to-face, a profound hope expressed in the hymn quoted. It signifies the blessed experience of being in the presence of the Savior, a moment of great anticipation for believers.

"His name shall be on their foreheads": This symbolic mark identifies believers as followers of Christ, demonstrating their eternal connection with God. It serves as a lasting reminder of their identity in Christ, which remains unchanging and everlasting.

"There shall be night no more": This verse reinforces the idea of a perfect and eternal existence, free from darkness and the need for external sources of light. In the Eternal Kingdom, God Himself will be the ultimate source of illumination.

"They shall reign forever and ever": Believers will participate in the reign of the Saints, symbolizing their unity with Christ and the truth that no one rules over them except God. While they won't rule over others, they will reign in the sense that no one will have dominion over them; only God will rule.

"These words are faithful and true": This phrase emphasizes the truth and reliability of every word in the book of Revelation. Believers can trust in God's promises of judgment for unbelievers and eternal blessings for the redeemed.

"The God of the spirits of the prophets": This phrase underscores that those who have passed away continue to exist as spirits and will one day experience bodily resurrection. It aligns with the biblical teaching that both unbelievers and believers will be resurrected, with the latter entering the Eternal Kingdom.

"Things which must shortly come to pass": This statement refers to the beginning of the events described in Revelation, which would soon commence during John's time and continue throughout the Church age. It rejects the notion that the entire book only pertains to a brief period before Christ's return.

"Seal not up the words of the prophecy of this book": John is instructed not to hide or conceal the prophetic words of this book. The phrase "for the time is at hand" indicates that these events are soon to commence, implying their relevance throughout the Church age, not just in the latter years preceding Christ's return.

(Revelation 22:11) – 11 Those who are unrighteous, let them continue in their unrighteousness, and those who are filthy, let them remain in their filthiness. And those who are righteous, let them continue in righteousness, and those who are holy, let them remain in holiness.

Explanation: This verse conveys the idea that people will continue in the state they have chosen. It emphasizes that individuals' actions and choices will align with their true nature and beliefs. In essence, it highlights the consistency between one's character and their behavior.

For those who are unrighteous and filthy, this verse implies that they will persist in their wickedness and impurity, demonstrating that their hearts remain unchanged. On the other hand, those who are righteous and holy will continue to live according to their godly nature and convictions, displaying their genuine faith.

The use of the word "still" emphasizes the continuation of these states. It suggests that one's character and choices are enduring and consistent over time.

Note: This verse does not negate the importance of repentance and transformation through faith in Christ. Instead, it underscores the idea that genuine faith will produce a life consistent with that faith.

(Revelation 22:12) – 12 Look, I am coming quickly, and My reward is with Me, to give to each one according to what they have done.

Explanation: In this verse, Jesus declares His imminent return, emphasizing the swiftness of His coming. He also announces that He will bring His rewards with Him to distribute to every individual based on their actions.

The phrase "I am coming quickly" underscores the certainty and promptness of Jesus' return. Believers are encouraged to be watchful and prepared for His coming.

The statement "My reward is with Me" suggests that Jesus will bring the rewards for both believers and non-believers when He returns. For believers, their rewards will be commensurate with their faithful service and obedience to Him. Non-believers will face judgment based on their deeds.

This verse highlights the importance of living a life of faithfulness and righteousness in anticipation of Christ's return, as the rewards or consequences will be justly distributed according to one's actions.

(Revelation 22:13) – 13 I am the Alpha and the Omega, the First and the Last, the Beginning and the End.

Explanation: This verse contains a powerful declaration by Jesus about His identity and divine attributes. He identifies Himself using three significant titles:

1. "I am the Alpha and the Omega": These are the first and last letters of the Greek alphabet, signifying that Jesus is the beginning and the end of all things. This declaration emphasizes His eternal existence and His role as the Creator and Sovereign over the entire universe.

2. "The First and the Last": This title further underscores Jesus' eternal nature, suggesting that He existed before all things and will exist after all things. He is the ultimate authority and source of all existence.

3. "The Beginning and the End": This reaffirms that Jesus is the origin and ultimate destination of all things. He is the one who initiates and completes God's plan for humanity and creation.

These titles collectively emphasize Jesus' divine nature, His omnipotence, and His central role in God's redemptive plan. He is the preeminent and eternal God, worthy of worship and obedience.

(Revelation 22:14) – 14 Blessed are those who wash their robes so that they may have the right to the tree of life and may enter the city by the gates.

Explanation: This verse conveys a message of blessing and assurance to those who have been cleansed from their sins and made righteous through faith in Jesus Christ. It uses symbolic language to illustrate the concept of salvation:

1. "Wash their robes": This phrase symbolizes the forgiveness of sins through faith in Jesus. Believers are cleansed and made righteous by His atoning sacrifice.
2. "Right to the tree of life": Access to the tree of life represents eternal life and fellowship with God. Believers have the privilege of partaking in the blessings of God's eternal kingdom.
3. "Enter the city by the gates": Entering the city signifies admission into God's heavenly kingdom. Believers will have the honor of dwelling with God in His presence forever.

Overall, this verse underscores the significance of faith in Christ as the means by which individuals can experience God's blessings, eternal life, and a place in His heavenly kingdom.

(Revelation 22:15) – 15 Outside are the dogs, those who practice magic arts, the sexually immoral, the murderers, the idolaters, and everyone who loves and practices falsehood.

Explanation: This verse describes those who are excluded from God's heavenly kingdom and remain outside its gates. It provides a list of sinful behaviors and characteristics that characterize the ungodly and unbelieving:

1. "Dogs": In biblical times, "dogs" were often associated with impurity and contempt. This term is used symbolically to represent those who are unclean or impure in heart and life.

2. "Those who practice magic arts": This refers to individuals involved in occult practices and sorcery, which are condemned in Scripture as idolatrous and spiritually dangerous.

3. "The sexually immoral": This includes those who engage in sexual immorality and impurity, violating God's moral standards for sexual conduct.

4. "The murderers": This refers to those who commit acts of murder and violence against others, disregarding the sanctity of human life.

5. "The idolaters": Idolatry involves the worship of false gods or the pursuit of false beliefs, rejecting the one true God.

6. "Everyone who loves and practices falsehood": Those who embrace lies and deceit and live dishonest lives, rejecting truth and righteousness.

This verse serves as a warning and a reminder of the consequences of unrepentant sin and unbelief. Those who persist in such behavior will remain separated from God's presence and the blessings of His kingdom.

(Revelation 22:16) – 16 I, Jesus, have sent my angel to bear witness to you about these things for the churches. I am the root and the descendant of David, the bright morning star.

Explanation: In Revelation 22:16, Jesus introduces Himself as the speaker and central figure of the book. His statement "I, Jesus" reaffirms His authority and emphasizes that He is the divine source of the revelations contained in the book. This underscores the authenticity and truthfulness of the entire book.

The phrase "for the churches" highlights that the messages conveyed in Revelation are not limited to a specific time or place but are relevant for all Christian communities, both then and in the future. It serves as a reminder that the book addresses the broader body of believers throughout history.

"I am the root and the descendant of David" points to Jesus' dual nature as both the originator and fulfillment of the Davidic line. He is the root, indicating His preexistence as the eternal Son of God, and the descendant of David, fulfilling the Messianic prophecies of the Old Testament.

Finally, Jesus describes Himself as "the bright morning star." This metaphor symbolizes His role as the bringer of light and hope, dispelling darkness and ignorance. It signifies His role in leading believers out of spiritual darkness into the light of salvation.

(Revelation 22:17) – 17 The Spirit and the bride say, "Come!" And let the one who hears say, "Come!" Let the one who is thirsty come; let the one who desires take the water of life without price.

Explanation: In Revelation 22:17, a compelling invitation is extended to all who are willing to receive it. It involves various participants:

"The Spirit and the bride" collectively represent the Church, indwelt and empowered by the Holy Spirit. Together, they invite others to come to Jesus. The Church, as the bride, serves as a witness to the world, offering the life-giving message of salvation.

"Let the one who hears say, 'Come!'" This phrase encourages those who have heard the message of the gospel to also extend the invitation to others. Believers are called to share the good news of Christ's salvation and invite others to partake in it.

"Let the one who is thirsty come; let the one who desires take the water of life without price." This emphasizes that anyone who recognizes their spiritual thirst and desire for salvation is welcome to come to Christ. The "water of life" symbolizes eternal life through faith in Jesus, and it is offered freely, without cost.

This verse highlights the inclusivity of God's invitation to salvation. It's open to all who are willing to come, hear, and respond to the gospel message.

(Revelation 22:18-19) – 18 I warn everyone who hears the words of the prophecy of this book: if anyone adds to them, God will add to him the plagues described in this book; 19 and if anyone takes away from the words of the book of this prophecy, God will take away his share in the tree of life and in the holy city, which are described in this book.

Explanation: Revelation 22:18-19 contains a solemn warning about tampering with the words of the book of Revelation. It emphasizes the sanctity and integrity of the prophecy:

"I warn everyone who hears the words of the prophecy of this book" indicates the seriousness of the warning and its applicability to all who encounter the book.

"If anyone adds to them" and "if anyone takes away from the words of the book of this prophecy" refer to any attempt to modify, distort, or misrepresent the content of Revelation. This applies to both additions and omissions.

"God will add to him the plagues described in this book" signifies severe judgment upon those who alter the words of Revelation. The plagues mentioned in the book represent divine judgment, and those who manipulate the message will face intensified consequences.

"God will take away his share in the tree of life and in the holy city" suggests that those who tamper with the book's content will forfeit their access to eternal life and citizenship in the holy city, which symbolize salvation and fellowship with God.

These verses emphasize the importance of preserving the integrity of God's Word and the seriousness of distorting His revealed truth. They serve as a stern warning against misrepresenting the message of Revelation.

(Revelation 22:20) – 20 He who testifies to these things says, "Surely I am coming soon." Amen. Come, Lord Jesus!

Explanation: In Revelation 22:20, Jesus, the One who has borne witness to the events and messages in the book, reaffirms His imminent return. His declaration, "Surely I am coming soon," underscores the certainty and swiftness of His return. Believers are encouraged to anticipate and eagerly await His coming.

The response "Amen" expresses agreement and affirmation of Jesus' promise. It is a heartfelt acknowledgment of the truth of His words.

"Come, Lord Jesus!" serves as a passionate plea and longing for the return of Christ. Believers express their desire for His arrival and the fulfillment of all that His coming entails, including the establishment of His eternal kingdom and the ultimate victory over evil.

This verse encapsulates the hopeful anticipation of the Church for the return of their Lord and Savior, Jesus Christ.

(Revelation 22:21) – 21 The grace of the Lord Jesus be with all. Amen.

Explanation: Revelation 22:21 concludes the book with a prayerful blessing. It imparts the grace of the Lord Jesus upon all who read and receive the message of Revelation. This grace represents God's unmerited favor, forgiveness, and empowerment for living as faithful followers of Christ.

The word "Amen" signifies agreement and underscores the sincerity of the prayer.

In essence, this final verse serves as a benediction, invoking God's grace and blessing upon every reader and believer. It highlights the importance of God's grace in enabling His people to navigate the challenges and uncertainties of life with the assurance of His presence and help.

CONCLUSION

The Book of Revelation, the final book of the New Testament, reaches its conclusion with a resounding proclamation of hope, triumph, and the ultimate fulfillment of God's divine plan for humanity. In Revelation Chapter 22, verses 16 to 21, we find the concluding words that bring this remarkable book to a close:

Verse 16: "I, Jesus, have sent my angel to testify to you about these things for the churches. I am the root and the descendant of David, the bright morning star."

Interpretation and Commentary:

In this verse, Jesus Himself speaks to confirm the authenticity and purpose of the revelations given in the book. He identifies Himself as the source and fulfillment of the messianic promises—the "root and descendant of David." Furthermore, He describes Himself as the "bright morning star," symbolizing His role as the One who brings light, hope, and guidance in the darkness of the world.

Bible References:

Jesus' identification as the "root of David" echoes prophecies such as Isaiah 11:1, where the Messiah is described as a shoot from the stump of Jesse, David's father.

Verse 17: "The Spirit and the Bride say, 'Come.' And let the one who hears say, 'Come.' And let the one who is thirsty come; let the one who desires take the water of life without price."

Interpretation and Commentary:

This verse underscores the invitation and accessibility of God's grace and salvation. It emphasizes that the Spirit and the Bride (often interpreted as the Church) join in a unified call for all to come to Christ. The offer of the "water of life" symbolizes eternal life and spiritual nourishment, freely available to all who thirst for it. Salvation is offered without cost, as it is a gift of God's grace.

Bible References:

The image of living water and the invitation to come can be traced back to passages like Isaiah 55:1 and John 4:13-14, where Jesus invites those who thirst to come to Him.

Verse 18: "I warn everyone who hears the words of the prophecy of this book: if anyone adds to them, God will add to him the plagues described in this book."

Interpretation and Commentary:

In this verse, a solemn warning is issued against tampering with or adding to the words of the Book of Revelation. It underscores the importance of preserving the integrity of God's Word and respecting the authenticity of the revelations contained within it. Those who distort or manipulate the prophecies face the consequences described within the book.

Bible References:

Similar warnings about not adding to God's words can be found in Deuteronomy 4:2 and Proverbs 30:6.

Verse 19: "And if anyone takes away from the words of the book of this prophecy, God will take away his share in the tree of life and in the holy city, which are described in this book."

Interpretation and Commentary:

This verse delivers another solemn warning, this time against subtracting or removing words from the Book of Revelation. The consequence for tampering with the prophecy is the forfeiture of one's share in the "tree of life" and exclusion from the "holy city." These symbols emphasize the eternal significance of obedience to God's Word.

Bible References:

The concept of losing access to the tree of life is reminiscent of Genesis 3:24, where Adam and Eve were barred from it.

Verse 20: "He who testifies to these things says, 'Surely I am coming soon.' Amen. Come, Lord Jesus!"

Interpretation and Commentary:

This verse affirms that the speaker is Jesus Himself, who testifies to the contents of this book. He reiterates His promise of coming soon, affirming the certainty of His return. The word "Amen" is an expression of agreement and affirmation, emphasizing the truth and certainty of Christ's return. The phrase "Come, Lord Jesus" is a prayer and expression of longing for Jesus' return, reflecting the eager anticipation of believers for the fulfillment of His promise.

Bible References:

The affirmation "Amen" is used throughout the Bible as a confirmation of truth and agreement (e.g., Numbers 5:22, Revelation 3:14).

Verse 21: "The grace of the Lord Jesus be with all. Amen."

Interpretation and Commentary:

This concluding verse offers a final blessing invoking the grace of the Lord Jesus upon all. It is a prayer for God's favor, mercy, and empowerment to rest upon believers. It emphasizes the universal reach of God's grace, extending to all who have encountered the message of Revelation.

Bible References:

Similar blessings invoking God's grace can be found in 2 Corinthians 13:14 and Romans 16:20.

In conclusion, the Book of Revelation reaches its climactic end with a powerful affirmation of Jesus' imminent return, a solemn warning against altering God's Word, and a universal blessing of God's grace. This book, with its vivid imagery and prophetic messages, reminds believers of the ultimate victory of Christ over evil and the hope of eternal life for those who remain faithful to Him. It is a fitting conclusion to a book that has challenged, inspired, and comforted generations of Christians throughout history.